Microsoft®

Excel 97

Illustrated Standard Edition,
A First Course

Microsoft®
Excel 97
Illustrated Standard Edition, A First Course

Elizabeth Eisner Reding
Tara Lynn O'Keefe

COURSE
TECHNOLOGY

ONE MAIN STREET, CAMBRIDGE, MA 02142

an International Thomson Publishing company I(T)P®

Cambridge • Albany • Bonn • Boston • Cincinnati • London • Madrid • Melbourne • Mexico City
New York • Paris • San Francisco • Singapore • Tokyo • Toronto • Washington

Microsoft Excel 97—Illustrated Standard Edition, A First Course

is published by Course Technology

Managing Editor:	Nicole Jones Pinard
Product Manager:	Jeanne Herring
Production Editor:	Nancy Ray
Developmental Editors:	Kim T. M. Crowley, Cynthia Anderson
Composition House:	GEX, Inc.
QA Manuscript Reviewers:	Chris Hall, John McCarthy, Brian McCooey, Jean-Claire Shiely
Text Designer:	Joseph Lee
Cover Designer:	Joseph Lee

© 1997 by Course Technology — I(T)P®

For more information contact:

Course Technology
One Main Street
Cambridge, MA 02142

ITP Europe
Berkshire House 168-173
High Holborn
London WC1V 7AA
England

Nelson ITP, Australia
102 Dodds Street
South Melbourne, 3205
Victoria, Australia

ITP Nelson Canada
1120 Birchmount Road
Scarborough, Ontario
Canada M1K 5G4

International Thomson Editores
Seneca, 53
Colonia Polanco
11560 Mexico D.F. Mexico

ITP GmbH
Königswinterer Strasse 418
53277 Bonn
Germany

ITP Asia
60 Albert Street, #15-01
Albert Complex
Singapore 189969

ITP Japan
Hirakawacho Kyowa Building, 3F
2-2-1 Hirakawacho
Chiyoda-ku, Tokyo 102
Japan

ISBN 0-7600-4695-6

Printed in the United States of America

6 7 8 9 BM 01 00 99

Illustrated Series™ Team

At Course Technology we believe that technology will transform the way that people teach and learn. We are very excited about bringing you, instructors and students, the most practical and affordable technology-related products available.

► The Development Process

Our development process is unparalleled in the educational publishing industry. Every product we create goes through an exacting process of design, development, review, and testing.

Reviewers give us direction and insight that shape our manuscripts and bring them up to the latest standards. Every manuscript is quality tested. Students whose backgrounds match the intended audience work through every keystroke, carefully checking for clarity and pointing out errors in logic and sequence. Together with our own technical reviewers, these testers help us ensure that everything that carries our name is as error-free and easy to use as possible.

► The Products

We show both how and why technology is critical to solving problems in the classroom and in whatever field you choose to teach or pursue. Our time-tested, step-by-step instructions provide unparalleled clarity. Examples and applications are chosen and crafted to motivate students.

► The Illustrated Series™ Team

The Illustrated Series™ Team is committed to providing you with the most visual introduction to microcomputer applications. No other series of books will get you up to speed faster in today's changing software environment. This book will suit your needs because it was delivered quickly, efficiently, and affordably. In every aspect of business, we rely on a commitment to quality and the use of technology. Each member of the Illustrated Series™ Team contributes to this process. The names of all our team members are listed below.

The Team

Cynthia Anderson	Mary-Terese Cozzola	Jeanne Herring	Elizabeth Eisner Reding
Chia-Ling Barker	Carol Cram	Meta Chaya Hirschl	Art Rotberg
Donald Barker	Kim T. M. Crowley	Jane Hosie-Bounar	Neil Salkind
Ann Barron	Catherine DiMassa	Steven Johnson	Gregory Schultz
David Beskeen	Stan Dobrawa	Bill Lisowski	Ann Shaffer
Ann Marie Buconjic	Shelley Dyer	Chet Lyskawa	Dan Swanson
Rachel Bunin	Linda Eriksen	Kristine O'Brien	Marie Swanson
Joan Carey	Jessica Evans	Tara O'Keefe	Jennifer Thompson
Patrick Carey	Lisa Friedrichsen	Harry Phillips	Sasha Vodnik
Sheralyn Carroll	Jeff Goding	Nicole Jones Pinard	Jan Weingarten
Brad Conlin	Michael Halvorson	Katherine T. Pinard	Christie Williams
Pam Conrad	Jamie Harper	Kevin Proot	Janet Wilson

Preface

Welcome to *Microsoft Excel 97 – Illustrated Standard Edition, A First Course*! This book in our highly visual new design offers new users a hands-on introduction to Microsoft Excel 97 and also serves as an excellent reference for future use.

▶ Organization and Coverage

This text contains eight units that cover basic Excel skills. In these units students learn how to design, create, edit, and enhance Excel workbooks. They also learn how to create meaningful charts, work with formulas and functions, design macros, and use lists.

▶ Microsoft Office User Specialist Program Approved Courseware

This book, when used as part of a two-course sequence with the companion textbook *Microsoft Excel 97-Illustrated Standard Edition, A Second Course*, has been approved by Microsoft as courseware for the Microsoft Office User Specialist program. After completing the lessons and exercises in these two books, the student will be prepared to take the Proficient level Microsoft Office User Specialist examination for Word 97. By passing the certification exam for a Microsoft software program, students demonstrate their proficiency in that program to employers. Microsoft Office User Specialist exams are offered at participating test centers, participating corporations, and participating employment agencies. For more information about certification, please visit the Microsoft Office User Specialist program World Wide Web site at http://www.microsoft.com/office/train_cert/.

▶ About this Approach

What makes the Illustrated approach so effective at teaching software skills? It's quite simple. Each skill is presented on two facing pages, with the step-by-step instructions on the left page, and large screen illustrations on the right. Students can focus on a single skill without having to turn the page. This unique design makes information extremely accessible and easy to absorb, and provides a great reference for after the course is over. This hands-on approach also makes it ideal for both self-paced or instructor-led classes. The modular structure of the book also allows for great flexibility; you can cover the units in any order you choose.
Each lesson, or "information display," contains the following elements:

This icon indicates a CourseHelp 97 slide show is available for this lesson. See the Instructor's Resource Kit page for more information.

Each 2-page spread focuses on a single skill.

Concise text that introduces the basic principles in the lesson and integrates the brief case study.

Changing Attributes and Alignment of Labels

Excel 97

Attributes are font styling features such as bold, italics, and underlining. You can apply bold, italics, and underlining from the Formatting toolbar or from the Font tab in the Format Cells dialog box. You can also change the alignment of text in cells. Left, right, or center alignment can be applied from the Formatting toolbar, or from the Alignment tab in the Format Cells dialog box. See Table C-2 for a description of the available attribute and alignment buttons on the Formatting toolbar. Excel also has predefined worksheet formats to make formatting easier. ▶ Now that he has applied the appropriate fonts and font sizes to his worksheet labels, Evan wants to further enhance his worksheet's appearance by adding bold and underline formatting and centering some of the labels.

Steps 123

CourseHelp
The camera icon indicates there is a CourseHelp available with this lesson. Click the Start button, point to programs, point to CourseHelp, then click Word 97 Illustrated. Choose the CourseHelp that corresponds to this lesson.

QuickTip
Highlighting information on a worksheet can be useful, but overuse of any attribute can be distracting and make a document less readable. Be consistent by adding emphasis the same way throughout a workbook.

Time To
✔ Save

1. Press [Ctrl][Home] to select cell A1, then click the Bold button **B** on the Formatting toolbar
   The title "Advertising Expenses" appears in bold.

2. Select the range A3:J3, then click the Underline button **U** on the Formatting toolbar
   Excel underlines the column headings in the selected range.

3. Click cell A3, click the Italics button **I** on the Formatting toolbar, then click **B**
   The word "Type" appears in boldface, italic type. Notice that the Bold, Italics, and Underline buttons on the Formatting toolbar are indented. You decide you don't like the italic formatting. You remove it by clicking **I** again.

4. Click **I**
   Excel removes italics from cell A3.

5. Add bold formatting to the rest of the labels in the range B3:J3
   You want to center the title over the data.

6. Select the range A1:F1, then click the Merge and Center button ⊞ on the Formatting toolbar
   The title Advertising Expenses is centered across six columns. Now you center the column headings in their cells.

7. Select the range A3:J3 then click the Center button ≡ on the Formatting toolbar
   You are satisfied with the formatting in the worksheet.
   Compare your screen to Figure C-8.

TABLE C-2: Attribute and Alignment buttons on the Formatting toolbar

icon	description	icon	description
B	Adds boldface	≣	Aligns left
I	Italicizes	≡	Aligns center
U	Underlines	≣	Aligns right
⸺	Adds lines or borders	⊞	Centers across columns, and combines two or more selected adjacent cells into one cell.

▶ EX C-6 **FORMATTING A WORKSHEET**

Quickly accessible summaries of key terms, toolbar buttons, or keyboard alternatives connected with the lesson material. Students can refer easily to this information when working on their own projects at a later time.

Hints as well as trouble-shooting advice right where you need it – next to the step itself.

Clear step-by-step directions, with what students are to type in red, explain how to complete the specific task.

Every lesson features large, full-color representations of what the screen should look like as students complete the numbered steps.

The innovative design draws the students' eyes to important areas of the screens.

Brightly colored tabs above the program name indicate which section of the book you are in. Useful for finding your place within the book and for referencing information from the index.

Other Features

The two-page lesson format featured in this book provides the new user with a powerful learning experience. Additionally, this book contains the following features:

▶ **Real-World Case**
The case study used throughout the textbook, a fictitious company called Nomad Ltd, is designed to be "real-world" in nature and introduces the kinds of activities that students will encounter when working with Microsoft Excel 97. With a real-world case, the process of solving problems will be more meaningful to students.

▶ **End of Unit Material**
Each unit concludes with a Concepts Review that tests students' understanding of what they learned in the unit. A Skills Review follows the Concepts Review and provides students with additional hands-on practice of the skills they learned in the unit. The Skills Review is followed by Independent Challenges, which pose case problems for students to solve. At least one Independent Challenge in each unit asks students to use the World Wide Web to solve the problem as indicated by a WebWork icon. The Visual Workshops that follow the Independent Challenges help students to develop critical thinking skills. Students are shown completed documents and are asked to recreate them from scratch.

FIGURE C-8: Worksheet with formatting attributes applied

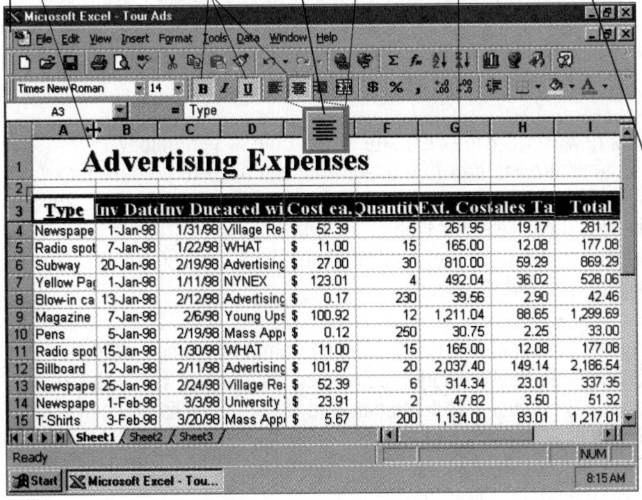

Title centered across columns

Buttons indented

Center button

Column headings centered, bold, and underlined

Excel 97

Using AutoFormat

Excel provides 16 preset formats called AutoFormats, which allow instant formatting of large amounts of data. AutoFormats are designed for worksheets with labels in the left column and top rows and totals in the bottom row or right column. To use AutoFormatting, select the data to be formatted—or place your mouse pointer anywhere within the range to be selected—click Format on the menu bar, click AutoFormat, then select a format from the Table Format list box, as shown in Figure C-9.

FIGURE C-9: AutoFormat dialog box

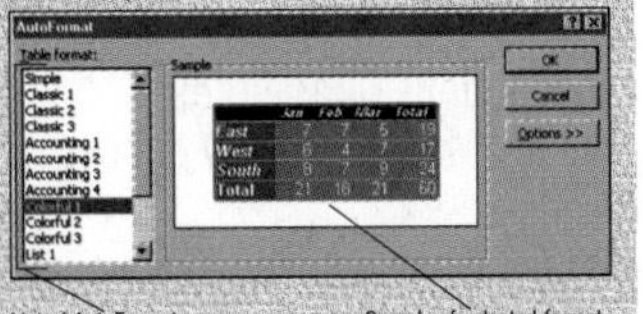

List of AutoFormats

Sample of selected format

FORMATTING A WORKSHEET   EX C-7

Clues to Use Boxes provide concise information that either expands on the major lesson skill or describes an independent task that in some way relates to the major lesson skill.

The page numbers are designed like a road map. EX indicates the Excel section, C indicates the Excel Unit C, and 7 indicates the page within the unit. This map allows for the greatest flexibility in content — each unit stands completely on its own.

Instructor's Resource Kit

The Instructor's Resource Kit is Course Technology's way of putting the resources and information needed to teach and learn effectively into your hands. With an integrated array of teaching and learning tools that offer you and your students a broad range of instructional options, we believe this kit represents the highest quality and most cutting edge resources available to instructors today. Many of these resources are available online at www.course.com. The resources available with this book are:

CourseHelp 97 CourseHelp 97 is a student reinforcement tool offering online annotated tutorials that are accessible directly from the Start menu in Windows 95. These on-screen "slide shows" help students understand the most difficult concepts in a specific program. Students are encouraged to view a CourseHelp 97 slide show before completing that lesson. This text includes the following CourseHelp 97 slide shows:
- Moving and Copying Text
- Relative versus Absolute Cell Referencing
- Choosing a Chart Type
- Using Macros

Adopters of this text are granted the right to post the CourseHelp 97 files on any standalone computer or network.

Course Test Manager Designed by Course Technology, this cutting edge Windows-based testing software helps instructors design and administer tests and pre-tests. This full-featured program also has an online testing component that allows students to take tests at the computer and have their exams automatically graded.

Course Faculty Online Companion This new World Wide Web site offers Course Technology customers a password-protected Faculty Lounge where you can find everything you need to prepare for class. These periodically updated items include lesson plans, graphic files for the figures in the text, additional problems, updates and revisions to the text, links to other Web sites, and access to Student Disk files. This new site is an ongoing project and will continue to evolve throughout the semester. Contact your Customer Service Representative for the site address and password.

Course Student Online Companion This book features its own Online Companion where students can go to access Web sites that will help them complete the WebWork Independent Challenges. This page also contains links to other Course Technology student pages where students can find task references for each of the Microsoft Office 97 programs, a graphical glossary of terms found in the text, an archive of meaningful templates, software, hot tips, and Web links to other sites that contain pertinent information. These new sites are also ongoing projects and will continue to evolve throughout the semester.

Student Files To use this book students must have the Student Files. See the inside front or inside back cover for more information on the Student Files. Adopters of this text are granted the right to post the Student Files on any stand-alone computer or network.

Instructor's Manual This is quality assurance tested and includes:
- Solutions to all lessons and end-of-unit material
- Unit notes with teaching tips from the author
- Extra Independent Challenges
- Transparency Masters of key concepts
- Student Files
- CourseHelp 97

The Illustrated Family of Products

This book that you are holding fits in the Illustrated Series – one series of three in the Illustrated family of products. The other two series are the Illustrated Projects Series and the Illustrated Interactive Series. The Illustrated Projects Series is a supplemental series designed to reinforce the skills learned in any skills-based book through the creation of meaningful and engaging projects. The Illustrated Interactive Series is a line of computer-based training multimedia products that offer the novice user a quick and interactive learning experience. All three series are committed to providing you with the most visual and enriching instructional materials.

Brief Contents

Contents

Excel 97

Contents

Formatting a Worksheet

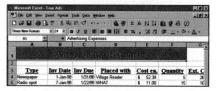

Working with Charts   EX D-1

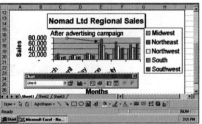

Contents

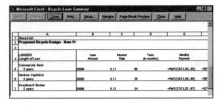

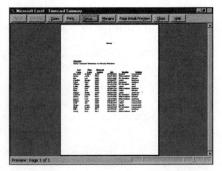

Automating Worksheet Tasks   EX G-1

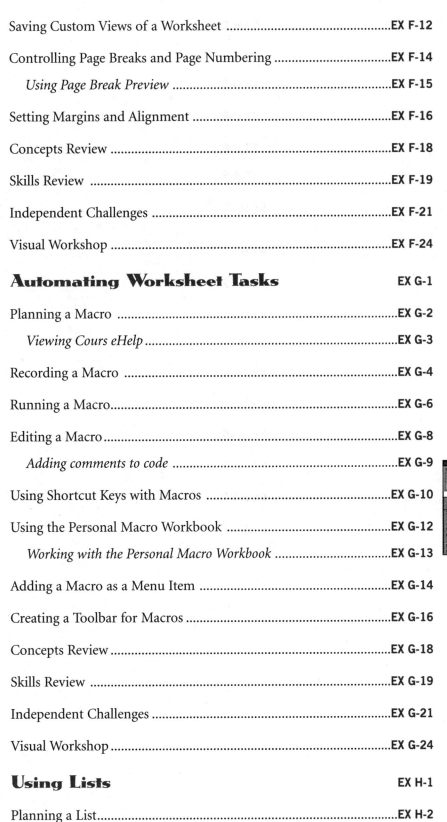

Using Lists   EX H-1

Contents

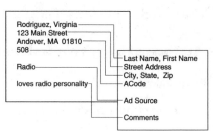

Getting
Started with Excel 97

Objectives

- ► **Define spreadsheet software**
- ► **Start Excel 97**
- ► **View the Excel window**
- ► **Open and save an existing workbook**
- ► **Enter labels and values**
- ► **Preview and print a worksheet**
- ► **Get Help**
- ► **Close a workbook and exit Excel**

In this unit, you will learn how to start Excel and recognize and use different elements of the Excel window and menus. You will also learn how to open existing files, enter data in a worksheet, and use the extensive online Help system. ◢━ Evan Brillstein works in the Accounting Department at Nomad Ltd, an outdoor sporting gear and adventure travel company. Evan will use Excel to complete a worksheet that summarizes budget information and create a workbook to track tour sales.

Defining Spreadsheet Software

Excel is an electronic spreadsheet that runs on Windows computers. An **electronic spreadsheet** uses a computer to perform numeric calculations rapidly and accurately. See Table A-1 for common ways spreadsheets are used in business. An electronic spreadsheet is also referred to as a **worksheet**, which is the document that you produce when you use Excel. A worksheet created with Excel allows Evan to work quickly and efficiently, and to update the results accurately and easily. He will be able to produce more professional-looking documents with Excel. Figure A-1 shows a budget worksheet that Evan and his manager created using pencil and paper. Figure A-2 shows the same worksheet that they can create using Excel.

Details

Excel is better than the paper system for the following reasons:

Enter data quickly and accurately

With Excel, Evan can enter information faster and more accurately than he could using the pencil-and-paper method. For example, in the Nomad Ltd. Budget, Evan can use Excel to calculate Total Expenses and Net Income for each quarter by simply supplying the data and formulas, and Excel calculates the rest.

Recalculate easily

Fixing errors using Excel is easy, and any results based on a changed entry are recalculated automatically. If Evan receives updated Expense figures for Qtr 4, he can simply enter the new numbers and Excel will recalculate the spreadsheet.

Perform what-if analysis

One of the most powerful decision-making features of Excel is the ability to change data and then quickly recalculate changed results. Anytime you use a worksheet to answer the question "what if," you are performing a what-if analysis. For instance, if the advertising budget for May were increased to $3,000, Evan could enter the new figure into the spreadsheet and immediately find out the impact on the overall budget.

Change the appearance of information

Excel provides powerful features for enhancing a spreadsheet so that information is visually appealing and easy to understand. Evan can use boldface type and shading to add emphasis to key data in the worksheet.

Create charts

Excel makes it easy to create charts based on information in a worksheet. With Excel, charts are automatically updated as data changes. The worksheet in Figure A-2 includes a pie chart that graphically shows the distribution of Nomad Ltd. expenses for the first quarter.

Share information with other users

Because everyone at Nomad is now using Microsoft Office, it's easy for Evan to share information with his colleagues. If Evan wants to use the data from someone else's worksheet, he accesses their files through the network or by disk. For example, Evan can complete the budget for Nomad Ltd. that his manager started creating in Excel.

Create new worksheets from existing ones quickly

It's easy for Evan to take an existing Excel worksheet and quickly modify it to create a new one. When Evan is ready to create next year's budget, he can use this budget as a starting point.

FIGURE A-1: Traditional paper worksheet

	Qtr 1	Qtr 2	Qtr 3	Qtr 4	Total
Nomad Ltd					
Net Sales	48,000	76,000	64,000	80,000	268,000
Expenses:					
Salary	8,000	8,000	8,000	8,000	32,000
Interest	4,800	5,600	6,400	7,200	24,000
Rent	2,400	2,400	2,400	2,400	9,600
Ads	3,600	8,000	16,000	20,000	47,600
COG	16,000	16,800	20,000	20,400	73,200
Total Exp	34,800	40,800	52,800	58,000	186,400
Net Income	13,200	35,200	11,200	22,000	81,600

FIGURE A-2: Excel worksheet

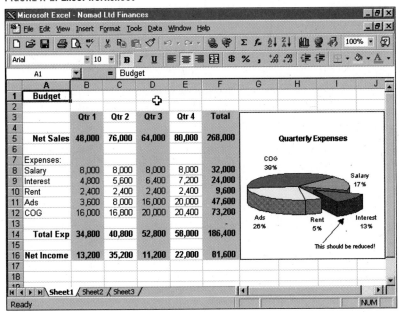

TABLE A-1: Common business spreadsheet uses

use	solution
Maintenance of values	Calculation of figures
Visual representation of values	Chart based on worksheet figures
Create consecutively numbered pages using multiple workbook sheets	Report containing workbook sheets
Organize data	Sort data in ascending or descending order
Analyze data	PivotTable or AutoFilter to create data summaries and short-lists
Create what-if data situations	Scenarios containing data outcomes using variable values

Starting Excel 97

To start Excel, you use the Start Button on the taskbar. Click Programs, then click the Microsoft Excel program icon. A slightly different procedure might be required for computers on a network and those that use utility programs to enhance Windows 95. If you need assistance, ask your instructor or technical support person for help. ✎ Evan's manager has started creating the Nomad Ltd budget and has asked Evan to finish it. He begins by starting Excel now.

1. Point to the **Start button** 🏁Start on the taskbar

The Start button is on the left side of the taskbar and is used to start, or launch, programs on your computer.

2. Click 🏁Start

Microsoft Excel is located in the Programs group—located at the top of the Start menu, as shown in Figure A-3.

Trouble?

If you don't see the Microsoft Excel icon, look for a program group called Microsoft Office.

3. Point to **Programs** on the Start menu

All the programs, or applications, found on your computer can be found in this area of the Start menu.

You can see the Microsoft Excel icon and other Microsoft programs, as shown in Figure A-4. Your desktop might look different depending on the programs installed on your computer.

Trouble?

If the Office Assistant appears on your screen, simply choose to start Excel.

4. Click the **Microsoft Excel program icon** on the Program menu

Excel opens and a blank worksheet appears. In the next lesson, you will familiarize yourself with the elements of the Excel worksheet window.

FIGURE A-3: **Start menu**

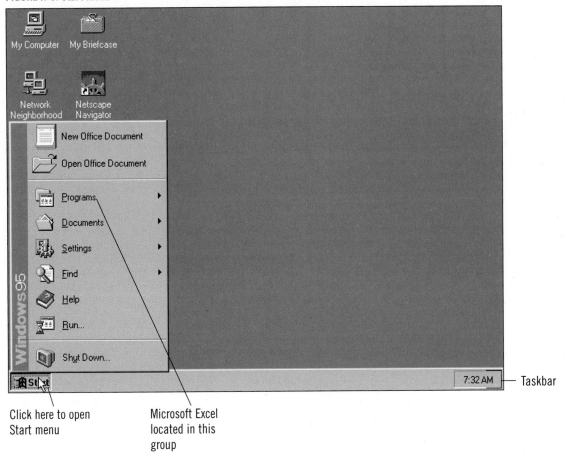

Click here to open
Start menu

Microsoft Excel
located in this
group

Taskbar

FIGURE A-4: **Programs available on your computer**

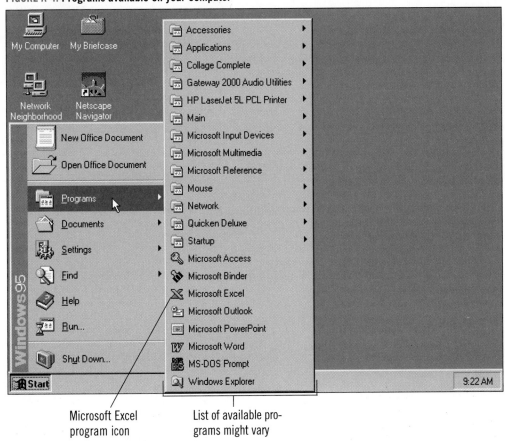

Microsoft Excel
program icon

List of available pro-
grams might vary

Excel 97

Viewing the Excel Window

When you start Excel, the computer displays the **worksheet window**, the area where you enter data, and the window elements that enable you to create and work with worksheets. Evan needs to familiarize himself with the Excel worksheet window and its elements before he starts working with the budget worksheet. Compare the descriptions below to Figure A-5.

Details

Trouble?

If your worksheet does not fill the screen as shown in Figure A-5, click the Maximize button in the worksheet window.

 The **worksheet window** contains a grid of columns and rows. Columns are labeled alphabetically (A, B, C, etc.) and rows are labeled numerically (1, 2, 3, etc.). The worksheet window displays only a tiny fraction of the whole worksheet, which has a total of 256 columns and 65,533 rows. The intersection of a column and a row is a **cell**. Cells can contain text, numbers, formulas, or a combination of all three. Every cell has its own unique location or **cell address**, which is identified by the coordinates of the intersecting column and row. For example, the cell address of the cell in the upper-left corner of a worksheet is A1.

 The **cell pointer** is a dark rectangle that highlights the cell you are working in, or the **active cell**. In Figure A-5, the cell pointer is located at A1, so A1 is the active cell. To make another cell active, click any other cell or press the arrow keys on your keyboard to move the cell pointer to another cell in the worksheet.

 The **title bar** displays the program name (Microsoft Excel) and the filename of the open worksheet (in this case, Book1). The title bar also contains a control menu box, a Close button, and resizing buttons.

 The **menu bar** contains menus from which you choose Excel commands. As with all Windows programs, you can choose a menu command by clicking it with the mouse or by pressing [Alt] plus the underlined letter in the menu name, referred to as the command's **shortcut key**.

 The **name box** displays the active cell address. In Figure A-5, "A1" appears in the name box, indicating that A1 is the active cell.

 The **formula bar** allows you to enter or edit data in the worksheet.

 The **toolbars** contain buttons for the most frequently used Excel commands. The **Standard** toolbar is located just below the menu bar and contains buttons corresponding to the most frequently used Excel features. The **Formatting** toolbar contains buttons for the most common commands used for improving the worksheet's appearance. To choose a button, simply click it with the left mouse button. The face of any button has a graphic representation of its function; for instance, the Printing button has a printer on its face.

 Sheet tabs below the worksheet grid enable you to keep your work in collections called **workbooks**. Each workbook contains 3 worksheets by default and can contain a maximum of 255 sheets. Sheet tabs can be given meaningful names. **Sheet tab scrolling buttons** help you move from one sheet to another.

The **status bar** is located at the bottom of the Excel window. The left side of the status bar provides a brief description of the active command or task in progress. The right side of the status bar shows the status of important keys, such as the Caps Lock key and the Num Lock key.

FIGURE A-5: **Excel worksheet window elements**

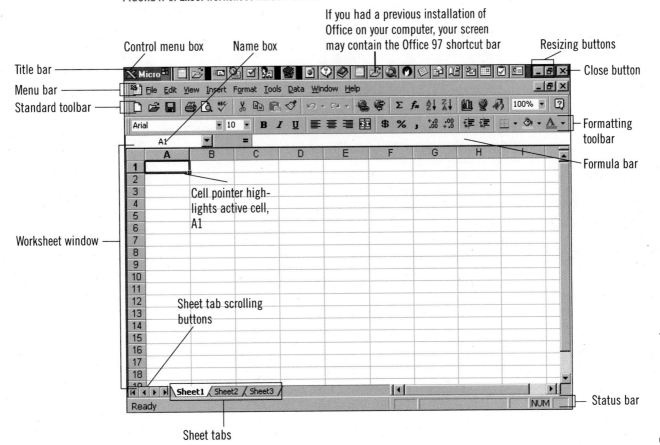

Control menu box   Name box   If you had a previous installation of Office on your computer, your screen may contain the Office 97 shortcut bar   Resizing buttons

Title bar

Menu bar

Standard toolbar

Close button

Formatting toolbar

Formula bar

Worksheet window

Cell pointer highlights active cell, A1

Sheet tab scrolling buttons

Sheet1   Sheet2   Sheet3

Ready   NUM

Status bar

Sheet tabs

Excel 97

Opening and Saving an Existing Workbook

Sometimes it's more efficient to create a new worksheet by modifying one that already exists. This saves you from having to retype information. Throughout this book, you will be instructed to open a file from your Student Disk, use the Save As command to create a copy of the file with a new name, and then modify the new file by following the lesson steps. Saving the files with new names keeps your original Student Disk files intact in case you have to start the lesson over again or you wish to repeat an exercise.  Evan's manager has asked Evan to enter information into the Nomad Ltd budget. Follow along as Evan opens the Budget workbook, then uses the Save As command to create a copy with a new name.

Steps

Trouble?

If necessary, you can download your student files from our Web Site at http:\\course.com.

1. Insert your Student Disk in the appropriate disk drive

2. Click the Open button 🖼 on the Standard toolbar
The Open dialog box opens. See Figure A-6.

3. Click the Look in list arrow
A list of the available drives appears. Locate the drive that contains your Student Disk.

4. Click the drive that contains your Student Disk
A list of the files on your Student Disk appears in the Look in list box, with the default filename placeholder in the File name text box already selected.

5. In the File name list box click XL A-1, then click Open
The file XL A-1 opens. You could also double-click the filename in the File name list box to open the file. To create and save a copy of this file with a new name, you use the Save As command.

6. Click File on the menu bar, then click Save As
The Save As dialog box opens.

QuickTip

You can also click 💾 on the Standard Toolbar or use the shortcut key [Ctrl][S] to save.

7. Make sure the Save in list box displays the drive containing your Student Disk
You should save all your files to your Student Disk, unless instructed otherwise.

8. In the File name text box, double-click the current file name to select it (if necessary), then type Nomad Budget as shown in Figure A-7.

QuickTip

Use the Save As command to create a new workbook from one that already exists; use the Save command to store any changes on your disk made to an existing file since the last time the file was saved.

9. Click Save to save the file and close the Save As dialog box, then click OK to close the Summary Info dialog box if necessary
The file XL A-1 closes, and a duplicate file named Nomad Budget opens, as shown in Figure A-8. To save the workbook in the future, you can click File on the menu bar, then click Save, or click the Save button on the Standard toolbar.

FIGURE A-6: Open dialog box

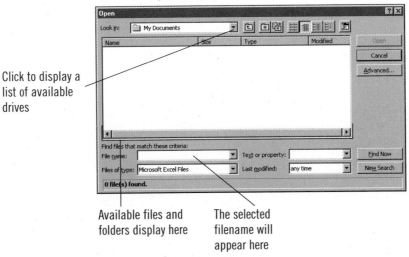

Click to display a
list of available
drives

Available files and
folders display here

The selected
filename will
appear here

FIGURE A-7: Save As dialog box

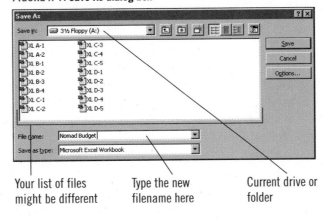

Your list of files
might be different

Type the new
filename here

Current drive or
folder

FIGURE A-8: Nomad Budget workbook

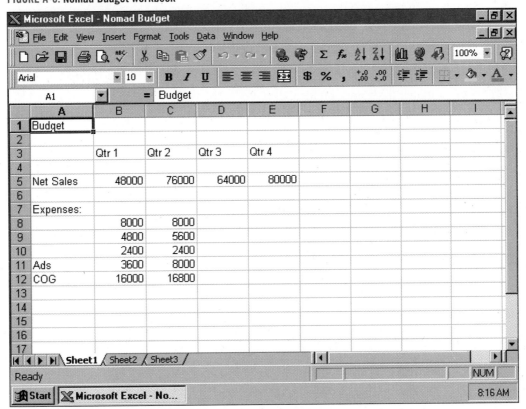

Entering Labels and Values

Labels are used to identify the data in the rows and columns of a worksheet. They are also used to make your worksheet readable and understandable. For these reasons, you should enter all labels in your worksheet first. Labels can contain text and numerical information not used in calculations, such as dates, times, or addresses. Labels are left-aligned by default. Values, which include numbers, formulas, and functions, are used in calculations. Excel recognizes an entry as a value when it is a number or begins with one of these symbols: +, -, =, @, #, or $. All values are right-aligned by default. When a cell contains both text and numbers, Excel recognizes the entry as a label. 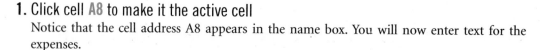 Evan needs to enter labels identifying expense categories, and the values for Qtr 3 and Qtr 4 into the Nomad budget worksheet.

1. Click cell A8 to make it the active cell
Notice that the cell address A8 appears in the name box. You will now enter text for the expenses.

Trouble?

If you notice a mistake in a cell entry after it has been confirmed, double-click the cell and use [Backspace] or [Delete] to make your corrections, then press [Enter].

2. Type Salary, as shown in Figure A-9, then click the Enter button ☑ on the formula bar
You must click ☑ to confirm your entry. You can also confirm a cell entry by pressing [Enter], pressing [Tab], or by pressing one of the arrow keys on your keyboard. If a label does not fit in a cell, Excel displays the remaining characters in the next cell to the right as long as it is empty. Otherwise, the label is truncated, or cut off. The contents of A8, the active cell, display in the formula bar.

3. Click cell A9, type Interest, then press [Enter] to complete the entry and move the cell pointer to cell A10; type Rent in cell A10, then press [Enter]
Now you enter the remaining expense values.

4. Drag the mouse over cells D8 through E12
Two or more selected cells is called a range. Since these entries cover multiple columns and rows, you can pre-select the range to make the data entry easier.

QuickTip

To enter a number, such as the year 1997, as a label so it will not be included in a calculation, type an apostrophe (') before the number.

5. Type 8000, then press [Enter]; type 6400 in cell D9, then press [Enter]; type 2400 in cell D10, then press [Enter]; type 16000 in cell D11, then press [Enter]; type 20000 in cell D12, then press [Enter]
You have entered all the values in the Qtr 3 column. The cell pointer is now in cell E8. Finish entering the expenses in column E.

6. Type the remaining values for cells E8 through E12 using Figure A-10 as a guide

7. Click the Save button 🖫 on the Standard toolbar
It is a good idea to save your work often. A good rule of thumb is to save every 15 minutes or so as you modify your worksheet, especially before making significant changes to the worksheet, or before printing.

FIGURE A-9: Worksheet with initial label entered

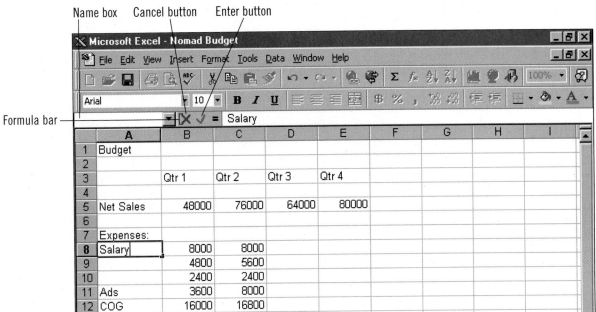

FIGURE A-10: Worksheet with labels and values entered

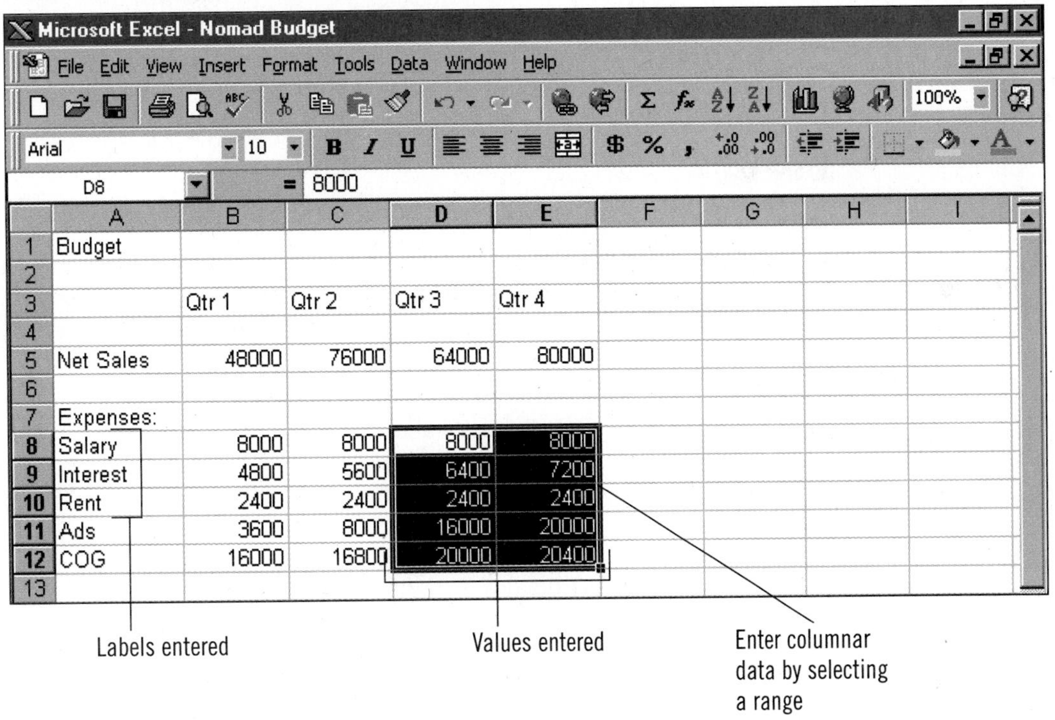

Labels entered   Values entered   Enter columnar data by selecting a range

CLUES TO USE

Navigating the worksheet

With over a billion cells available to you, it is important to know how to move around, or navigate, the worksheet. You can use the pointer-movement keys ([↑], [↓], [←], [→]) to move a cell or two at a time, or the [Page Up] or [Page Down] to move a screenful at a time. You can also simply use your mouse pointer to click the desired cell. If the desired cell is not visible in the worksheet window, you can use the scroll bars, or the Go To command to move the location into view. To return to the top of the worksheet, cell A1, press [Ctrl][Home].

Previewing and Printing a Worksheet

When a worksheet is completed, you print it to have a paper copy to reference, file, or send to others. You can also print a worksheet that is not complete to review it or work on when you are not at a computer. Before you print a worksheet, you should first save it, as you did at the end of the previous lesson. That way, if anything happens to the file as it is being sent to the printer, you will have a clean copy saved to your disk. Then you should preview it to make sure that it will fit on the page the way you want. When you preview a worksheet, you see a copy of the worksheet exactly as it will appear on paper. Table A-2 provides printing tips. Evan is finished entering the labels and values into the Nomad Ltd budget as his manager asked him to. Before he submits it to her for review, he previews it and then prints a copy.

Steps

1. Make sure the printer is on and contains paper

If a file is sent to print and the printer is off, an error message appears. You preview the worksheet to check its overall appearance.

2. Click the Print Preview button on the Standard toolbar

You could also click File on the menu bar, then click Print Preview. A miniature version of the worksheet appears on the screen, as shown in Figure A-11. If there was more than one page, you could click Next and Previous to move between pages. You can also enlarge the image by clicking the Zoom button. After verifying that the preview image is correct, print the worksheet.

3. Click Print

The Print dialog box opens, as shown in Figure A-12.

4. Make sure that the Active Sheet(s) radio button is selected and that 1 appears in the Number of Copies text box

Now you are ready to print the worksheet.

5. Click OK

The Printing dialog box appears while the file is sent to the printer. Note that the dialog box contains a Cancel button that you can use to cancel the print job.

TABLE A-2: Worksheet printing tips

before you print	recommendation
Check the printer	Make sure that the printer is turned on and online, that it has paper, and that there are no error messages or warning signals
Preview the worksheet	Check the formatted image for page breaks, page setup (vertical or horizontal), and overall appearance of the worksheet
Check the printer selection	Use the Printer setup command in the Print dialog box to verify that the correct printer is selected

FIGURE A-11: **Print Preview screen**

Move to another page | Enlarge the screen image | Print the worksheet | Change print options | Return to worksheet

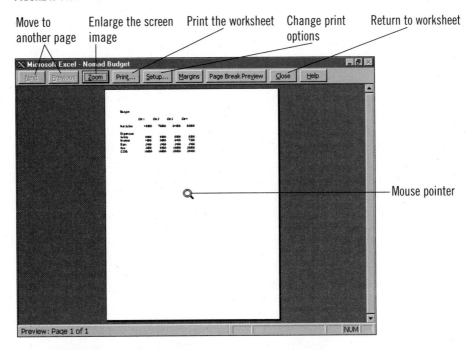

Mouse pointer

FIGURE A-12: **Print dialog box**

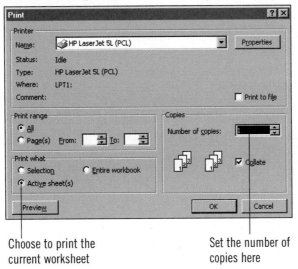

Choose to print the current worksheet

Set the number of copies here

Using Zoom in Print Preview

When you are in the Print Preview window, you can make the image of the page larger by clicking the Zoom button. You can also position the mouse pointer over a specific part of the worksheet page, then click to view that section of the page. While the image is zoomed in, use the scroll bars to view different sections of the page. See Figure A-13.

FIGURE A-13: **Enlarging the view using Zoom**

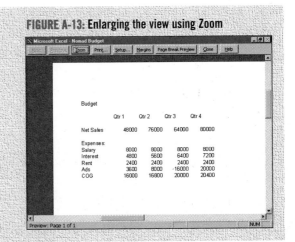

Excel 97

Getting Help

Excel features an extensive online Help system that gives you immediate access to definitions, explanations, and useful tips. The Office Assistant provides this information using a question and answer format. As you are working, the Office Assistant provides tips—indicated by a light bulb you can click—in response to your own working habits. Help appears in a separate balloon-shaped dialog box that you can resize and refer to as you work. You can press the F1 key at any time to get immediate help. ▶ Evan knows the manager will want to know the grand total of the expenses in the budget, and he thinks Excel can perform this type of calculation. He decides to use the animated Office Assistant to learn how to see the sum of a range using the AutoCalculate feature, located in the Status bar.

1. **Click the Office Assistant button 🔁 on the Standard toolbar**
   The Office Assistant helps you find information using a question and answer format.

2. **Once the Office Assistant is displayed, click its window to activate the query box**
   You want information on calculating the sum of a range.

3. **Type How can I calculate a range?**
   See Figure A-15. Once you type a question, the Office Assistant can search for relevant topics from the help files in Excel, from which you can choose.

4. **Click Search**
   The Office Assistant displays several topics related to making quick calculations. See Figure A-16.

QuickTip

Information in Help can be printed by clicking the Options button, then clicking Print Topic.

5. **Click Quick calculations on a worksheet**
   The Quick calculations on a worksheet help window opens.

6. **Click View the total for a selected range, press [Esc] once you've read the text, then click the Close button on the dialog box title bar**
   The Help window closes and you return to your worksheet.

QuickTip

You can close the Office Assistant at any time by clicking its Close button.

7. **Click the Close button in the Office Assistant window**

Changing the Office Assistant

The default Office Assistant is Clippit, but there are eight others from which you can choose. To change the appearance of the Office Assistant, right-click the Office Assistant window, then click Choose Assistant. Click the Gallery tab, click the Back and Next buttons until you find an Assistant you want to use, then click OK. (You may need your Microsoft Office 97 CD-ROM to change Office Assistants.) Each Office Assistant makes its own unique sounds and can be animated by right-clicking its window and clicking Animate! Figure A-16 displays the Office Assistant dialog box.

FIGURE A-14: Office Assistant dialog box

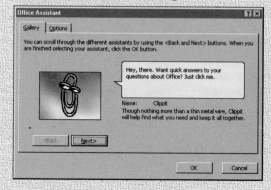

FIGURE A-15: Office Assistant

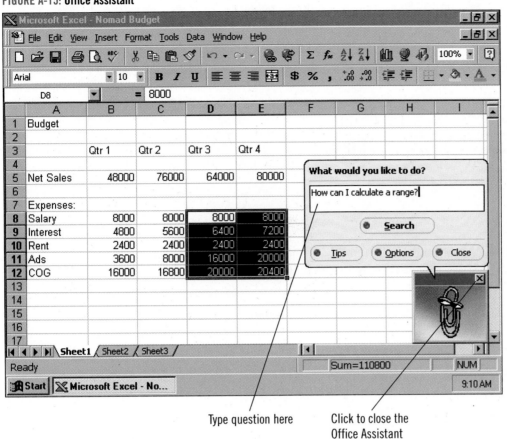

Type question here

Click to close the
Office Assistant

FIGURE A-16: Relevant Help Assistant topics

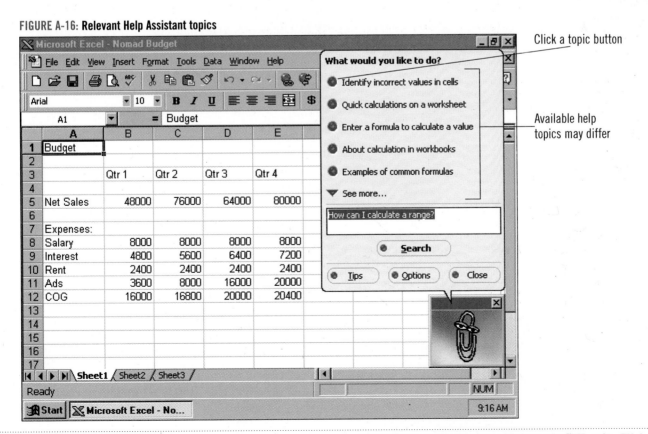

Click a topic button

Available help
topics may differ

Closing a Workbook and Exiting Excel

When you have finished working on a workbook, you need to save the file and close it. Once you have saved a file and are ready to close it, click Close on the File menu. When you have completed all your work in Excel, you need to exit the program. To exit Excel, click Exit on the File menu. ◢ Evan is done adding the information to the Budget worksheet, and he is ready to pass the printout to his manger to review, so he closes the workbook and then exits Excel.

Steps

1. **Click File on the menu bar**
   The File menu opens as displayed in Figure A-17.

2. **Click Close**
   You could also click the workbook Close button instead of choosing File, then Close. Excel closes the workbook and asks you to save your changes; be sure that you do. A blank worksheet window appears.

3. **Click File, then click Exit**
   You could also click the program Close button to exit the program. Excel closes and computer memory is freed up for other computing tasks.

Trouble?

To exit Excel and close several files at once, choose Exit from the File menu. Excel will prompt you to save changes to each workbook before exiting.

FIGURE A-17: **Closing a workbook using the File menu**

Program control
menu box

Workbook control
menu box

Close command

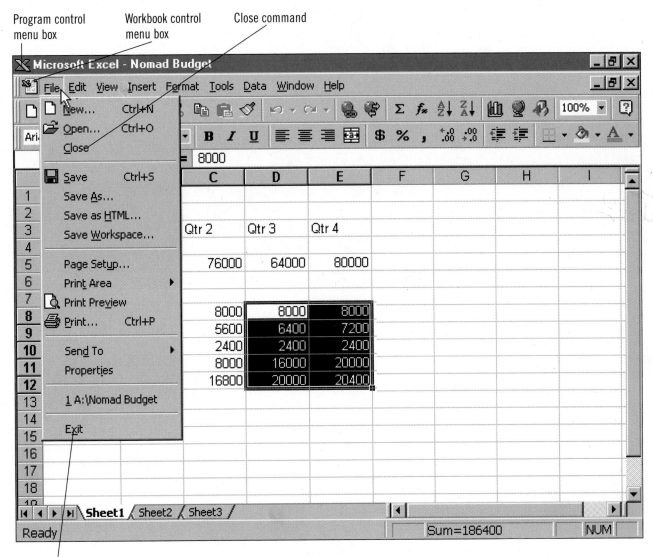

Exit command

Practice

► Concepts Review

Label each of the elements of the Excel worksheet window shown in Figure A-18.

FIGURE A-18

Title bar 1
Menu bar 2
toolbars 3
Name box 4

Sheet tabs 5

6
Status bar

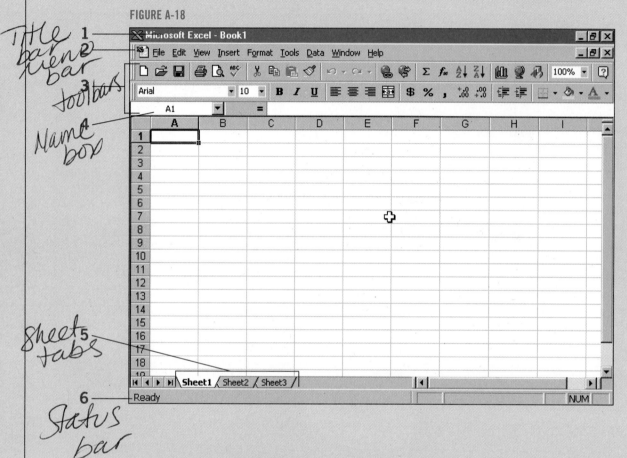

Match each of the terms with the statement that describes its function.

7. Cell pointer E
8. Button C
9. Worksheet window A
10. Name box F
11. Cell B
12. Workbook D

a. Area that contains a grid of columns and rows
b. The intersection of a column and row
c. Graphic symbol that depicts a task or function
d. Collection of worksheets
e. Rectangle that indicates the cell you are currently working in
f. Displays the active cell address

Select the best answer from the list of choices.

13. An electronic spreadsheet can perform all of the following tasks, *except*
   a. Display information visually
   b. Calculate data accurately
   c. Plan worksheet objectives
   d. Recalculate updated information

14. Each of the following is true about labels, *except*
   a. They are left-aligned, by default
   b. They are not used in calculations
   c. They are right-aligned, by default
   d. They can include numerical information

15. Each of the following is true about values, *except*
   a. They can include labels
   b. They are right-aligned, by default
   c. They are used in calculations
   d. They can include formulas

16. What symbol is typed before a number to make the number a label?
   a. "   b. !   c. '   d. ;

17. You can get Excel Help by any of the following ways, *except*
   a. Clicking Help on the menu bar
   b. Pressing [F1]
   c. Clicking the Help button 🔲 on the Standard toolbar
   d. Minimizing the application window

18. Each key(s) can be used to confirm cell entries, *except*
   a. [Enter]   b. [Tab]   c. [Esc]   d. [Shift][Enter]

19. Which button is used to preview a worksheet?
   a. 🔲   b. 🔲   c. 🔲   d. 🔲

20. Which feature is used to enlarge a print preview view?
   a. Magnify   b. Enlarge   c. Amplify   d. Zoom

21. Each of the following is true about the Office Assistant, *except*
   a. It provides tips based on your work habits
   b. It provides help using a question and answer format
   c. You can change the appearance of the Office Assistant
   d. It can complete certain tasks for you

▶ Skills Review

1. Start Excel and identify the elements in the worksheet window.
a. Point to Programs in the Start menu.
b. Click the Microsoft Excel program icon.
c. Try to identify as many elements in the Excel worksheet window as you can without referring to the unit material.

2. Open an existing workbook.
a. Open the workbook XL A-2 by clicking the Open button on the Standard toolbar.
b. Save the workbook as "Country Duds" by clicking File on the menu bar, then clicking Save As.

3. Enter labels and values.
a. Enter labels shown in Figure A-19.
b. Enter values shown in Figure A-19.
c. Save the workbook by clicking the Save button on the Standard toolbar.

FIGURE A-19

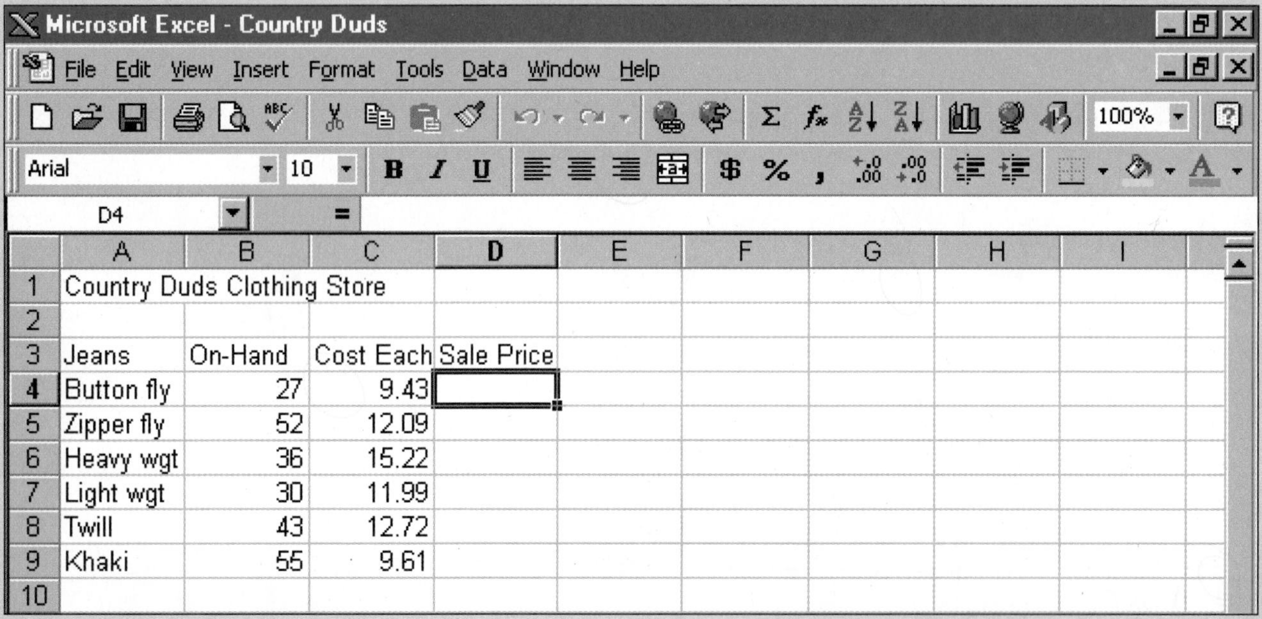

4. Previewing and printing a worksheet.
a. Click the Print Preview button on the Standard toolbar.
b. Use the Zoom button to see more of your worksheet.
c. Print one copy of the worksheet.
d. Hand in your printout.

5. Get Help.
a. Click the Office Assistant button on the Standard toolbar if the Assistant is not displayed.
b. Ask the Office Assistant for information about changing the Office Assistant character in Excel.
c. Print information offered by the Office Assistant using the Print topic command on the Options menu.
d. Close the Help window.
e. Hand in your printout.

6. **Close the workbook and exit Excel.**
   a. Click File on the menu bar, then click Close.
   b. If asked if you want to save the worksheet, click No.
   c. If necessary, close any other worksheets you might have opened.
   d. Click File on the menu bar, then click Exit.

► Independent Challenges

1. Excel's online Help provides definitions, explanations, procedures, and other helpful information. It also provides examples and demonstrations to show you how Excel features work. Topics include elements such as the active cell, status bar, buttons, and dialog boxes, as well as detailed information about Excel commands and options.

   To complete this independent challenge:

   1. Open a new workbook
   2. Click the Office Assistant.
   3. Type a question that will give you information about opening and saving a worksheet. (Hint: you may have to ask the Office Assistant more than one question.)
   4. Print out the information and hand it in.
   5. Return to your workbook when you are finished.

2. Spreadsheet software has many uses that can affect the way work is done. Some examples of how Excel can be used are discussed in the beginning of this unit. Use your own personal or business experiences to come up with five examples of how Excel could be used in a business setting.

To complete this independent challenge:

1. Open a new workbook.
2. Think of five business tasks that you could complete more efficiently by using an Excel worksheet.
3. Sketch a sample of each worksheet. See Figure A-20, a sample payroll worksheet.
4. Submit your sketches.

FIGURE A-20

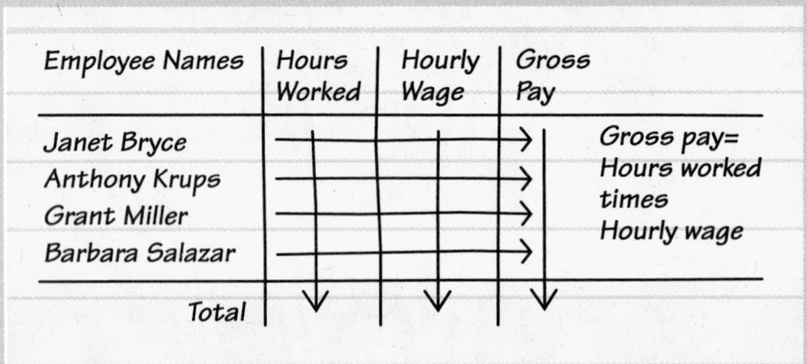

Employee Names	Hours Worked	Hourly Wage	Gross Pay	
Janet Bryce			→	Gross pay=
Anthony Krups			→	Hours worked
Grant Miller			→	times
Barbara Salazar			→	Hourly wage
Total	↓	↓	↓	

3. You are the office manager for Blossoms and Greens, a small greenhouse and garden center. Although the company is just three years old, it is expanding rapidly, and you are continually looking for ways to make your job easier. Last year you began using Excel to manage and maintain data on inventory and sales, which has greatly helped you to track this information accurately and efficiently. However, the job is still overwhelming for just one person. Fortunately, the owner of the company has just approved the hiring of an assistant for you. This person will need to learn how to use Excel. Create a short training document that your new assistant can use as a reference while becoming familiar with Excel.

To complete this independent challenge:

1. Draw a sketch of the Excel worksheet window, and label the key elements, such as toolbars, title bar, formula bar, scroll bars, etc.
2. For each labeled element, write a short description of its use.
3. List the main ways to get Help in Excel. (Hint: use the Office Assistant to learn of all the ways to get help in Excel..)
4. Identify five different ways to use spreadsheets in business.

4. Data on the World Wide Web is current and informative. It is a useful tool that can be used to gather the most up-to-date information which you can use to make smart buying decisions. Imagine that your supervisor has just told you that due to your great work, she has just found money in the budget to buy you a new computer. You can have whatever you want, but she wants you to justify the expense by creating a spreadsheet using data found on the World Wide Web to support your purchase decision.

To complete this independent challenge:

1. Open a new workbook and save it on your Student Disk as "New Computer Data."
2. Decide which features you want your ideal computer to have, and list these features.
3. Log on to the Internet and use your browser to go to the http://www.course.com. From there, click the link Student On Line Companions, then click the Microsoft Office 97 Professional Edition—Illustrated: A First Course page, then click on the Excel link for Unit A.
4. Use any of the following sites to compile your data: IBM [www.ibm.com], Gateway [www.gw2k.com], Dell [www.dell.com], or any other site you can find with related information.
5. Compile data for the components you want.
6. Make sure all components are listed and totaled. Include any tax and shipping costs the manufacturer charges.
7. Indicate on the worksheet your final purchase decision.
8. Save, print, and hand in your work.

▶ Visual Workshop

Create a worksheet similar to Figure A-21 using the skills you learned in this unit. Save the workbook as "Bea's Boutique" on your Student Disk. Preview, then print the worksheet.

FIGURE A-21

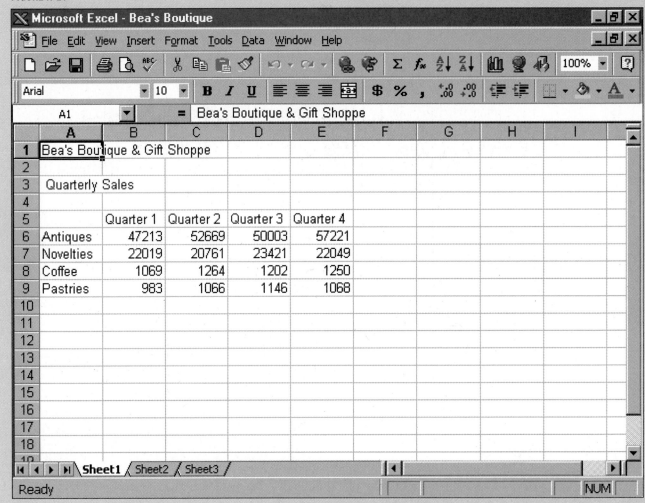

Building
and Editing Worksheets

Objectives

▶ **Plan, design, and create a worksheet**
▶ **Edit cell entries and work with ranges**
▶ **Enter formulas**
▶ **Introduce functions**
▶ **Copy and move cell entries**
▶ **Copy formulas with relative cell references**
▶ **Copy formulas with absolute cell references**
▶ **Name and move a sheet**

You will now plan and build your own worksheets. When you build a worksheet, you enter text, values, and formulas into worksheet cells. Once you create a worksheet, you can save it in a workbook file and then print it. ✐ Evan Brillstein has received a request from the Marketing Department for a forecast of this year's summer tour business, and an estimate of the average tour sales for each type of tour. Marketing hopes that the tour business will increase 20% over last year's figures. Evan needs to create a worksheet that summarizes tour sales for last year and a worksheet that forecasts the summer tour sales for this year.

Planning, Designing, and Creating a Worksheet

Before you start entering data into a worksheet, you need to know the purpose and approximate layout of the worksheet. Evan wants to forecast Nomad's 1998 summer tour sales. The sales goal, already identified by the Marketing Department, is to increase the 1997 summer sales by 20%. Using Figure B-1 and the planning guidelines below, work with Evan as he plans his worksheet.

Details

 Determine the purpose of the worksheet and give it a meaningful title
Evan needs to forecast summer tour sales for 1998. Evan titles the worksheet "1998 Summer Tour Sales Forecast."

 Determine your worksheet's desired results, sometimes called output
Evan needs to determine what the 1998 sales totals will be if sales increase by 20% over the 1997 sales totals, as well as the average number of tours per type.

 Collect all the information, sometimes called input, that will produce the results you want to see
Evan gathers together the sales data for the 1997 summer tour season. The season ran from June through August. The types of tours sold in these months included Bike, Raft, Horse, and Bus.

 Determine the calculations, or formulas, necessary to achieve the desired results
First, Evan needs to total the number of tours sold for each month of the 1997 summer season. Then he needs to add these totals together to determine the grand total of summer tour sales. Finally, the 1997 monthly totals and grand total must be multiplied by 1.2 to calculate a 20% increase for the 1998 summer tour season. He'll use the Paste Function to determine the average number of tours per type.

 Sketch on paper how you want the worksheet to look; that is, identify where the labels and values will go
Evan decides to put tour types in rows and the months in columns. He enters the tour sales data in his sketch and indicates where the monthly sales totals and the grand total should go. Below the totals, he writes out the formula for determining a 20% increase in sales for 1997. He also includes a label for the location of the tour averages. Evan's sketch of his worksheet is shown in Figure B-1.

 Create the worksheet
Evan enters his labels first to establish the structure of his worksheet. He then enters the values, the sales data into his worksheet. These values will be used to calculate the output Evan needs. The worksheet Evan creates is shown in Figure B-2.

1998 Summer Tours Sales Forecast

	June	July	August	Totals	Average
Bike	14	10	6	3 month total	
Raft	7	8	12		
Horse	12	7	6		
Bus	1	2	9		
Totals	June Total	July Total	August Total	Grand Total for 1997	
1998 Sales	Total X 1.2				

FIGURE B-2: **Evan's forecasting worksheet**

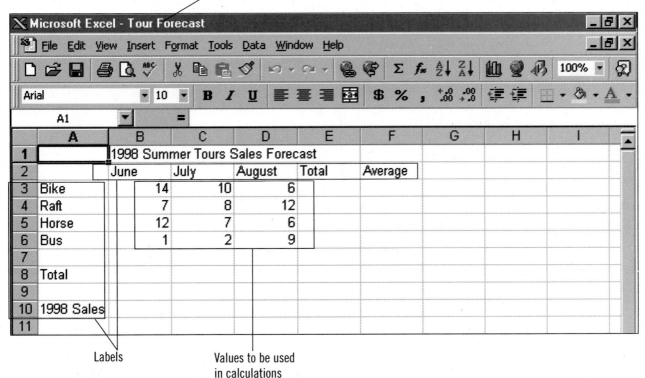

Check title bar for correct title

Labels

Values to be used in calculations

Excel 97

Editing Cell Entries and Working with Ranges

You can change the contents of any cells at any time. To edit the contents of a cell, you first select the cell you want to edit, then click the formula bar, double-click the selected cell, or press [F2]. This puts Excel into Edit mode. To make sure you are in Edit mode, check the **mode indicator** on the far left of the status bar. The mode indicator identifies the current Excel command or operation in progress. After planning and creating his worksheet, Evan notices that he entered the wrong value for the June bus tours and forgot to include the canoe tours. He fixes the bus tours figure, and he decides to add the canoe sales data to the raft sales figures.

Steps 1 2 3 4

1. Start Excel, open the workbook XL B-1 from your Student Disk, then save it as **Tour Forecast**

2. Click cell **B6**
   This cell contains June bus tours, which Evan needs to change to 2.

3. Click anywhere in the formula bar
   Excel goes into Edit mode, and the mode indicator displays "Edit." A blinking vertical line, called the **insertion point**, appears in the formula bar, and if you move the mouse pointer to the formula bar, the pointer changes to I as displayed in Figure B-3.

4. Press [Backspace], type 2, then press [Enter] or click the Enter button ☑ on the formula bar
   Evan now needs to add "/Canoe" to the Raft label.

5. Click cell **A4** then press [F2]
   Excel is in Edit mode again, but this time, the insertion point is in the cell.

6. Type **/Canoe** then press [Enter]
   The label changes to Raft/Canoe.

7. Double-click cell **B4**
   Double-clicking a cell also puts Excel into Edit mode with the insertion point in the cell.

8. Press [Delete], then type 9
   See Figure B-4.

9. Click ☑ to confirm the entry

QuickTip

If you make a mistake, you can either click the Cancel button ☒ on the formula bar before accepting the cell entry, or click the Undo button ↶ on the Standard toolbar if you notice the mistake after you have accepted the cell entry. The Undo button allows you to reverse up to 16 previous actions, one at a time.

FIGURE B-3: Worksheet in Edit mode

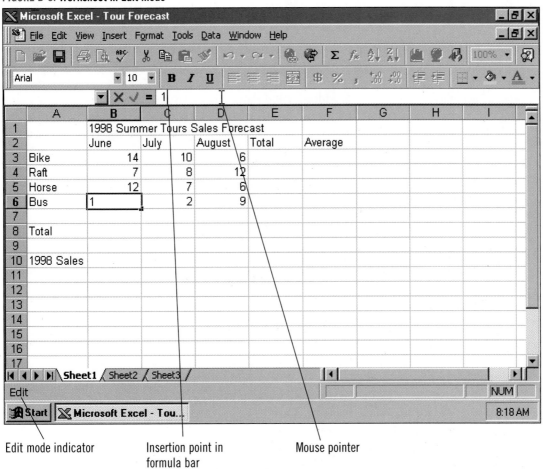

Edit mode indicator

Insertion point in formula bar

Mouse pointer

FIGURE B-4: Edited worksheet

Insertion point in cell

 Using range names in a workbook

Any group of cells (two or more) is called a range. To select a range, click the first cell and drag to the last cell you want included in the range. The range address is defined by noting the first and last cells in the range. Give a meaningful name to a range by selecting cells, clicking the name box, and then typing a name. Range names—meaningful English names

that Evan uses in this worksheet—are usually easier to remember than cell addresses, they can be used in formulas, and they also help you move around the workbook quickly. Click the name box list arrow, then click the name of the range you want to go to. The cell pointer moves immediately to that range.

Entering Formulas

Formulas are used to perform numeric calculations such as adding, multiplying, and averaging. Formulas in an Excel worksheet start with the formula prefix—the equal sign (=). All formulas use one or more **arithmetic operators** to perform calculations. See Table B-1 for a list of Excel operators. Formulas often contain cell addresses and range names. Using a cell address or range name in a formula is called **cell referencing**. Using cell references keeps your worksheet up-to-date and accurate. If you change a value in a cell, any formula containing that cell reference will be automatically recalculated using the new value. In formulas using more than one arithmetic operator, Excel decides which operation to perform first. Evan needs to add the monthly tour totals for June, July, and August, and calculate a 20% increase in sales. He can perform these calculations using formulas.

1. Click cell **B8**
This is the cell where you want to put the calculation that will total the June sales.

2. Type = (the equal sign)
Placing an equal sign at the beginning of an entry tells Excel that a formula is about to be entered rather than a label or a value. The total June sales is equal to the sum of the values in cells B3, B4, B5, and B6.

3. Type **b3+b4+b5+b6**, then click the **Enter button** ☑ on the formula bar
The result of 37 appears in cell B8, and the formula appears in the formula bar. See Figure B-5. Next, you add the number of tours in July and August.

> **Trouble?**
> If the formula instead of the result appears in the cell after you click ☑, make sure you began the formula with = (the equal sign).

4. Click cell **C8**, type =c3+c4+c5+c6, then press [Tab]; in cell D8, type =d3+d4+d5+d6, then press [Enter]
The total tour sales for July, 27, and for August, 33, appear in cells C8 and D8 respectively.

5. Click cell **B10**, type =B8*1.2, then click ☑ on the formula bar
To calculate the 20% increase, you multiply the total by 1.2. This formula calculates the result of multiplying the total monthly tour sales for June, cell B8, by 1.2. The result of 44.4 appears in cell B10.
Now you need to calculate the 20% increase for July and August. You can use the **pointing method**, by which you specify cell references in a formula by selecting the desired cell with your mouse instead of typing its cell reference into the formula.

> **QuickTip**
> It does not matter if you type the column letter in lower case or upper case when entering formulas. Excel is not case-sensitive—B3 and b3 both refer to the same cell.

6. Click cell **C10**, type =, click cell **C8**, type *1.2, then press [Tab]

7. Click cell **D10**, type =, click cell **D8**, type *1.2, then click ☑
Compare your results with Figure B-6.

TABLE B-1: Excel arithmetic operators

operator	purpose	example
+	Performs addition	=A5+A7
–	Performs subtraction	=A5-10
*	Performs multiplication	=A5*A7
/	Performs division	=A5/A7

FIGURE B-5: Worksheet showing formula and result

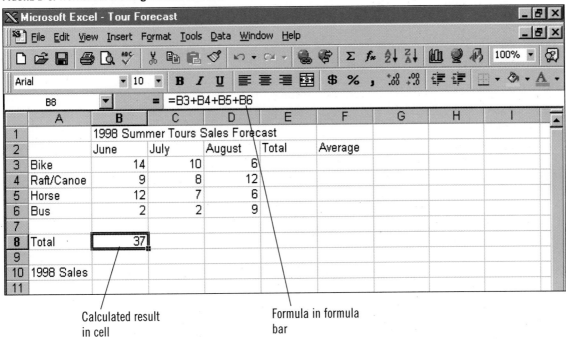

Calculated result
in cell

Formula in formula
bar

FIGURE B-6: Calculated results for 20% increase

Order of precedence in Excel formulas

A formula can include several operations. When you work with formulas that have more than one operator, the order of precedence is very important. If a formula contains two or more operators, such as 4 + .55/4000 * 25, the computer performs the calculations in a particular sequence based on these rules:

Calculated 1st — Calculation of exponents
Calculated 2nd — Multiplication and division, left to right
Calculated 3rd — Addition and subtraction, left to right

In the example 4 + .55/4000 * 25, Excel performs the arithmetic operations by first dividing 4000 into .55, then multiplying the result by 25, then adding 4. You can change the order of calculations by using parentheses. For example, in the formula (4+.55)/4000 * 25, Excel would first add 4 and .55, then divide that amount by 4000, then finally multiply it by 25. Operations inside parentheses are calculated before any other operations.

Introducing Excel Functions

Functions are predefined worksheet formulas that enable you to do complex calculations easily. Like formulas, functions always begin with the formula prefix = (the equal sign). You can enter functions manually, or you can use the Paste Function. Evan uses the SUM function to calculate the grand totals in his worksheet, and the AVERAGE function to calculate the average number of tours per type.

Steps 1 2 3 4

1. **Click cell E3**
   This is the cell where you want to display the total of all bike tours for June, July, and August. You use the AutoSum button to create the totals. AutoSum sets up the SUM function to add the values in the cells above the cell pointer. If there are no values in the cells above the cell pointer, AutoSum adds the values in the cells to the left of the cell pointer—in this case, the values in cells B3, C3, and D3.

2. **Click the AutoSum button** Σ **on the Standard toolbar, then click the Enter button** ✓ **on the formula bar**
   The formula =SUM(B3:D3) appears in the formula bar. The information inside the parentheses is the **argument**, or the information to be used in calculating a result of the function. An argument can be a value, a range of cells, text, or another function.
   The result appears in cell E3. Next, you calculate the total of raft and canoe tours.

3. **Click cell E4, click** Σ **, then click** ✓
   Now you calculate the three-month total of the horse tours.

4. **Click cell E5 then click** Σ
   AutoSum sets up a function to sum the two values in the cells above the active cell, which is not what you intended. You need to change the argument.

5. **Click cell B5, then drag to select the range B5:D5, then click** ✓ **to confirm the entry**
   As you drag, the argument in the SUM function changes to reflect the range being chosen, and a tip box appears telling you the size of the range you are selecting.

6. **Enter the SUM function in cells E6, E8, and E10**
   Make sure you add the values to the left of the active cell, not the values above it. See Figure B-7. Next, you calculate the average number of Bike tours using the Paste Function.

7. **Click cell F3, then click the Paste Function button** ƒ✱ **on the Standard toolbar**
   The Paste Function dialog box opens. See Table B-2 for frequently used functions.
   The function needed to calculate averages—named AVERAGE—is included in the Most Recently Used category.

8. **Click the function name AVERAGE in the Function name list box, click OK, then in the AVERAGE dialog box type B3:D3 in the Number 1 text box, as shown in Figure B-8**

Time To

✔ Save

9. **Click OK, then repeat steps 7, 8 and 9 to calculate the Raft/Canoe (cell F4), Horse (cell F5), and Bus tours (cell F6) averages**
   The Time To checklist in the left margin contains Steps for routine actions. Everytime you see a Time To checklist, perform the actions listed.

FIGURE B-7: Worksheet with SUM functions entered

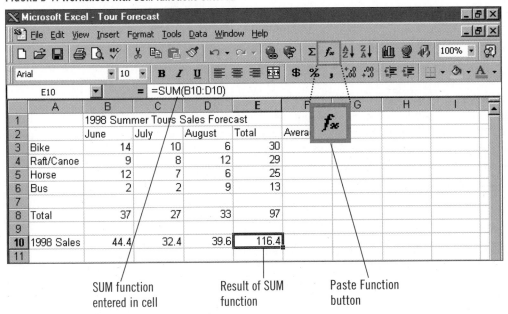

SUM function
entered in cell

Result of SUM
function

Paste Function
button

FIGURE B-8: Using the Paste Function to create a formula

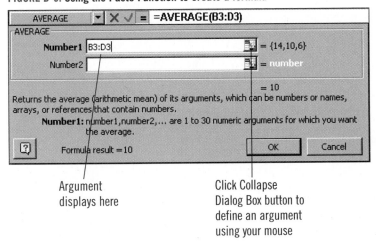

Argument
displays here

Click Collapse
Dialog Box button to
define an argument
using your mouse

TABLE B-2: Frequently Used Functions

function	description
SUM(*argument*)	Calculates the sum of the arguments
AVERAGE(*argument*)	Calculates the average of the arguments
MAX(*argument*)	Displays the largest value among the arguments
MIN(*argument*)	Displays the smallest value among the arguments
COUNT(*argument*)	Calculates the number of values in the arguments

CLUES TO USE

Introducing the Paste Function

The Paste Function button *f* is located to the right of the AutoSum button on the Standard toolbar. To use the Paste Function, click *f*. In the Paste Function dialog box, click the category containing the function you want, then click the desired function. The function appears in the formula bar. Click OK to fill in values or cell addresses for the arguments, then click OK.

Copying and Moving Cell Entries

Using the Cut, Copy, and Paste buttons or Excel's drag-and-drop feature, you can copy or move information from one cell or range in your worksheet to another. You can also cut, copy, and paste data from one worksheet to another. Evan included the 1998 forecast for spring and fall tours sales in his Tour Info workbook. He already entered the spring report in Sheet2 and will finish entering the labels and data for the fall report. Using the Copy and Paste buttons and drag-and-drop, Evan copies information from the spring report to the fall report.

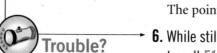 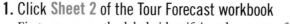

CourseHelp

The camera icon indicates there is a CourseHelp available with this lesson. Click the Start button, point to programs, point to CourseHelp, then click Excel 97 Illustrated. Choose the CourseHelp that corresponds to this lesson.

1. **Click Sheet 2 of the Tour Forecast workbook**
   First, you copy the labels identifying the types of tours from the Spring report to the Fall report.

2. **Select the range A4:A9, then click the Copy button 🗐 on the Standard toolbar**
   The selected range (A4:A9) is copied to the **Clipboard**, a temporary storage file that holds all the selected information you copy or cut. The Cut button ✂ removes the selected information from the worksheet and places it on the Clipboard. To copy the contents of the Clipboard to a new location, you click the new cell and then use the Paste command.

3. **Click cell A13, then click the Paste button 📋 on the Standard toolbar**
   The contents of the Clipboard are copied into the range A13:A18. When pasting the contents of the Clipboard into the worksheet, you need to specify only the first cell of the range where you want the copied selection to go. Next, you decide to use drag-and-drop to copy the Total label.

4. **Click cell E3, then position the pointer on any edge of the cell until the pointer changes to ᐟ**

5. **While the pointer is ᐟ, press and hold down [Ctrl]**
   The pointer changes to ᐟ.

Trouble?

When you drag-and-drop into occupied cells, Excel asks if you want to replace the existing cells. Click OK to replace the contents with the cells you are moving.

6. **While still pressing [Ctrl], press and hold the left mouse button, then drag the cell contents to cell E12**
   As you drag, an outline of the cell moves with the pointer, as shown in Figure B-9, and a tip box appears tracking the current position of the item as you move it. When you release the mouse button, the Total label appears in cell E12. You now decide to move the worksheet title over to the left. To use drag-and-drop to move data to a new cell without copying it, do not press [Ctrl] while dragging.

7. **Click cell C1, then position the mouse on the edge of the cell until it changes to ᐟ, then drag the cell contents to A1**
   You now enter fall sales data into the range B13:D16.

8. **Using the information shown in Figure B-10, enter the sales data for the fall tours into the range B13:D16**
   Compare your worksheet to Figure B-10.

FIGURE B-9: Using drag-and-drop to copy information

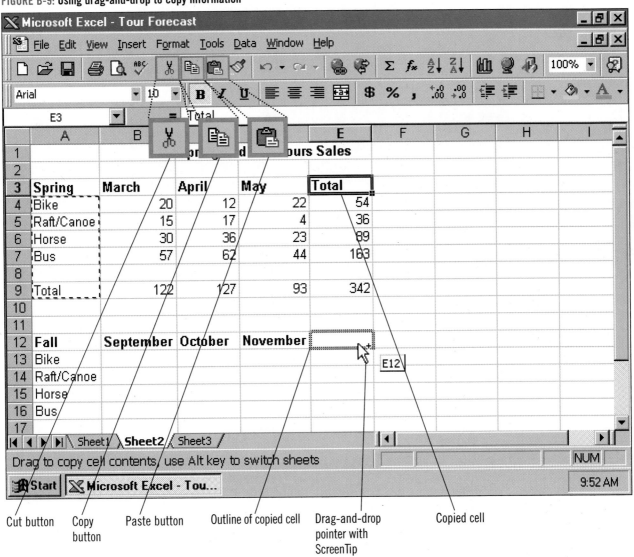

Cut button   Copy   Paste button   Outline of copied cell   Drag-and-drop   Copied cell
             button   pointer with
                                                            ScreenTip

FIGURE B-10: Worksheet with Fall tours data entered

	A	September	October	November	Total			
11								
12	Fall	September	October	November	Total			
13	Bike	17	15	18				
14	Raft/Canoe	21	8	5				
15	Horse	12	21	14				
16	Bus	25	12	18				
17								

Sheet1 \ Sheet2 / Sheet3 /

Ready   Sum=186   NUM

Start   Microsoft Excel - Tou...   9:55 AM

Copying Formulas with Relative Cell References

Copying and moving formulas allows you to reuse formulas you've already created. Copying formulas, rather than retyping them, helps to prevent typing errors. ▬▬▬▬▬ Evan wants to copy from the Spring tours report to the Fall tours report the formulas that total the tours by type and by month. He can use Copy and Paste commands and the Fill right method to copy this information.

CourseHelp

If you have trouble with the concepts in this lesson, be sure to view the CourseHelp entitled Relative versus Absolute Cell Referencing

1. Click cell E4, then click the Copy button 🗐 on the Standard toolbar
The formula for calculating the total number of spring Bike tours is copied to the Clipboard. Notice that the formula in the formula bar appears as =SUM(B4:D4).

2. Click cell E13, then click the Paste button 🗐 on the Standard toolbar
The formula from cell E4 is copied into cell E13, where the new result of 50 appears. Notice in the formula bar that the cell references have changed, so that the range B13:D13 appears in the formula. Formulas in Excel contain **relative cell references**. A relative cell reference tells Excel to copy the formula to a new cell, but to substitute new cell references so that the relationship of the cells to the formula in its new location remains unchanged. In this case, Excel inserted cells D13, C13, and B13, the three cell references immediately to the left of E13.

Notice that the bottom right corner of the active cell contains a small square, called the **fill handle**. Evan uses the fill handle to copy the formula in cell E13 to cells E14, E15, and E16. You can also use the fill handle to copy labels.

QuickTip

You can fill cells with sequential months, days of the week, years, and text plus a number (Quarter 1, Quarter 2, . . .) by dragging the fill handle. As you drag the fill handle, the contents of the last filled cell appears in the name box.

3. Position the pointer over the fill handle until it changes to ＋, then drag the fill handle to select the range E13:E16
See Figure B-11.

4. Release the mouse button
Once you release the mouse button, the fill handle copies the formula from the active cell (E13) and pastes it into each cell of the selected range. Again, because the formula uses relative cell references, cells E14 through E16 correctly display the totals for Raft and Canoe, Horse, and Bus tours

5. Click cell B9, click Edit on the menu bar, then click Copy
The Copy command on the Edit menu has the same effect as clicking the Copy button 🗐 on the Standard toolbar.

6. Click cell B18, click Edit on the menu bar, then click Paste
See Figure B-12. The formula for calculating the September tours sales appears in the formula bar. Now you use the Fill Right command to copy the formula from cell B18 to cells C18, D18, and E18.

7. Select the range B18:E18

QuickTip

Use the Fill Series command on the Edit menu to examine all of Excel's available fill series options.

8. Click Edit on the menu bar, point to Fill, then click Right
The rest of the totals are filled in correctly. Compare your worksheet to Figure B-13.

9. Click the Save button 🖫 on the Standard toolbar
Your worksheet is now saved.

FIGURE B-11: Selected range using the fill handle

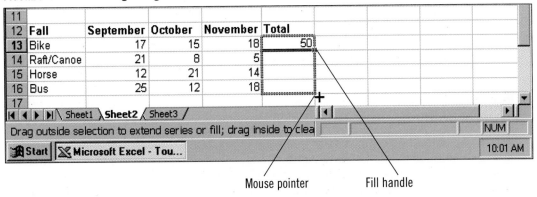

Mouse pointer   Fill handle

FIGURE B-12: Worksheet with copied formula

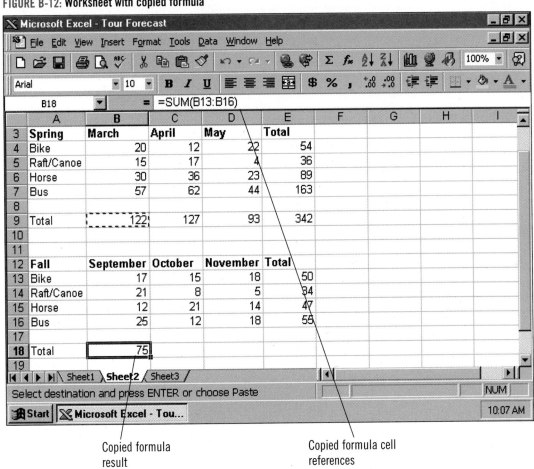

Copied formula
result

Copied formula cell
references

FIGURE B-13: Completed worksheet with all formulas copied

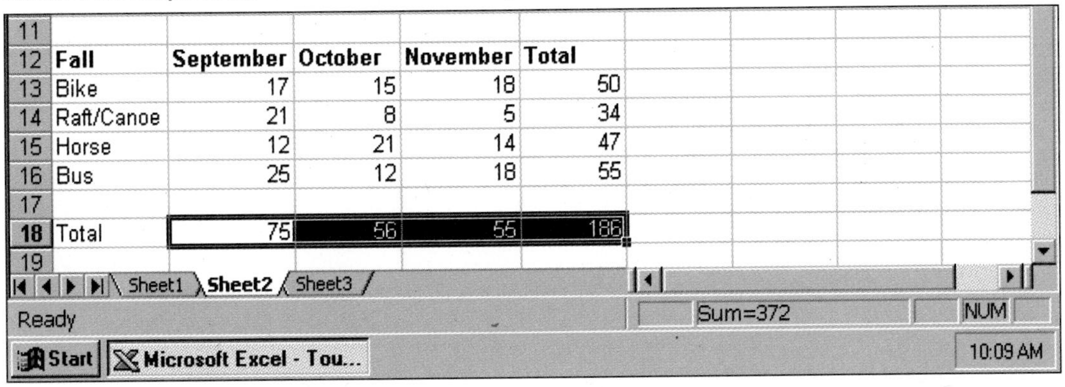

Copying Formulas with Absolute Cell References

Sometimes you might want a cell reference to always refer to a particular cell address. In such an instance, you would use an **absolute cell reference**. An absolute cell reference is a cell reference that always refers to a specific cell address, even if you move the formula to a new location. You identify an absolute reference by placing a dollar sign ($) before the column letter and row number of the address (for example A1). Marketing hopes the tour business will increase by 20% over last year's figures. Evan decides to add a column that calculates a possible increase in the number of spring tours in 1998. He wants to do a what-if analysis and recalculate the spreadsheet several times, changing the percentage that the tours might increase each time.

1. Click cell **G1**, type **Change**, and then press [→]

You can store the increase factor that will be used in the what-if analysis in cell H1.

2. Type **1.1** in cell **H1**, then press [Enter]

This represents a 10% increase in sales.

3. Click cell **F3**, type **1998?**, then press [Enter]

Now, you create a formula that references a specific address: cell H1.

4. In cell **F4**, type **=E4*H1**, then click the **Enter button** ☑ on the formula bar

The result of 59.4 appears in cell F4. Now use the fill handle to copy the formula in cell F4 to F5:F7.

5. Drag the fill handle to select the range **F4:F7**

The resulting values in the range F5:F7 are all zeros. When you look at the formula in cell F5, which is =E5*H2, you realize you need to use an absolute reference to cell H1. You can correct this error by editing cell F4 using [F4], a shortcut key, to change the relative cell reference to an absolute cell reference.

6. Click cell **F4**, press [F2] to change to Edit mode, then press [F4]

When you pressed [F2], the **range finder** outlined the equations arguments in blue and green. When you pressed [F4], dollar signs appeared, changing the H1 cell reference to an absolute reference. See Figure B-14.

7. Click the ☑ on the formula bar

Now that the formula correctly contains an absolute cell reference, use the fill handle to copy the formula in cell F4 to F5:F7.

8. Drag the fill handle to select the range **F4:F7**

Now you can complete your what-if analysis by changing the value in cell H1 from 1.1 to 1.25 to indicate a 25% increase in sales.

9. Click cell **H1**, type **1.25**, then click the ☑ on the formula bar

The values in the range F4:F7 change. Compare your worksheet to Figure B-15.

FIGURE B-14: Absolute cell reference in cell F4

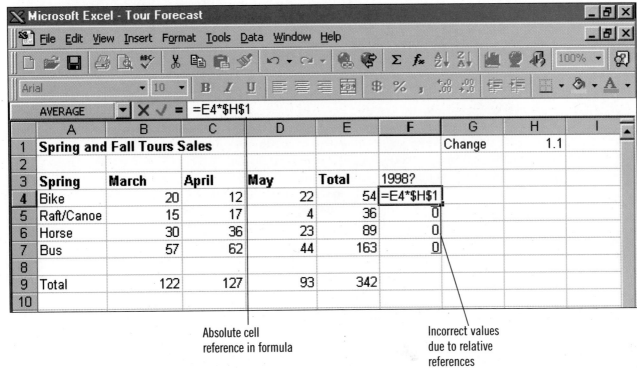

Absolute cell
reference in formula

Incorrect values
due to relative
references

FIGURE B-15: Worksheet with what-if value

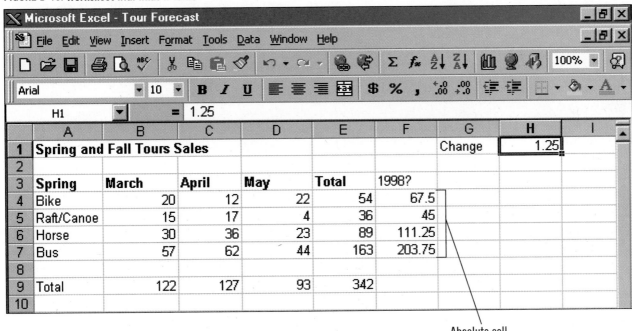

Absolute cell
reference in
formulas

Project a What-If Analysis

The ability to "plug in" values in a worksheet means you can create countless what-if analyses. A what-if analysis occurs when you insert different values into a worksheet model. This type of analysis can help you determine budgetary constraints, and can influence corporate economic decisions.

Naming and Moving a Sheet

Each workbook initially contains three worksheets. When the workbook is opened, the first worksheet is the active sheet. To move from sheet to sheet, click the desired sheet tab located at the bottom of the worksheet window. Sheet tab scrolling buttons, located to the left of the sheet tabs, allow rapid movement among the sheets. To make it easier to identify the sheets in a workbook, you can name each sheet. The name appears on the sheet tab. For instance, sheets within a single workbook could be named for individual sales people to better track performance goals. To better organize a workbook, you can easily rearrange sheets within it. Evan wants to be able to easily identify the Tour Information and the Tour Forecast sheets. He decides to name the two sheets in his workbook, then changes their order.

Steps 1234

1. **Click the Sheet1 tab**
   Sheet1 becomes active; this is the worksheet that contains the Fall Tour Forecast information you compiled for the Marketing department. Its tab moves to the front, and the tab for Sheet2 moves to the background.

2. **Click the Sheet2 tab**
   Sheet2, containing last year's Tour Information, becomes active. Now that you have confirmed which sheet is which, rename Sheet1 so it has a name that identifies its contents.

3. **Double-click the Sheet1 tab**
   The Sheet1 text ("Sheet1") is selected. You could also click Format in the menu bar, point to Sheet, then click Rename to select the sheet name.

4. **Type Forecast, then press [Enter]**
   See Figure B-16. The new name automatically replaced the default name on the tab. Worksheet names can have up to 31 characters, including spaces and punctuation.

5. **Double-click the Sheet2 tab, then rename this sheet Information**
   You decide to rearrange the order of the sheets, so that Forecast comes after Information.

6. **Drag the Forecast sheet after the Information sheet**
   As you drag, the pointer changes to a sheet relocation indicator.
   See Figure B-17.

7. **Save and close the workbook, then exit Excel**

FIGURE B-16: Renamed sheet in workbook

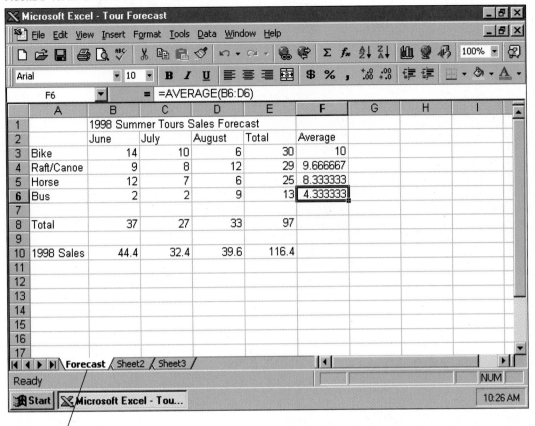

Sheet 1 renamed

FIGURE B-17: Moving Forecast after Information sheet

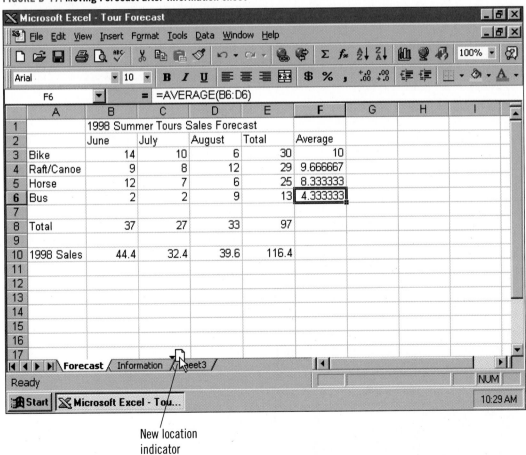

New location
indicator

Practice

► Concepts Review

Label each of the elements of the Excel worksheet window shown in Figure B-18.

FIGURE B-18

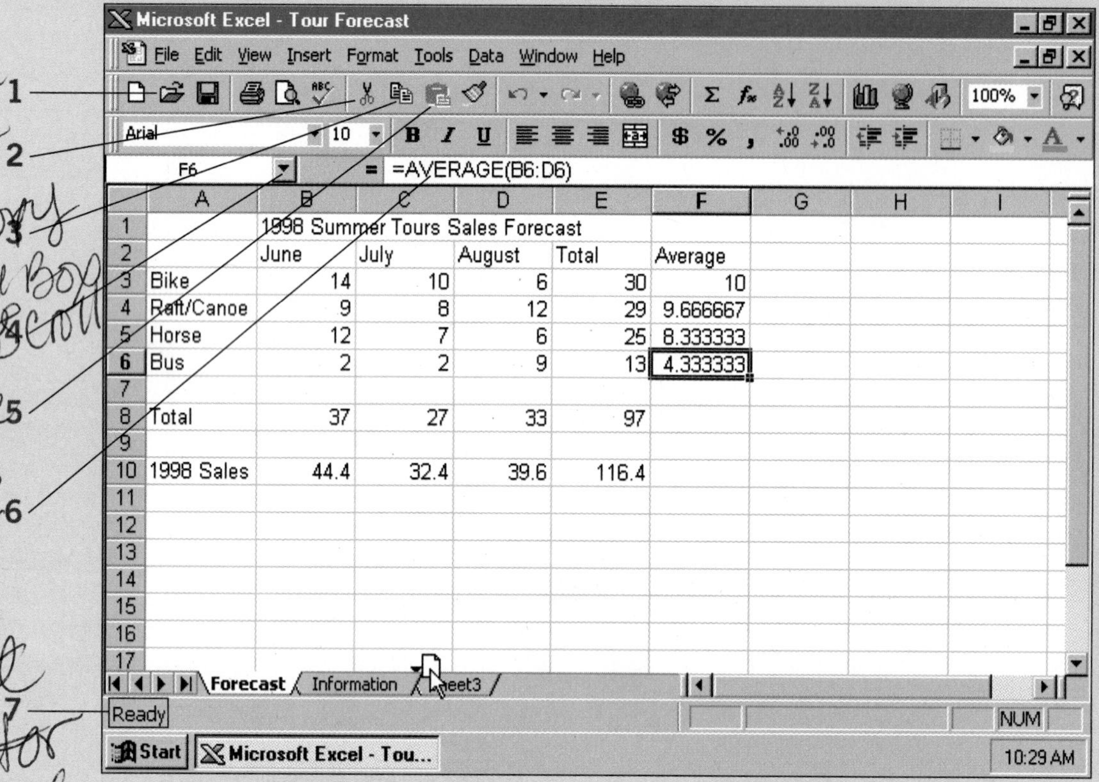

Handwritten labels:
- open — 1
- Cut — 2
- Copy — 3
- Name Box — Cell Scroll
- Paste — 5
- Form. bar — 6
- mode indicator / Status bar — 7

```
Microsoft Excel - Tour Forecast

File  Edit  View  Insert  Format  Tools  Data  Window  Help

F6         = =AVERAGE(B6:D6)

        A          B        C        D        E        F        G        H        I
1    1998 Summer Tours Sales Forecast
2               June     July    August   Total   Average
3   Bike          14       10        6       30       10
4   Raft/Canoe     9        8       12       29    9.666667
5   Horse         12        7        6       25    8.333333
6   Bus            2        2        9       13    4.333333
7
8   Total         37       27       33       97
9
10  1998 Sales   44.4     32.4     39.6    116.4
11
12
13
14
15
16
17

Forecast / Information / Sheet3

Ready                                            NUM

Start   Microsoft Excel - Tou...                 10:29 AM
```

Match each of the terms with the statement that describes its function.

8. Range C
9. Function A
10. (paste icon) E
11. (copy icon) D
12. Formula B

a. A predefined formula that provides a shortcut for commonly used calculations

b. A cell entry that performs a calculation in an Excel worksheet

c. A specified group of cells, which can include the entire worksheet

d. Used to copy cells

e. Used to paste cells

Select the best answer from the list of choices.

13. **What type of cell reference changes when it is copied?**
    a. Absolute
    b. Circular
    c. Looping
    d. Relative

14. **Which character is used to make a reference absolute?**
    a. &
    b. ^
    c. $
    d. @

▶ Skills Review

1 Edit cell entries and work with ranges.
   a. Open workbook XL B-2 and save it as "Mutual Funds" on your Student Disk.
   b. Change the number of Arch shares to 210.
   c. Change the price per share of RST stock to 18.45.
   d. Change the number of United shares to 100.
   e. Name the range B2:B5 "Shares".
   f. Name the range C2:C5 "Price".
   g. Save, preview, and print your worksheet.

2 Enter formulas.
   a. Click cell B6.
   b. Enter the formula B2+B3+B4+B5.
   c. Click cell C6.
   d. Enter the formula C2+C3+C4+C5.
   e. Save your work, then preview and print the data in the Mutual Funds worksheet.

3 Introduce functions.
   a. Click cell C7.
   b. Enter the MIN function for the range C2:C5.
   c. Type the label Min Price in cell A7.
   d. Save your work.
   e. Preview and print this worksheet.

4 Copy and move cell entries.
   a. Select the range A1:E6.
   b. Use drag-and-drop to copy the range to cell A10.
   c. Delete the range B11:C14.
   d. Save your work.
   e. Preview and print this worksheet.

5 Copy formulas with relative cell references.

 a. Click cell D2.

 b. Create a formula that multiplies B2 and C2.

 c. Copy the formula in D2 into cells D3:D5.

 d. Copy the formula in D2 into cells D11:D14.

 e. Save, preview, and print this worksheet.

6 Copy formulas with absolute cell references.

 a. Click cell G2.

 b. Type the value 1.375.

 c. Click cell E2.

 d. Create a formula containing an absolute reference that multiplies D2 and G2.

 e. Copy the formula in E2 into cells E3:E5.

 f. Copy the formula in E2 into cells E11:E14.

 g. Change the amount in cell G2 to 2.873.

 h. Save, preview, and print this worksheet.

7 Name a sheet.

 a. Name the Sheet1 tab "Funds".

 b. Move the Funds sheet so it comes after Sheet3.

 c. Save and close this worksheet.

▶ Independent Challenges

1. You are the box-office manager for Lightwell Players, a regional theater company. Your responsibilities include tracking seasonal ticket sales for the company's main stage productions and anticipating ticket sales for the next season. Lightwell Players sells four types of tickets: reserved seating, general admission, senior citizen tickets, and student tickets. The 1993–94 season included productions of *Hamlet*, *The Cherry Orchard*, *Fires in the Mirror*, *The Shadow Box*, and *Heartbreak House*.

Open a new workbook and save it as "Theater" on your Student Disk. Plan and build a worksheet that tracks the sales of each of the four ticket types for all five of the plays. Calculate the total ticket sales for each play, the total sales for each of the four ticket types, and the total sales for all tickets.

Enter your own sales data, but assume the following: the Lightwell Players sold 800 tickets during the season; reserved seating was the most popular ticket type for all of the shows except for *The Shadow Box*; no play sold more than 10 student tickets. Plan and build a second worksheet in the workbook that reflects a 5% increase in sales of all ticket types.

To complete this independent challenge:

1. Think about the results you want to see, the information you need to build into these worksheets, and what types of calculations must be performed.
2. Sketch sample worksheets on a piece of paper to indicate how the information should be laid out. What information should go in the columns? In the rows?
3. Build the worksheets by entering a title, row labels, column headings, and formulas. Use named ranges to make the worksheet easier to use, and rename the sheet tabs to easily identify the contents of each sheet. (Hint: If your columns are too narrow, position the cell pointer in the column you want to widen. To widen the column, click Format on the menu bar, click Column, click Width, choose a new column width, and then click OK.)
4. Use separate worksheets for existing ticket sales and projected sales showing the 5% increase.
5. Save your work, then preview and print the worksheets.
6. Submit your sketches and printed worksheets.

2. You have been promoted to computer lab manager at your school, and it is your responsibility to make sure there are enough computers for students during scheduled classes. Currently, you have four classrooms: three with IBM PCs and one with Macintoshes. Classes are scheduled Monday, Wednesday, and Friday in two-hour increments from 9 a.m. to 5 p.m. (the lab closes at 7 p.m.), and each room can currently accommodate 20 computers.

Open a new workbook and save it as "Lab Manager" on your Student Disk. Plan and build a worksheet that tracks the number of students who can currently use available computers per two-hour class. Create your enrollment data, but assume that current enrollment averages 85% of each room's daily capacity. Using an additional worksheet, show the impact of an enrollment increase of 25%.

To complete this independent challenge:

1. Think about how to construct these worksheets to create the desired output.
2. Sketch sample paper worksheets, to indicate how the information should be laid out.
3. Build the worksheets by entering a title, row labels, column headings, and formulas. Use named ranges to make the worksheet easier to use, and rename the sheets to identify their contents easily.
4. Use separate sheets for actual enrollment and projected changes.
5. Save your work, then preview and print the worksheets.
6. Submit your sketches and printed worksheets.

3. Nuts and Bolts is a small but growing hardware store that has hired you to organize its accounting records using Excel. The store hopes to track its inventory using Excel once its accounting records are under control. Before you were hired, one of the accounting staff started to enter expenses in a workbook, but the work was never completed. Open the workbook XL B-3 and save it as "Nuts and Bolts Finances" on your Student Disk. Include functions such as the Average, Maximum, and Minimum amounts of each of the expenses in the worksheet.

To complete this independent challenge:

1. Think about what information would be important for the accounting staff to know.
2. Use the existing worksheet to create a paper sketch of the types of functions and formulas you will use and of where they will be located. Indicate where you will have named ranges.
3. Create your sketch using the existing worksheet as a foundation. Your worksheet should use range names in its formulas and functions.
4. Rename Sheet1 "Expenses".
5. Save your work, and then preview and print the worksheet.
6. Submit your sketches and printed worksheets.

4. The immediacy of the World Wide Web allows you to find comparative data on any service or industry of interest to you. Your company is interested in investing in one of any of the most actively traded stocks in the three primary trading houses, and you have been asked to retrieve this information. To complete this independent challenge:

1. Open a new workbook and save it on your Student Disk as Stock Data.
2. Log on to the Internet and use your browser to go to the http://www.course.com. From there, click the link Student On Line Companions, then click the Microsoft Office 97 Professional Edition — Illustrated: A First Course page, then click on the Excel link for Unit B.
3. Use each of the following sites to compile your data: NASDAQ [www.nasdaq.com], the New York Stock Exchange [www.nyse.com], and the American Stock Exchange [www.amex.com].
4. Using one worksheet per exchange, locate data for the 10 most actively traded stocks.
5. Make sure all stocks are identified using their commonly known names.
6. Your company will invest a total of $100,000 and wants to make that investment in only one exchange. Still, they are asking you to research the types of stocks that could be purchased in each exchange.
7. Assume an even distribution of the original investment in the stocks, and total pertinent columns. Determine the total number of shares that will be purchased.
8. Save, print, and hand in a print of your work.

▶ Visual Workshop

Create a worksheet similar to Figure B-19 using the skills you learned in this unit. Save the workbook as "Annual Budget" on your Student Disk. Preview, and then print the worksheet.

FIGURE B-19

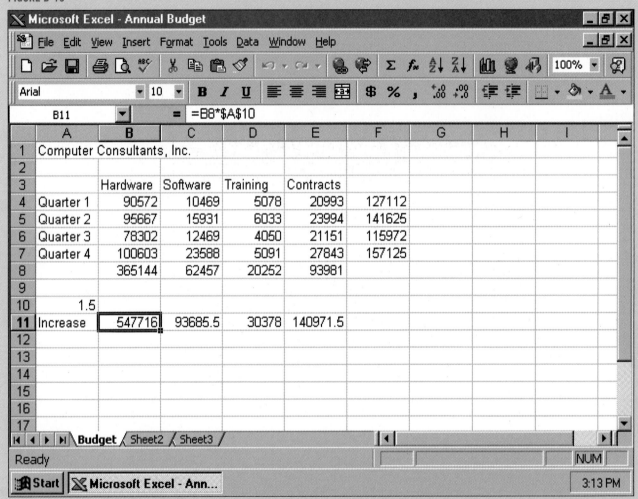

Formatting
a Worksheet

Objectives

► **Format values**
► **Select fonts and point sizes**
► **Change attributes and alignment of labels**
► **Adjust column widths**
► **Insert and delete rows and columns**
► **Apply colors, patterns, and borders**
► **Use conditional formatting**
► **Check spelling**

Now you will learn how to format a worksheet to make it easier to read and to emphasize key data. You do this by formatting cell contents, adjusting column widths, and inserting and deleting columns and rows. ✐ The marketing managers at Nomad Ltd have asked Evan Brillstein to create a worksheet that tracks tour advertising expenses. Evan has prepared a worksheet containing this information, and now he needs to use formatting techniques to make the worksheet easier to read and to call attention to important data.

Formatting Values

Formatting is how information appears in cells; it does not alter the data in any way. To format a cell, you select it, then apply the formatting you want. You can also format a range of cells. Cells and ranges can be formatted before or after data is entered. If you enter a value in a cell, and the cell appears to display the data incorrectly, you need to format the cell to display the value correctly. You might also want more than one cell to have the same format. ✐ The Marketing Department has requested that Evan track tour advertising expenses. Evan developed a worksheet that tracks invoices for tour advertising. He has entered all the information and now wants to format some of the labels and values in the worksheet. Because some of the format changes he will make to labels and values might also affect column widths, Evan decided to make all his formatting changes before changing the column widths. He formats his values first.

Steps 1234

1. **Open the worksheet XL C-1 from your Student Disk, then save it as Tour Ads**
   The tour advertising worksheet appears in Figure C-1.
   You want to format the data in the Cost ea. column so it displays with a dollar sign.

2. **Select the range E4:E32, then click the Currency Style button 🖲 on the Formatting toolbar**
   Excel adds dollar signs and two decimal places to the Cost ea. column data. When the new format is applied, Excel automatically resizes the columns to display all the information. Columns G, H, and I contain dollar values also, but you decide to apply the comma format instead of currency.

3. **Select the range G4:I32, then click the Comma Style button 🖲 on the Formatting toolbar**
   Column J contains percentages.

4. **Select the range J4:J32, click the Percent Style button 🖲 on the Formatting toolbar, then click the Increase Decimal button 🖲 on the Formatting toolbar to show one decimal place**
   Data in the % of Total column is now formatted in Percent style. Next, you reformat the invoice dates.

5. **Select the range B4:B31, click Format on the menu bar, then click Cells**
   The Format Cells dialog box appears with the Number tab in front and the Date format already selected. See Figure C-2. You can also use this dialog box to format ranges with currency, commas, and percentages.

6. **Select the format 4-Mar-97 in the Type list box, then click OK**
   You decide you don't need the year to appear in the Inv Due column.

7. **Select the range C4:C31, click Format on the menu bar, click Cells, click 4-Mar in the Type list box, then click OK**
   Compare your worksheet to Figure C-3.

8. **Save your work**

FIGURE C-1: Tour advertising worksheet

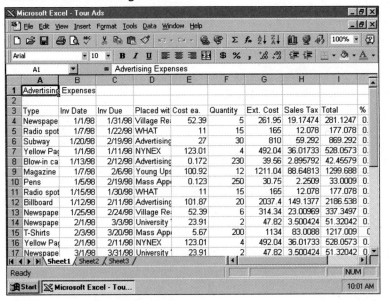

FIGURE C-2: Format Cells dialog box

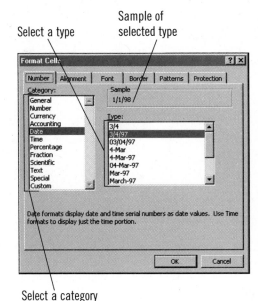

Select a type

Sample of selected type

Select a category

FIGURE C-3: Worksheet with formatted values

Currency Style button

Percent Style button

Comma Style button

Increase decimal button

Decrease decimal button

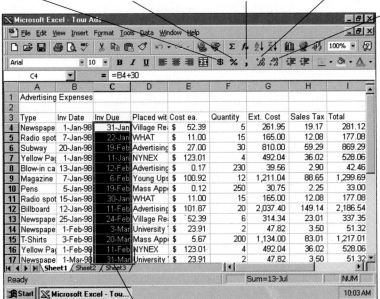

Modified date formats

Using the Format Painter

A cell's format can be "painted" into other cells using the Format Painter button ✍ on the Formatting toolbar. This is similar to using drag-and-drop to copy information, but instead of copying cell contents, you copy only the cell format. Select the cell containing the desired format, then click ✍. The pointer changes to ⊕🖌, as shown in Figure C-4. Use this pointer to select the cell or range you want to contain the painted format.

FIGURE C-4: Using the Format Painter

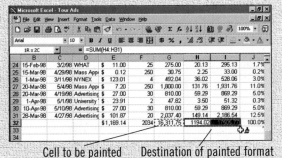

Cell to be painted   Destination of painted format

FORMATTING A WORKSHEET   EX C-3

Excel 97

Selecting Fonts and Point Sizes

A **font** is the name given to a collection of characters (letters, numerals, symbols, and punctuation marks) with a specific design. The **point size** is the physical size of the text, measured in points. The default font in Excel is 10 point Arial. You can change the font, the size, or both of any entry or section in a worksheet by using the Format command on the menu bar or by using the Formatting toolbar. Table C-1 shows several fonts in different sizes. Now that the data is formatted, Evan wants to change the font and size of the labels and the worksheet title so that they stand out.

Steps 123 4

QuickTip

You can also open the Format Cells dialog box by right-clicking the mouse after selecting cells, then selecting Format Cells.

1. Press **[Ctrl][Home]** to select cell A1

2. Click **Format** on the menu bar, click **Cells**, then click the **Font tab** in the Format Cells dialog box
   See Figure C-5.
   You decide to change the font of the title from Arial to Times New Roman, and increase the font size to 24.

Trouble?

If you don't have Times New Roman in your list of fonts, choose another font.

3. Click **Times New Roman** in the Font list box, click **24** in the Size list box, then click **OK**
   The title font appears in 24 point Times New Roman, and the Formatting toolbar displays the new font and size information. Next, you make the column headings larger.

4. Select the range **A3:J3**, click **Format** on the menu bar, then click **Cells**
   The Font tab should still be the front-most tab in the Format Cells dialog box.

QuickTip

The Format Cells dialog box displays a sample of the selected font. Use the Format Cells command to access the Format Cells dialog box if you're unsure of a font's appearance.

5. Click **Times New Roman** in the Font list box, click **14** in the Size list box, then click **OK**
   Compare your worksheet to Figure C-6.

6. Save your work

TABLE C-1: Types of fonts

font	12 point	24 point
Arial	Excel	Excel
Helvetica	Excel	Excel
Palatino	Excel	Excel
Times	Excel	Excel

FIGURE C-5: Font tab in the Format Cells dialog box

Available fonts on your computer— yours may differ

Currently selected font

Font attribute options

Type a custom font size or select from the list

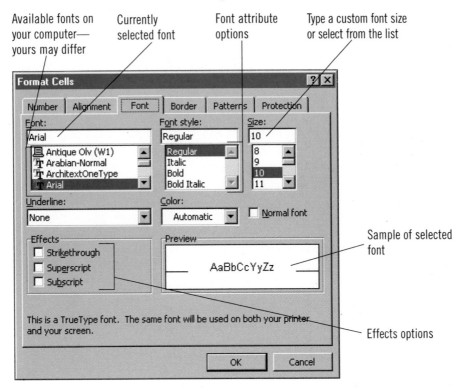

Sample of selected font

Effects options

FIGURE C-6: Worksheet with enlarged title and labels

Column headings now 14 point Times New Roman

Font and size of active cell

Title after changing to 24 point Times New Roman

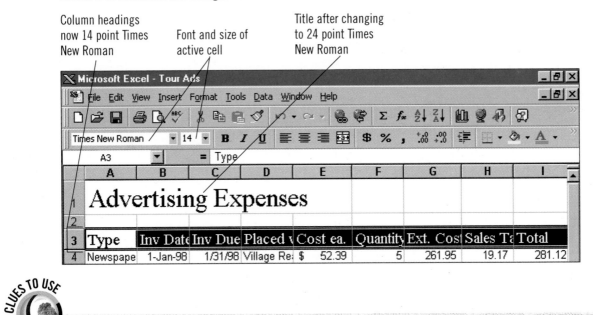

Using the Formatting toolbar to change fonts and sizes

The font and size of the active cell appear on the Formatting toolbar. Click the Font list arrow, as shown in Figure C-7, to see a list of available fonts. If you want to change the font, first select the cell, click the Font list arrow, then choose the font you want. You can change the size of selected text in the same way, by clicking the Size list arrow on the Formatting toolbar to display a list of available point sizes.

FIGURE C-7: Available fonts on the Formatting toolbar

Available fonts installed on your computer—yours may differ

FORMATTING A WORKSHEET   EX C-5

Changing Attributes and Alignment of Labels

Attributes are font styling features such as bold, italics, and underlining. You can apply bold, italics, and underlining from the Formatting toolbar or from the Font tab in the Format Cells dialog box. You can also change the alignment of text in cells. Left, right, or center alignment can be applied from the Formatting toolbar, or from the Alignment tab in the Format Cells dialog box. See Table C-2 for a description of the available attribute and alignment buttons on the Formatting toolbar. Excel also has predefined worksheet formats to make formatting easier. ✐ Now that he has applied the appropriate fonts and font sizes to his worksheet labels, Evan wants to further enhance his worksheet's appearance by adding bold and underline formatting and centering some of the labels.

1. Press **[Ctrl][Home]** to select cell A1, then click the **Bold button** **B** on the Formatting toolbar
   The title "Advertising Expenses" appears in bold.

2. Select the range **A3:J3**, then click the **Underline button** **U** on the Formatting toolbar
   Excel underlines the column headings in the selected range.

QuickTip

Highlighting information on a worksheet can be useful, but overuse of any attribute can be distracting and make a document less readable. Be consistent by adding emphasis the same way throughout a workbook.

3. Click cell **A3**, click the **Italics button** **I** on the Formatting toolbar, then click **B**
   The word "Type" appears in boldface, italic type. Notice that the Bold, Italics, and Underline buttons on the Formatting toolbar are indented. You decide you don't like the italic formatting. You remove it by clicking **I** again.

4. Click **I**
   Excel removes italics from cell A3.

5. Add bold formatting to the rest of the labels in the range **B3:J3**
   You want to center the title over the data.

6. Select the range **A1:F1**, then click the **Merge and Center button** on the Formatting toolbar
   The title Advertising Expenses is centered across six columns. Now you center the column headings in their cells.

Time To

✔ Save

7. Select the range **A3:J3** then click the **Center button** on the Formatting toolbar
   You are satisfied with the formatting in the worksheet.
   Compare your screen to Figure C-8.

FIGURE C-8: Worksheet with formatting attributes applied

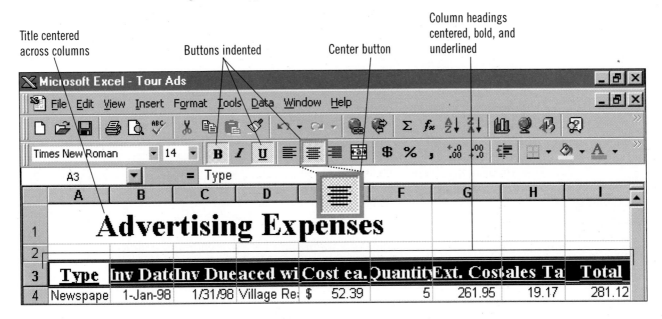

Title centered across columns

Buttons indented

Center button

Column headings centered, bold, and underlined

TABLE C-2: Attribute and Alignment buttons on the Formatting toolbar

icon	description	icon	description
B	Adds boldface		Aligns left
I	Italicizes		Aligns center
U	Underlines		Aligns right
	Adds lines or borders		Centers across columns, and combines two or more selected adjacent cells into one cell.

 CLUES TO USE

Using AutoFormat

Excel provides 16 preset formats called AutoFormats, which allow instant formatting of large amounts of data. AutoFormats are designed for worksheets with labels in the left column and top rows and totals in the bottom row or right column. To use AutoFormatting, select the data to be formatted—or place your mouse pointer anywhere within the range to be selected—click Format on the menu bar, click AutoFormat, then select a format from the Table Format list box, as shown in Figure C-9.

FIGURE C-9: AutoFormat dialog box

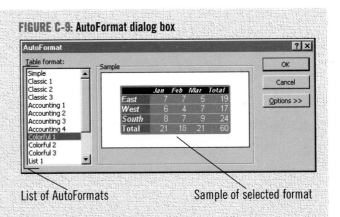

List of AutoFormats

Sample of selected format

Adjusting Column Widths

As you work with a worksheet, you might need to adjust the width of the columns to make your worksheet more usable. The default column width is 8.43 characters wide, a little less than one inch. With Excel, you can adjust the column width for one or more columns using the mouse or the Column command on the Format menu. Table C-3 describes the commands available on the Format Column menu. You can also adjust the height of rows. Evan notices that some of the labels in column A don't fit in the cells. He decides to adjust the widths of columns so that the labels fit in the cells.

Steps 1234

1. Position the pointer on the column line between columns **A** and **B** in the column header area
The pointer changes to ↔, as shown in Figure C-10. You make the column wider.

2. Drag the line to the right until column A is wide enough to accommodate all of the labels for types of advertising
You decide to resize the columns so they automatically accommodate the widest entry in a cell.

3. Position the pointer on the column line between columns B and C in the column header area until it changes to ↔, then double-click the left mouse button
The width of column B is automatically resized to fit the widest entry, in this case, the column head. This feature is called **AutoFit**.

4. Repeat step 3 to use AutoFit to automatically resize columns C, D, and J
You can also use the Column Width command on the Format menu to adjust several columns to the same width.

5. Select the range F5:I5
Any cells in the columns you want to resize can be selected.

6. Click Format on the menu bar, point to Column, then click Width
The Column Width dialog box appears. Move the dialog box, if necessary, by dragging it by its title bar so you can see the contents of the worksheet.

7. Type 12 in the Column Width text box, then click OK
The column widths change to reflect the new settings. See Figure C-11. You are satisfied and decide to save the worksheet.

8. Save your work

QuickTip

To reset columns to the default width, select the range of cells, then use the Column Standard Width command on the Format menu. Click OK in the Standard Width dialog box to accept the default width.

TABLE C-3: Format Column commands

command	description
Width	Sets the width to a specific number of characters
AutoFit Selection	Fits the widest entry
Hide	Hide(s) column(s)
Unhide	Unhide(s) column(s)
Standard Width	Resets to default widths

FIGURE C-10: Preparing to change the column width

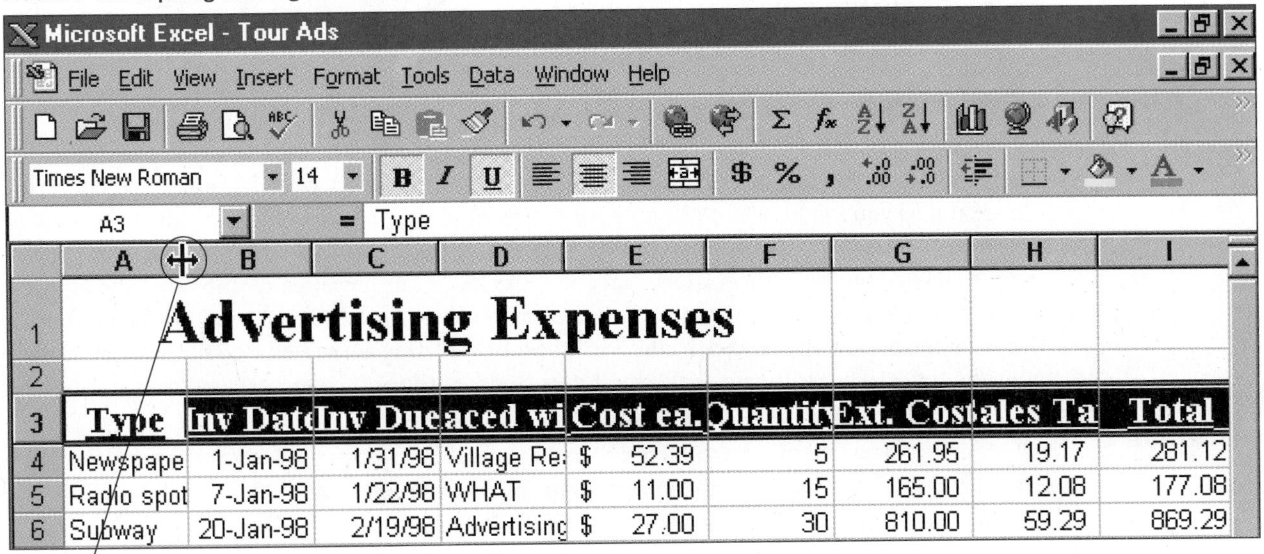

Microsoft Excel - Tour Ads

File Edit View Insert Format Tools Data Window Help

Times New Roman · 14 · B I U · $ % , · · · · · · A ·

A3 · = Type

	A	B	C	D	E	F	G	H	I
1	**Advertising Expenses**								
2									
3	**Type**	**Inv Date**	**Inv Due**	**aced wi**	**Cost ea.**	**Quantity**	**Ext. Cost**	**ales Ta**	**Total**
4	Newspape	1-Jan-98	1/31/98	Village Re:	$ 52.39	5	261.95	19.17	281.12
5	Radio spot	7-Jan-98	1/22/98	WHAT	$ 11.00	15	165.00	12.08	177.08
6	Subway	20-Jan-98	2/19/98	Advertising	$ 27.00	30	810.00	59.29	869.29

Resize pointer
between columns
A and B

FIGURE C-11: Worksheet with column widths adjusted

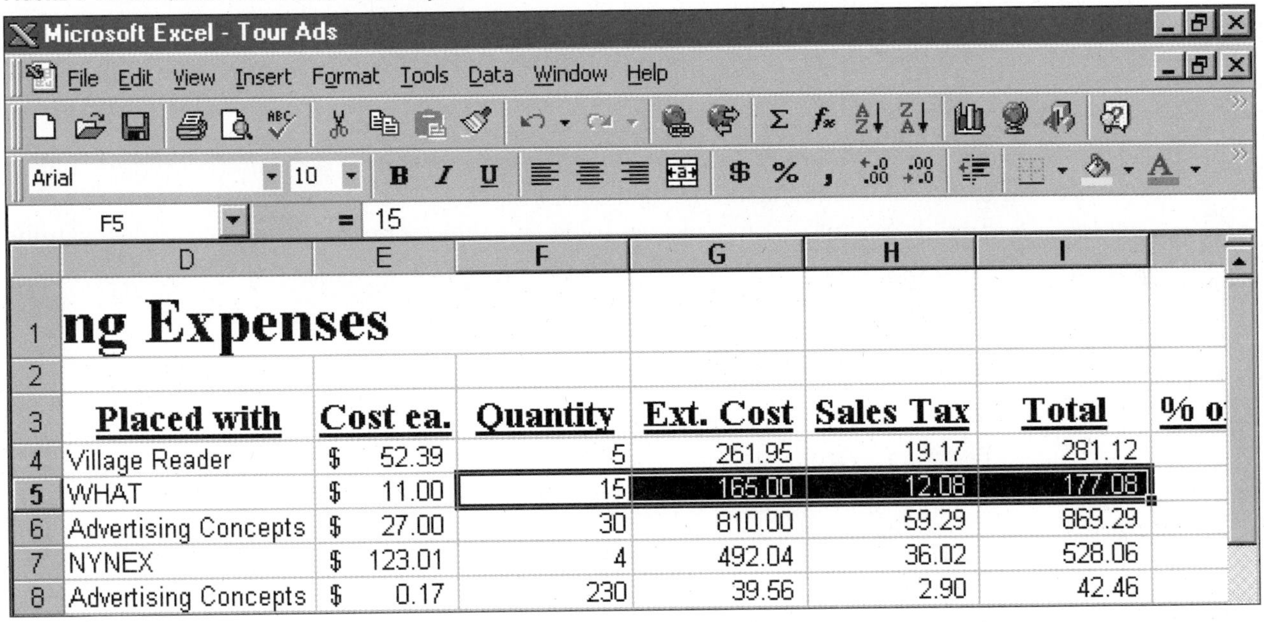

Microsoft Excel - Tour Ads

File Edit View Insert Format Tools Data Window Help

Arial · 10 · B I U · $ % , · · · · · · A ·

F5 · = 15

	D	E	F	G	H	I	
1	**ng Expenses**						
2							
3	**Placed with**	**Cost ea.**	**Quantity**	**Ext. Cost**	**Sales Tax**	**Total**	**% o**
4	Village Reader	$ 52.39	5	261.95	19.17	281.12	
5	WHAT	$ 11.00	15	165.00	12.08	177.08	
6	Advertising Concepts	$ 27.00	30	810.00	59.29	869.29	
7	NYNEX	$ 123.01	4	492.04	36.02	528.06	
8	Advertising Concepts	$ 0.17	230	39.56	2.90	42.46	

Specifying row height

The Row Height command on the Format menu allows you to customize row height to improve readability. Row height is calculated in points, units of measure also used for fonts—one inch equals 72 points. The row height must exceed the size of the font you are using. For example, if you are using a 12 point font, the row height must be more than 12 points. Normally, you don't need to adjust row heights manually. If you format something in a row to be a larger point size, Excel will adjust the row height to fit the largest point size in the row.

Inserting and Deleting Rows and Columns

As you modify a worksheet, you might find it necessary to insert or delete rows and columns. For example, you might need to insert rows to accommodate new inventory products or remove a column of yearly totals that are no longer current. Inserting or deleting rows or columns can help to make your worksheet more readable. Evan has already improved the appearance of his worksheet by formatting the labels and values in the worksheet. Now he decides to improve the overall appearance of the worksheet by inserting a row between the last row of data and the totals. This will help make the totals stand out more. Evan has also located a row of inaccurate data that should be deleted.

1. Click cell **A32**, click **Insert** on the menu bar, then click **Cells**

The Insert dialog box opens. See Figure C-12. You can choose to insert a column or a row, or you can shift the data in the cells in the active column right or in the active row down. You want to insert a row to add some space between the last row of data and the totals.

2. Click the **Entire Row radio button**, then click **OK**

A blank row is inserted between the title and the month labels. When you insert a new row, the contents of the worksheet shift down from the newly inserted row. When you insert a new column, the contents of the worksheet shift to the right from the point of the new column. Now delete the row containing information about hats, as this information is inaccurate.

3. Click the **row 27 selector button** (the gray box containing the row number to the left of the worksheet)

All of row 27 is selected as shown in Figure C-13.

4. Click **Edit** on the menu bar, then click **Delete**

Excel deletes row 27, and all rows below this shift up one row. You are satisfied with the appearance of the worksheet.

5. Save your work

QuickTip

Inserting or deleting rows or columns can also cause problems with formulas that reference cells in that area, so be sure to consider this when inserting or deleting rows or columns.

FIGURE C-12: Insert dialog box

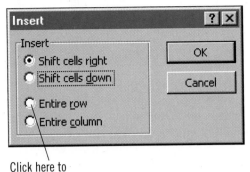

Click here to
insert a row

FIGURE C-13: Worksheet with row 27 selected

25	Pens	15-Mar-98	4/29/98	Mass Appeal, Inc.	$ 0.12	250	3
26	Yellow Pages	1-Mar-98	3/11/98	NYNEX	$ 123.01	4	49
27	Hats	20-Mar-98	5/4/98	Mass Appeal, Inc.	$ 7.20	250	1,80
28	Subway	20-Mar-98	4/19/98	Advertising Concepts	$ 27.00	30	81
29	Newspaper	1-Apr-98	5/1/98	University Voice	$ 23.91	2	4
30	Subway	10-Apr-98	5/10/98	Advertising Concepts	$ 27.00	30	81
31	Billboard	28-Mar-98	4/27/98	Advertising Concepts	$ 101.87	20	2,03
32							
33					$1,169.14	2034	16,31
34							
35							

Sheet1 / Sheet2 / Sheet3 /

Ready   Sum=75913.83035   NUM

Start   Microsoft Excel - Tou...   8:26 AM

Row 27 selector
button

Inserted row

Excel 97

Using dummy columns and rows

You use cell references and ranges in formulas. When you add or delete a column or row within a range used in a formula, Excel automatically adjusts the formula to reflect the change. However, when you add a column or row at the end of a range used in a formula, you must modify the formula to reflect the additional column or row. To avoid having to edit the formula, you can include a dummy column and dummy row within the range you use for that formula. A dummy column is a blank column included to the right of but within a range. A dummy row is a blank row included at the bottom of but within a range, as shown in Figure C-14. Then if you add another column or row to the end of the range, the formula will automatically be modified to include the new data.

FIGURE C-14: Formula with dummy row

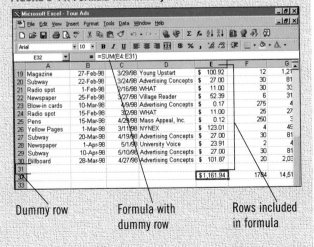

Dummy row

Formula with
dummy row

Rows included
in formula

Applying Colors, Patterns, and Borders

You can use colors, patterns, and borders to enhance the overall appearance of a worksheet and to improve its readability. You can add these enhancements using the Patterns tab in the Format Cells dialog box or by using the Borders and Color buttons on the Formatting toolbar. When you use the Format Cells dialog box, you can see what your enhanced text will look like in the Sample box. You can apply color to the background of a cell or range or to cell contents. If you do not have a color monitor, the colors appear in shades of gray. You can apply patterns to the background of a cell or range. And, you can apply borders to all the cells in a worksheet or only to selected cells. See Table C-4 for a list of border buttons and their functions. Evan decides to add a pattern, a border, and color to the title of the worksheet. This will give the worksheet a more professional appearance.

Steps 1 2 3 4

QuickTip

Use color sparingly. Excessive use can divert the reader's attention away from the data in the worksheet.

1. Click cell **A1**, then click the **Fill Color button list arrow** on the Formatting toolbar
   The color palette appears, as shown in Figure C-15.

2. Click **Turquoise** (fourth row, fourth color from the right)

3. Click **Format** on the menu bar, then click **Cells**
   The Format Cells dialog box opens.

4. Click the **Patterns tab**, as shown in Figure C-16, if it is not already displayed
   When choosing a background pattern, consider that the more cell contents contrast with the background, the more readable the contents will be. You choose the diamond pattern.

5. Click the **Pattern list arrow**, click the **thin diagonal crosshatch pattern** (third row, last pattern on the right), then click **OK**
   Now you add a border.

6. Click the **Borders button list arrow** on the Formatting toolbar, then click the **heavy bottom border** (second row, second border from the left)
   Next, you change the font color.

7. Click the **Font Color button list arrow** on the Formatting toolbar, then click **blue** (second row, third color from the right)
   The text changes color, as shown in Figure C-17.

Time To

▶ Save

8. Preview and print the first page of the worksheet

TABLE C-4: Border buttons

button	description	button	description
	No border		Thin border around range
	Single underline		Left border
	Double underline		Right border
	Thick bottom, thin top border		Double bottom, single top
	Outline all in range		Thick bottom border
	Thick border around range		

FIGURE C-15: **Fill Color palette**

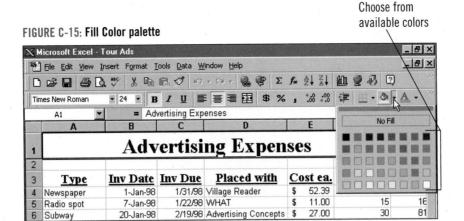

FIGURE C-16: **Patterns tab in the Format Cells dialog box**

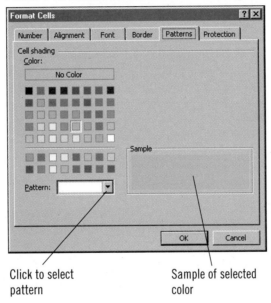

Click to select
pattern

Sample of selected
color

FIGURE C-17: **Worksheet with color, patterns, and border**

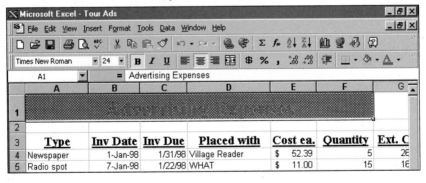

Using color to organize a worksheet

You can use color to give a distinctive look to each part of a worksheet. For example, you might want to apply a light blue to all the rows containing the subway data and a light green to all the rows containing the newspaper data. Be consistent throughout a group of worksheets, and try to avoid colors that are too bright and distracting.

Using Conditional Formatting

Formatting attributes make worksheets look professional, and these same attributes can be applied depending on specific outcomes in cells. Automatically applying formatting attributes based on cell values is called **conditional formatting**. You might, for example, want advertising costs above a certain number to display in red boldface, and lower values to display in blue. Evan wants his worksheet to include conditional formatting so that extended advertising costs greater than $175 display in red boldface. He creates the conditional format in the first cell in the extended cost column.

Steps

Trouble?

If the Office Assistant appears, click the No, don't provide help now button to close the Office Assistant.

1. Click cell **G4**

Use the scroll bars if necessary, to make column G visible.

2. Click **Format** on the menu bar, then click **Conditional Formatting**

The Conditional Formatting dialog box opens, as shown in Figure C-18. The number of input fields varies depending on which operator is selected. You can define up to 3 different conditions that let you determine outcome parameters and then assign formatting attributes to each one.

You begin by defining the first part of the condition.

3. Click the **Operator list arrow**, then click **greater than or equal to**

Next, you define the value in this condition that must be met for the formatting to be applied.

4. Click the **Value text box**, then type **175**

Once the value has been assigned, you define this condition's formatting attributes.

5. Click **Format**, click the **Color list arrow**, click **Red** (third row, first color from the left), click **Bold** in the Font Style list box, click **OK**, then click **OK** again to close the Conditional Formatting dialog box

Next, you copy the formatting to the other cells in the column.

6. Click the **Format Painter button** 🖌 on the Formatting toolbar, then select the range **G5:G30**

Once the formatting is copied, you reposition the cell pointer to review the results.

7. Click cell **G4**

Compare your results to Figure C-19.

8. Press **[Ctrl][Home]** to move to cell Al

9. Save your work

FIGURE C-18: Conditional Formatting dialog box

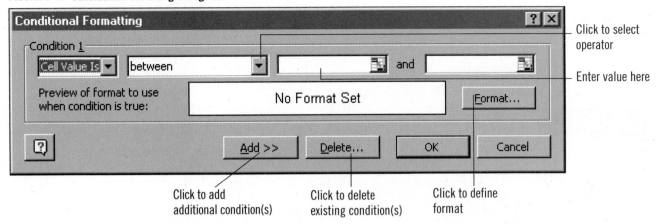

Click to select operator

Enter value here

Click to add additional condition(s)

Click to delete existing condition(s)

Click to define format

FIGURE C-19: Worksheet with conditional formatting

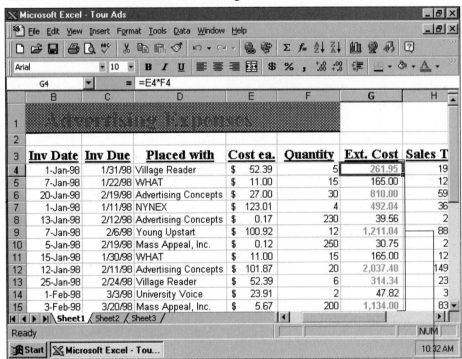

Results of conditional formatting

CLUES TO USE

Deleting conditional formatting

Because its likely that the conditions you define will change, any of the conditional formats defined can be deleted. Select the cell(s) containing conditional formatting, click Format, click Conditional Formatting, then click the Delete button. The Delete Conditional Format dialog box opens, as shown in Figure C-20. Click the checkboxes for any of the conditions you want to delete, then click OK. The previously assigned formatting is deleted—leaving the cell's contents intact.

FIGURE C-20: Delete Conditional Format dialog box

Click the existing condition(s) to delete

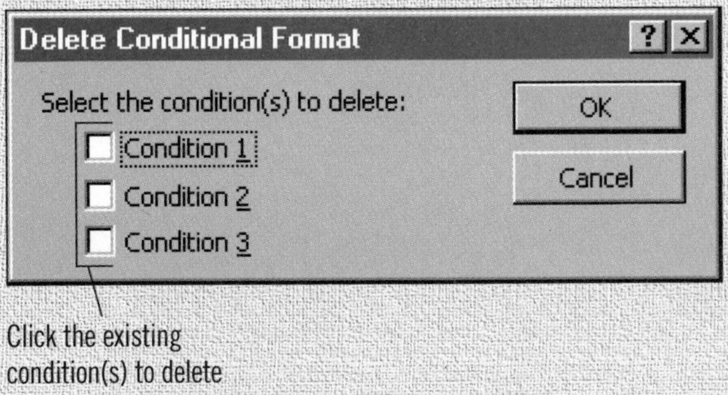

Checking Spelling

You may think your worksheet is complete, but if you haven't checked for spelling errors, you risk undermining the professional effect of your work. A single misspelled word can ruin your work. The spell checker in Excel is also shared by Word, PowerPoint, and Access, so any words you've added to the dictionary using those programs are also available in Excel. ✐━━ Evan has completed the formatting for his worksheet and is ready to check its spelling.

Steps

1. **Click the Spelling button 🔤 on the Standard toolbar**
   The Spelling dialog opens, as shown in Figure C-21, with the abbreviation Inv selected as the first misspelled word in the worksheet. The spell checker starts from the active cell and compares words in the worksheet to those in its dictionary. Any word not found in the dictionary causes the spell checker to stop. At that point, you can decide to Ignore, Change, or Add the word.
   You decide to Ignore All cases of Inv, the abbreviation of invoice.

2. **Click Ignore All, then click Ignore All again when the spell checker stops on T-Shirts**
   The spell checker found the word 'cards' misspelled. You find the correct spelling and fix the error.

3. **Scroll through the Suggestions list, click Cards, then click Change**
   The word 'Concepts' is also misspelled. Make this correction.

4. **Click Concepts in the Suggestions list, then click Change**
   When no more incorrect words are found, Excel displays the message box shown in Figure C-22.

5. **Click OK**

6. **Press [Ctrl][Home] to move to cell A1**

7. **Save your work**

8. **Preview and print the worksheet, then close the workbook and exit Excel**

FIGURE C-21: Spelling dialog box

Misspelled word

Type replacement
word here or click
a suggestion

Click to add word to
dictionary

Click to ignore all
occurrences of
misspelled word

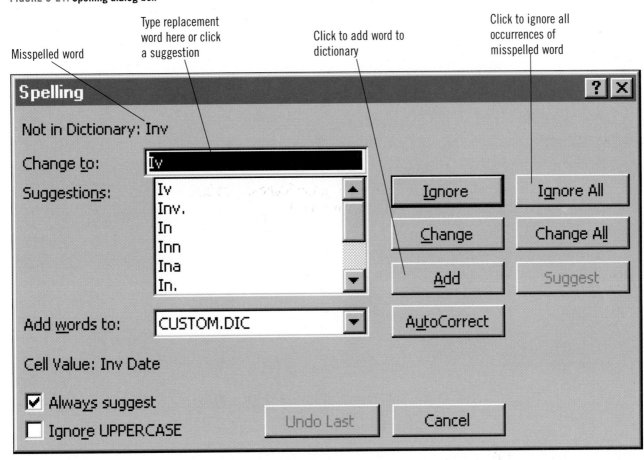

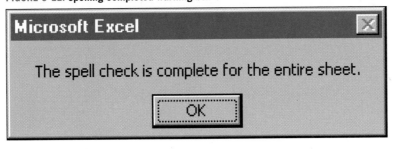

FIGURE C-22: Spelling completed warning box

CLUES TO USE

Modifying the spell checker

Each of us use words specific to our profession or task. Because the dictionary supplied with Microsoft Office cannot possibly include all the words that each of us needs, it is possible to add words to the dictionary shared by all the components in the suite.

To customize the Microsoft Office dictionary used by the spell checker, click Add when a word not in the dictionary is found. From then on, that word will no longer be considered misspelled by the spell checker.

Practice

▶ Concepts Review

Label each of the elements of the Excel worksheet window shown in Figure C-23.

FIGURE C-23

[Handwritten labels:] Format painter 3, Percent Style button 2, increase dec 1 button, Merge & Center 4, Currency Style button 5, Comma Style button 6, decrease dec. button 7

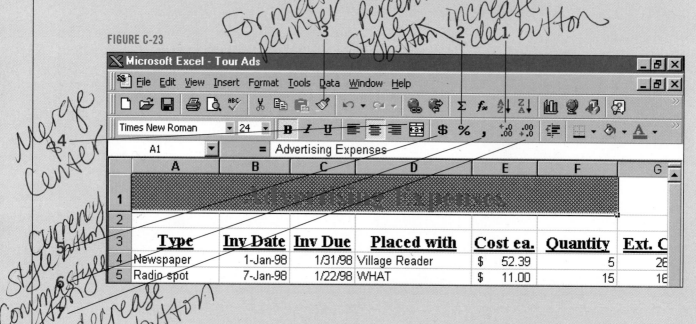

Match each of the statements to the command or button it describes.

8. **Format Cells** *D*		**a.** Adds a new row or column
9. **Edit Clear** *B*		**b.** Erases the contents of a cell
10. **Insert Row/Column** *A*		**c.** Checks the spelling in a worksheet
11. ⧉ *E*		**d.** Changes the point size of selected cells
12. $ *F*		**e.** Pastes the contents of the Clipboard in the current cell
13. ABC✓ *C*		**f.** Changes the format to Currency

Select the best answer from the list of choices.

14. Which button increases the number of decimal places in selected cells?

   a. `’`   **b.** `.00 .0`   **c.** `◇`   **d.** `.0 .00`

15. Each of the following operators can be used in conditional formatting, *except*

   a. equal to   **b.** greater than   **c.** similar to   **d.** not between

16. How many conditional formats can be created in any cell?

   a. 1   **b.** 2   **c.** 3   **d.** 4

▶ Skills Review

1. Format values.

   a. Open a new workbook.
   b. Enter the information from Table C-5 in your worksheet. Make sure you put "Quarterly Sales Sheet" on the next line.
   c. Select the range of values in the Price and Totals columns.
   d. Click the Currency Style button.
   e. Calculate the Totals column by multiplying the price by the number sold.
   f. Save this workbook as Chairs on your Student Disk.

TABLE C-5

Country Oak Chairs, Inc.
Quarterly Sales Sheet

Description	Price	Sold	Totals
Rocker	1299	1104	
Recliner	800	1805	
Bar stool	159	1098	
Dinette	369	1254	

2. Select fonts and point sizes.

   a. Select the range of cells containing the column titles.
   b. Change the font of the column titles to Times New Roman.
   c. Increase the point size of the column titles to 14 point.
   d. Resize columns as necessary.
   e. Save your workbook changes.

3. Change attributes and alignment of labels.

   a. Select the worksheet title Country Oak Chairs, Inc.
   b. Click the Bold button to apply boldface to the title.
   c. Select the label Quarterly Sales Sheet.
   d. Click the Underline button to apply underlining to the label.
   e. Add the bold attribute to the furniture descriptions, as well as the Totals label.
   f. Make the Price and Sold labels italics.
   g. Select the range of cells containing the column titles.
   h. Click the Center button to center the column titles.
   i. Save your changes, then preview and print the worksheet.

4. Adjust column widths.

   a. Change the width of the Price column to 11.
   b. Use the Format menu to make the Description and Sold columns the same size as the Price column.
   c. Save your workbook changes.

5. Insert and delete rows and columns.

  a. Insert a new row between rows 4 and 5.

  b. Add Country Oak Chairs' newest product—a Shaker bench—in the newly inserted row. Enter "239" for the price and "360" for the number sold.

  c. Use the fill handle to copy the formula in cell D4 to D5.

  d. Save your changes, then preview and print the workbook.

6. Apply colors, patterns, and borders.

  a. Add a border around the data entered from Table C-5.

  b. Apply a light green background color to the Descriptions column.

  c. Apply a light pattern to the Descriptions column.

  d. Apply a dark green background to the column labels.

  e. Change the color of the font in the first row of the data to light green.

  f. Save your work.

  g. Preview and print the worksheet, then close the workbook.

7. Use conditional formatting.

  a. Open the file XL C-2 from your Student Disk.

  b. Save it as "Recap" on your Student Disk.

  c. Create conditional formatting that changes values to blue if they are greater than 35000, and changes values to green if they are less than 21000.

  d. Use the Bold button and Center button to format the column headings and row titles.

  e. Autofit the other columns as necessary.

  f. Save your changes.

8. Check spelling.

  a. Open the spell checker.

  b. Check the spelling in the worksheet.

  c. Correct any spelling errors.

  d. Save your changes, then preview and print the workbook.

  e. Close the workbook, then exit Excel.

▶ Independent Challenges

1. Nuts and Bolts is a small but growing hardware store that has hired you to organize its accounting records using Excel. Now that the Nuts and Bolts hardware store's accounting records are on Excel, they would like you to work on the inventory. Although more items will be added later, enough have been entered in a worksheet for you to begin your modifications.

Open the workbook XL C-3 on your Student Disk, and save it as "NB Inventory."

To complete this independent challenge:

1. Create a formula that calculates the Value of the inventory on-hand for each item.
2. Use an absolute reference to calculate the Sale Price of each item.
3. Use enhancements to make the title, column headings, and row headings more attractive.
4. Make sure all columns are wide enough to see the data.
5. Before printing, preview the file so you know what the worksheet will look like. Adjust any items as needed, check spelling, and print a copy. Save your work before closing the file.
6. Submit your final printout.

2. You recently moved to a small town and joined the Chamber of Commerce. Since the other members are not computer-literate, you volunteered to organize the member organizations in a worksheet. As part of your efforts with the Chamber of Commerce, you need to examine more closely the membership in comparison to the community. To make the existing data more professional-looking and easier to read, you've decided to use attributes and your formatting abilities.

Open the workbook XL C-4 on your Student Disk, and save it as "Community."

To complete this independent challenge:

1. Remove any blank columns.
2. Format the Annual Revenue column using the Currency format.
3. Make all columns wide enough to fit their data.
4. Use formatting enhancements, such as fonts, font sizes, and text attributes, to make the worksheet more attractive.
5. Before printing, preview the file so you know what the worksheet will look like. Adjust any items as needed, check spelling, and print a copy. Save your work before closing the file.
6. Submit your final printout.

3. Write Brothers is a Houston-based company that manufactures high-quality pens and markers. As the finance manager, one of your responsibilities is to analyze the monthly reports from your five district sales offices. Your boss, Joanne Parker, has just told you to prepare a quarterly sales report for an upcoming meeting. Because several top executives will be attending this meeting, Joanne reminds you that the report must look professional. In particular, she asks you to emphasize the company's surge in profits during the last month and to highlight the fact that the Northeastern district continues to outpace the other districts.

Plan and build a worksheet that shows the company's sales during the last three months. Make sure you include:

- The number of pens sold (units sold) and the associated revenues (total sales) for each of the five district sales offices. The five Write Brothers sales districts include: Northeastern, Midwestern, Southeastern, Southern, and Western.
- Calculations that show month-by-month totals and a three-month cumulative total.
- Calculations that show each district's share of sales (percent of units sold).
- Formatting enhancements to emphasize the recent month's sales surge and the Northeastern district's sales leadership.

To complete this independent challenge:

1. Prepare a worksheet plan that states your goal, lists the worksheet data you'll need, and identifies the formulas for the different calculations.
2. Sketch a sample worksheet on a piece of paper, indicating how the information should be organized and formatted. How will you calculate the totals? What formulas can you copy to save time and keystrokes? Do any of these formulas need to use an absolute reference? How will you show dollar amounts? What information should be shown in bold? Do you need to use more than one font? More than one point size?
3. Build the worksheet with your own sales data. Enter the titles and labels first, then enter the numbers and formulas. Save the workbook as Write Brothers on your Student Disk.
4. Make enhancements to the worksheet. Adjust the column widths as necessary. Format labels and values, and change attributes and alignment.
5. Add a column that calculates a 10% increase in sales. Use an absolute cell reference in this calculation.
6. Before printing, preview the file so you know what the worksheet will look like. Adjust any items as needed, check spelling, and print a copy. Save your work before closing the file.
7. Submit your worksheet plan, preliminary sketches, and the final printout.

4. As the manager of your company's computer lab, you've been asked to assemble data on currently available software for use in a business environment. Using the World Wide Web, you can retrieve information about current software and create an attractive worksheet for distribution to department managers. To complete this independent challenge:

1. Open a new workbook and save it on your Student Disk as Software Comparison.
2. Log on to the Internet and use your browser to go to http://www.course.com. From there, click the link Student On Line Companions, then click the Microsoft Office 97 Professional Edition—Illustrated: A First Course page, then click the Excel link for Unit C.
3. Use each of the following sites to compile your data.
   Microsoft Corporation [www.microsoft.com], and Lotus Corporation [www.lotus.com].
4. Retrieve information on word processors, spreadsheets, presentation graphics, and database programs manufactured by both companies. The software must be Windows 95 compatible.
5. Create a worksheet that includes the information in step 4 above, as well as a retail price for each component, and whether all the programs can be purchased as a suite.
6. Use formatting attributes to make this data look attractive.
7. Use conditional formatting so that individual programs that cost over $100 display in red.
8. Save, print, and hand in a print out of your work.

▶ Visual Workshop

Create the following worksheet using the skills you learned in this unit. Open the file XL C-5 on your Student Disk, and save it as January Invoices. Create a conditional format in the Cost ea. column where entries greater than 50 are displayed in red. (Hint: The only additional font used in this exercise is Times New Roman. It is 22 points in row 1, and 14 points in row 3.)

FIGURE C-24

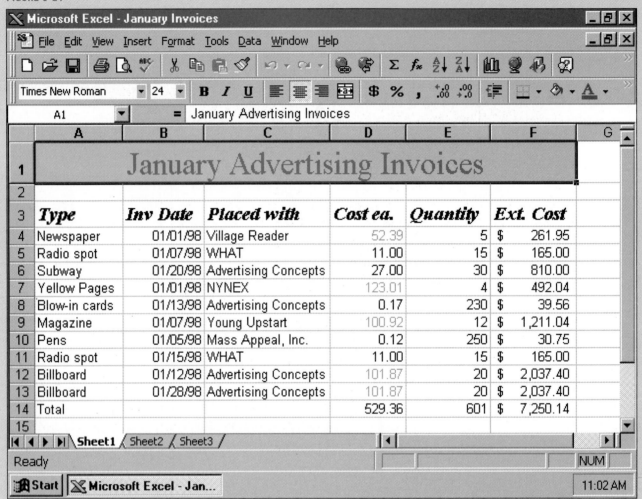

Working
with Charts

► **Plan and design a chart**
► **Create a chart**
► **Move and resize a chart and its objects**
► **Edit a chart**
► **Change the appearance of a chart**
► **Enhance a chart**
► **Add text annotations and arrows to a chart**
► **Preview and print a chart**

Worksheets provide an effective way to organize information, but they are not always the best format for presenting data to others. Information in a selected range or worksheet can be easily converted to the visual format of a chart. Charts quickly communicate the relationships of data in a worksheet. In this unit, you will learn how to create a chart, edit a chart and change the chart type, add text annotations and arrows to a chart, then preview and print it. ✐══ Evan Brillstein needs to create a chart showing the six-month sales history of Nomad Ltd for the annual meeting. He wants to illustrate the impact of an advertising campaign that started in June.

Planning and Designing a Chart

Before creating a chart, you need to plan what you want your chart to show and how you want it to look. Evan wants to create a chart to be used at the annual meeting. The chart will show the spring and summer sales throughout the Nomad Ltd regions. In early June, the Marketing Department launched a national advertising campaign. The results of the campaign were increased sales for the summer months. Evan wants his chart to illustrate this dramatic sales increase. Evan uses the worksheet shown in Figure D-1 and the following guidelines to plan the chart:

Steps 1234

CourseHelp

The camera icon indicates there is a CourseHelp for this lesson. Click the Start button, point to Programs, then click Excel 97 Illustrated. Choose the CourseHelp that corresponds to this lesson.

1. Determine the purpose of the chart, and identify the data relationships you want to communicate visually

You want to create a chart that shows sales throughout Nomad's regions in the spring and summer months (March through August). In particular, you want to highlight the increase in sales that occurred in the summer months as a result of the advertising campaign.

2. Determine the results you want to see, and decide which chart type is most appropriate to use; Table D-1 describes several different types of charts

Because you want to compare related data (sales in each of the regions) over a time period (the months March through August), you decide to use a column chart.

3. Identify the worksheet data you want the chart to illustrate

You are using data from the worksheet titled "Nomad Ltd Regions, Spring and Summer Sales," as shown in Figure D-1. This worksheet contains the sales data for the five regions from March through August.

4. Sketch the chart, then use your sketch to decide where the chart elements should be placed

You sketch your chart as shown in Figure D-2. You put the months on the horizontal axis (the **X-axis**) and the monthly sales figures on the vertical axis (the **Y-axis**). The **tick marks** on the Y-axis create a scale of measure for each value. Each value in a cell you select for your chart is a **data point**. In any chart, each data point is visually represented by a **data marker**, which in this case is a column. A collection of related data points is a **data series**. In this chart, there are five data series (Midwest, Northeast, Northwest, South, and Southwest), so you have included a **legend** to identify them.

FIGURE D-1: Worksheet containing sales data

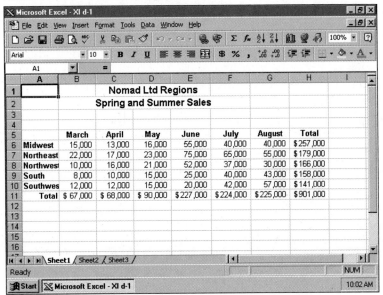

FIGURE D-2: Sketch of the column chart

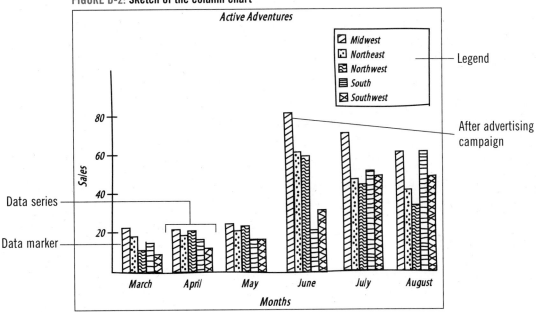

TABLE D-1: Commonly used chart types

type	button	description
Area		Shows how volume changes over time
Bar		Compares distinct, unrelated objects over time using a horizontal format; sometimes referred to as a horizontal bar chart in other spreadsheet programs
Column		Compares distinct, unrelated objects over time using a vertical format; the Excel default; sometimes referred to as a bar chart in other spreadsheet programs
Line		Compares trends over even time intervals; similar to an area chart
Pie		Compares sizes of pieces as part of a whole; can have slices pulled away from the pie, or "exploded"
XY (scatter)		Compares trends over uneven time or measurement intervals; used in scientific and engineering disciplines for trend spotting and extrapolation
Combination	none	Combines a column and line chart to compare data requiring different scales of measure

Excel 97

Creating a Chart

To create a chart in Excel, you first select the range containing the data you want to chart. Once you've selected a range, you can use Excel's Chart Wizard to lead you through the chart creation process. ✏️ Using the worksheet containing the spring and summer sales data for the five regions, Evan will create a chart that shows the monthly sales of each region from March through August.

Steps 1234

1. **Open the workbook XL D-1 from your Student Disk, then save it as Nomad Regions**
   First, you need to select the cells you want to chart. You want to include the monthly sales figures for each of the regions, but not the totals. You also want to include the month and region labels.

QuickTip

When selecting a large, unnamed range, select the upper left-most cell in the range, press and hold [Shift], then click the lower right-most cell in the range.

2. **Select the range A5:G10, then click the Chart Wizard button 📊 on the Standard toolbar**
   When you click 📊 the Chart Wizard opens. The first Chart Wizard dialog box lets you choose the type of chart you want to create. See Figure D-3. You can see a preview of the chart by clicking the Press and hold to view sample button.

3. **Click Next to accept the default chart type of column**
   The second dialog box lets you choose the data being charted and whether the series are in rows or columns. Currently, the rows are selected as the data series. You could switch this by clicking the Columns radio button located under the Data range. Since you selected the data before clicking the Chart Wizard button, the correct range A5:G10 displays in the Data range text box. Satisfied with the selections, you accept the default choices.

4. **Click Next**
   The third Chart Wizard dialog box shows a sample chart using the data you selected. Notice that the regions (the rows in the selected range) are plotted according to the months (the columns in the selected range), and that the months were added as labels for each data series. Notice also that there is a legend showing each region and its corresponding color on the chart. Here, you can choose to keep the legend, add a chart title, and add axis titles. You add a title.

5. **Click the Chart title text box, then type Nomad Ltd Regional Sales**
   After a moment, the title appears in the Sample Chart box. See Figure D-4.

6. **Click Next**
   In the last Chart Wizard dialog box, you determine the location of the chart. A chart can be displayed on the same sheet as the data, or a separate sheet in the workbook. You decide to display the chart on the current sheet.

Trouble?

If you want to delete a chart, select it then press [Delete].

7. **Click Finish**
   The column chart appears, as shown in Figure D-5. Your chart might look slightly different. Just as you had hoped, the chart shows the dramatic increase in sales between May and June. The **selection handles**, the small squares at the corners and sides of the chart borders, indicate that the chart is selected. Anytime a chart is selected (as it is now), the Chart toolbar appears. It might be floating, as shown in Figure D-5, or it might be fixed at the top or bottom of the worksheet window.

FIGURE D-3: First Chart Wizard dialog box

Chart types   Chart sub-types

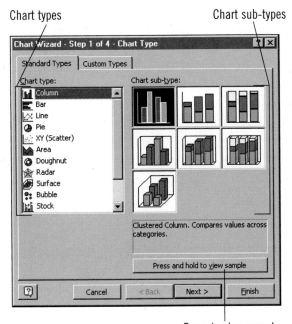

Press to view sample

FIGURE D-4: Third Chart Wizard dialog box

Sample chart   Title added   Legend

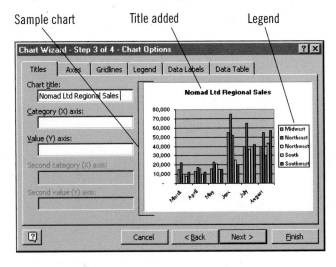

FIGURE D-5: Worksheet with column chart

Floating chart
toolbar   Title   Legend

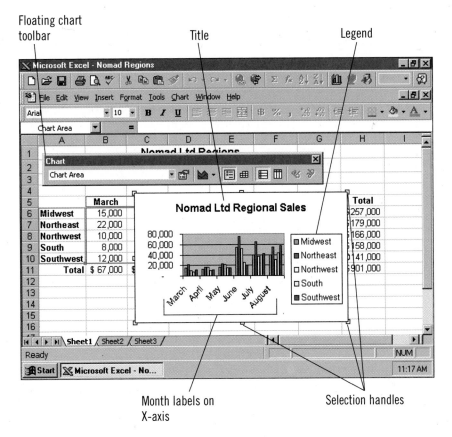

Month labels on   Selection handles
X-axis

Excel 97

Moving and Resizing a Chart and its Objects

Charts are graphics, or drawn **objects**, and have no specific cell or range address. You can move charts anywhere on a worksheet without affecting formulas or data in the worksheet. You can even put them on another sheet. You can also easily resize a chart to improve its appearance by dragging the selection handles. Drawn objects such as charts can contain other objects that you can move and resize. To move an object, select it then drag it or cut and copy it to a new location. To resize an object, use the selection handles. ◀▬▬ Evan wants to increase the size of the chart and position it below the worksheet data. He also wants to change the position of the legend.

Trouble?

If the Chart toolbar is in the way of the legend, move it out of your way first.

1. Make sure the chart is still selected. Scroll the worksheet until **row 28** is visible, then position the pointer over the white space around the chart
   The pointer shape ▧ indicates that you can move the chart or use a selection handle to resize it.

2. Press and hold the mouse button and drag the chart until the lower edge of the chart is in **row 28** and the left edge of the chart is in **column A**, then release the mouse button
   A dotted outline of the chart perimeter appears as the chart is being moved, the pointer changes to ✛, and the chart moves to the new location.

3. Position the pointer over one of the selection handles on the right border until it changes to ↔, then drag the right edge of the chart to the **middle of column I**
   The chart is widened. See Figure D-6.

4. Position the pointer over the top middle selection handle until it changes to ↕, then drag it to the **top of row 12**
   Now, you move the legend up so that it is slightly lower than the chart title.

5. Click the **legend** to select it, then drag it to the upper-right corner of the chart until it is slightly lower than the chart title
   Selection handles appear around the legend when you click it, and a dotted outline of the legend perimeter appears as you drag.

6. Press **[Esc]** to deselect the legend. The legend is now repositioned. See Figure D-7.

7. Save your work

FIGURE D-6: Worksheet with reposition and resized chart

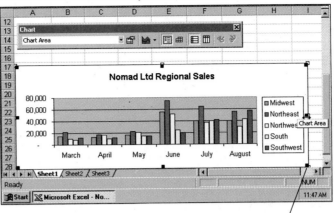

Widened to column I

FIGURE D-7: Worksheet with repositioned legend

Chart menu   Repositioned legend

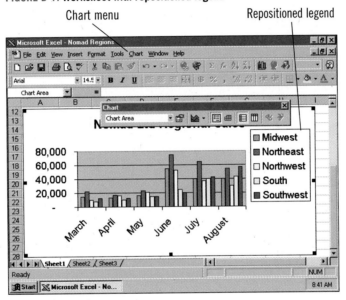

CLUES TO USE

Viewing multiple worksheets

A workbook can be organized with a chart on one sheet and the data on another sheet. With this organization, you can still see the data next to the chart by opening multiple windows of the same workbook. This allows you to see portions of multiple sheets at the same time. Click Window on the menu bar, then click New Window. A new window containing the current workbook opens. To see the windows next to each other, click Window on the menu bar, click Arrange, then choose one of the options in the Arrange Windows dialog box. You can open one worksheet in one window and a different worksheet in the second window. See Figure D-8. To close one window without closing the worksheet, double-click the control menu box on the window you want to close.

FIGURE D-8: Workbook with two windows open

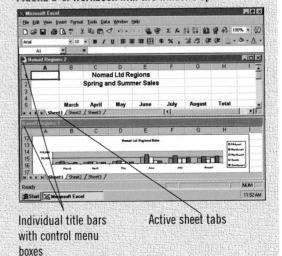

Individual title bars with control menu boxes

Active sheet tabs

Editing a Chart

Once you've created a chart, it's easy to modify it. You can change data values in the worksheet, and the chart will automatically be updated to reflect the new data. You can also easily change chart types using the buttons on the Chart toolbar. Table D-2 shows and describes the Chart toolbar buttons. Evan looks over his worksheet and realizes he entered the wrong data for the Northwest region in July and August. After he corrects this data, he wants to find out what percentage of total sales the month of June represents. He will convert the column chart to a pie chart to find this out.

Steps 1 2 3 4

1. **Scroll the worksheet so that you can see both the chart and row 8, containing the Northwest region's sales figures, at the same time**
As you enter the correct values, watch the columns for July and August in the chart change.

2. **Click cell F8, type 49000 to correct the July sales figure, press [→], type 45000 in cell G8, then press [Enter]**
The Northwest columns for July and August reflect the increased sales figures. See Figure D-9.

3. **Select the chart by clicking anywhere within the chart border, then click the Chart Type list arrow on the Chart toolbar**
The chart type buttons appear, as shown in Figure D-10.

4. **Click the 2-D Pie Chart button**
The column chart changes to a pie chart showing total sales by month (the columns in the selected range). See Figure D-11. (You may need to scroll up to see the chart.) You look at the pie chart, takes some notes, and then decide to convert it back to a column chart. You now want to see if the large increase in sales would be better presented with a three-dimensional column chart.

5. **Click , then click the 3-D Column Chart button to change the chart type**
A three-dimensional column chart appears. You note that the three-dimensional column format is too crowded, so you switch back to the two-dimensional format.

6. **Click , then click the 2-D Column Chart button to change the chart type**

Time To
✔ Save

TABLE D-2: Chart Type buttons

button	description	button	description
	Displays 2-D area chart		Displays 3-D area chart
	Displays 2-D bar chart		Displays 3-D bar chart
	Displays 2-D column chart		Displays 3-D column chart
	Displays 2-D line chart		Displays 3-D line chart
	Displays 2-D pie chart		Displays 3-D pie chart
	Displays 2-D scatter chart		Displays 3-D surface chart
	Displays 2-D doughnut chart		Displays 3-D cylinder chart
	Displays radar chart		Displays 3-D cone chart

FIGURE D-9: Worksheet with new data entered for the Northwest region

New data

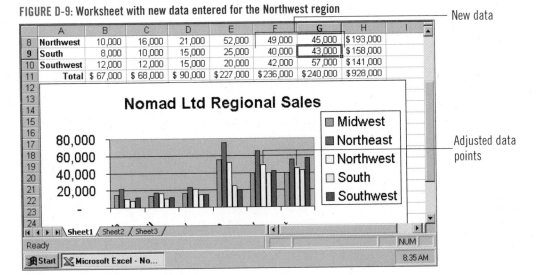

	A	B	C	D	E	F	G	H	I
8	Northwest	10,000	16,000	21,000	52,000	49,000	45,000	$193,000	
9	South	8,000	10,000	15,000	25,000	40,000	43,000	$158,000	
10	Southwest	12,000	12,000	15,000	20,000	42,000	57,000	$141,000	
11	Total	$ 67,000	$ 68,000	$ 90,000	$227,000	$236,000	$240,000	$928,000	

Adjusted data points

FIGURE D-10: Chart Type list box

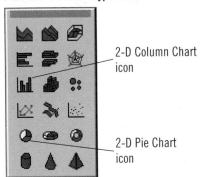

2-D Column Chart icon

2-D Pie Chart icon

FIGURE D-11: Pie chart

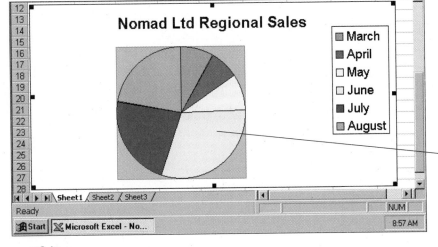

June sales pie slice

Rotating a chart

In a three-dimensional chart, columns or bars can sometimes be obscured by other data series within the same chart. You can rotate the chart until a better view is obtained. Double-click the chart, click the tip of one of its axes, then drag the handles until a more pleasing view of the data series appears. See Figure D-12.

FIGURE D-12: 3-D chart rotated with improved view of data series

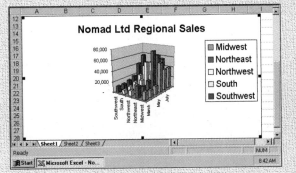

Changing the Appearance of a Chart

After you've created a chart using the Chart Wizard, you can modify its appearance by changing the colors of data series and adding or eliminating a legend and gridlines using the Chart toolbar and the Chart menu. **Gridlines** are the horizontal lines in the chart that enable the eye to follow the value on an axis. The corresponding Chart toolbar buttons are listed in Table D-3. Evan wants to make some changes in the appearance of his chart. He wants to see if the chart looks better without gridlines, and he wants to change the color of a data series.

Steps 1 2 3 4

> **QuickTip**
>
> Experiment with different formats for your charts until you get just the right look.

1. Make sure the chart is still selected

You want to see how the chart looks without gridlines. Gridlines currently appear on the chart.

2. Click Chart on the menu bar, then click Chart Options

3. Click the Gridlines tab in the Chart Options dialog box, then click the Major Gridlines checkbox for the Value (Y) Axis to remove the check and deselect this option

The gridlines disappear from the sample chart in the dialog box, as shown in Figure D-13. You decide that the gridlines are necessary to the chart's readability.

4. Click the Major Gridlines checkbox for the Value (Y) Axis, then click OK

The gridlines reappear. You are not happy with the color of the columns for the South data series and would like the columns to stand out more.

5. With the chart selected, double-click any column in the South data series

Handles appear on all the columns in the South data series, and the Format Data Series dialog box opens, as shown in Figure D-14. Make sure the Patterns tab is the front-most tab.

6. Click the dark green box (in the third row, fourth from the left), then click OK

All the columns in the series are dark green. Compare your finished chart to Figure D-15. You are pleased with the change.

7. Save your work

TABLE D-3: Chart enhancement buttons

button	use	button	use
📷	Displays formatting dialog box for the selected chart element	⊞	Charts data by row
📈▾	Selects chart type	⊞	Charts data by column
📋	Adds/Deletes legend	✂	Angles selected text downward
⊞	Creates a data table within the chart	✍	Angles selected text upward

FIGURE D-13: Chart Options dialog box

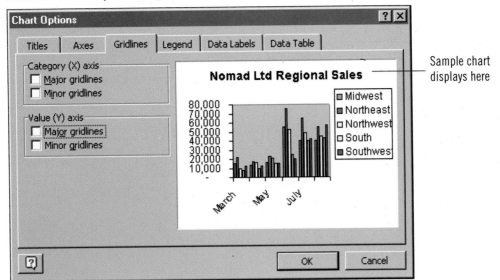

Sample chart
displays here

FIGURE D-14: Format Data Series dialog box

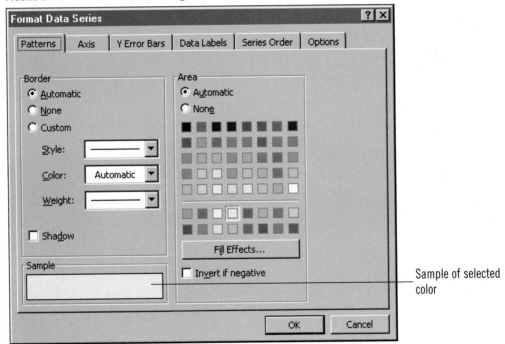

Sample of selected
color

FIGURE D-15: Chart with formatted data series

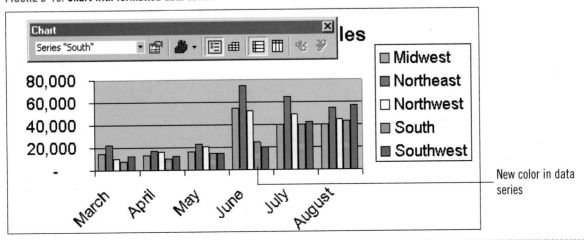

New color in data
series

Excel 97

Enhancing a Chart

There are many ways to enhance a chart to make it easier to read and understand. You can create titles for the X-axis and Y-axis, add graphics, or add background color. You can even format the text you use in a chart. Evan wants to improve the appearance of his chart by creating titles for the X-axis and Y-axis. He also decides to add a drop shadow to the title.

1. Make sure the chart is selected

You want to add descriptive text to the X-axis.

2. Click Chart on the menu bar, click Chart Options, click the Titles tab in the Chart Options dialog box, then type Months in the Category (X) Axis text box

The word "Months" appears below the month labels in the sample chart, as shown in Figure D-16. You now add text to the Y-axis.

3. Click the Value (Y) Axis text box, type Sales, then click OK

A selected text box containing "Sales" appears to the left of the Y-axis. Once the Chart Options dialog box is closed, you can move the axis title to a new position, by clicking on an edge of the selection and dragging it. If you wanted to edit the axis title, position the pointer over the selected text box until it becomes Ⅰ and click, then edit the text.

4. Press [Esc] to deselect the Y-axis label

Next you decide to draw a rectangle with a drop shadow around the title.

5. Click the chart title to select it

If necessary, you may have to move the Chart toolbar. You use the Format button on the Chart toolbar to create a drop shadow.

QuickTip

The Format button 📝 opens a dialog box with the appropriate formatting options for the selected chart element.

6. Click the Format button 📝 on the Chart toolbar to open the Format Chart Title dialog box, make sure the Patterns tab is active, click the Shadow checkbox, then click OK

A drop shadow appears around the title.

7. Press [Esc] to deselect the chart title and view the drop shadow

Compare your chart to Figure D-17.

8. Save your work

FIGURE D-16: Sample chart with X-axis text

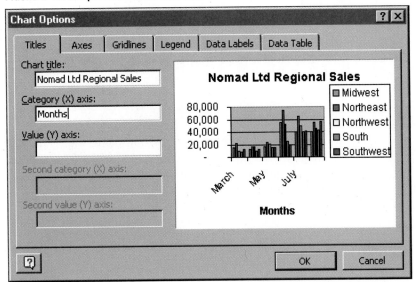

FIGURE D-17: Enhanced chart

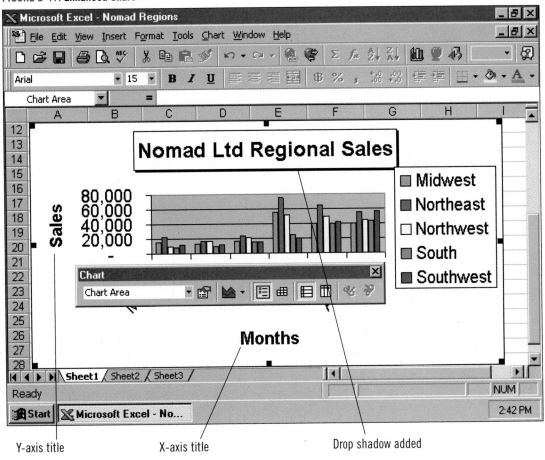

Y-axis title   X-axis title   Drop shadow added

Changing text font and alignment in charts

The font and the alignment of axis text can be modified to make it more readable or to better fit within the plot area. With a chart selected, double-click the text to be modified. The Format Axis dialog box appears. Click the Font or the Alignment tab, make the desired changes, then click OK.

Excel 97

Adding Text Annotations and Arrows to a Chart

You can add arrows and text annotations to highlight information in your charts. Text annotations are labels that you add to a chart to draw attention to a certain part of it. Evan wants to add a text annotation and an arrow to highlight the June sales increase.

1. Make sure the chart is selected

You want to call attention to the June sales increase by drawing an arrow that points to the top of the June data series with the annotation, "After advertising campaign." To enter the text for an annotation, you simply start typing.

2. Type After advertising campaign then click the Enter button ✓ on the formula bar

As you type, the text appears in the formula bar. After you confirm the entry, the text appears in a floating selected text box within the chart window.

3. Point to an edge of the text box, then press and hold the left mouse button

The pointer should be ✛. If the pointer changes to] or ↔, release the mouse button, click outside the text box area to deselect it, then select the text box and repeat Step 3.

4. Drag the text box above the chart, as shown in Figure D-18, then release the mouse button

You are ready to add an arrow.

5. Click the Drawing button 🖉 on the Standard toolbar

The Drawing toolbar appears.

6. Click the Arrow button ◥ on the Drawing toolbar

The pointer changes to +.

7. Position + under the word "advertising" in the text box, click the left mouse button, drag the line to the June sales, then release the mouse button

An arrowhead appears pointing to the June sales. Compare your finished chart to Figure D-19.

8. Click the Drawing button 🖉 to close the Drawing toolbar

9. Save your work

QuickTip

You can also insert text and an arrow in the data section of a worksheet by clicking the Text Box button 🔳 on the Drawing toolbar, drawing a text box, typing the text, and then adding the arrow.

FIGURE D-18: Repositioning text annotation

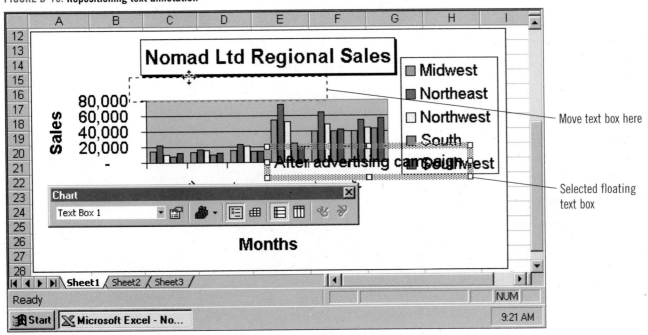

Move text box here

Selected floating text box

FIGURE D-19: Completed chart with text annotation and arrow

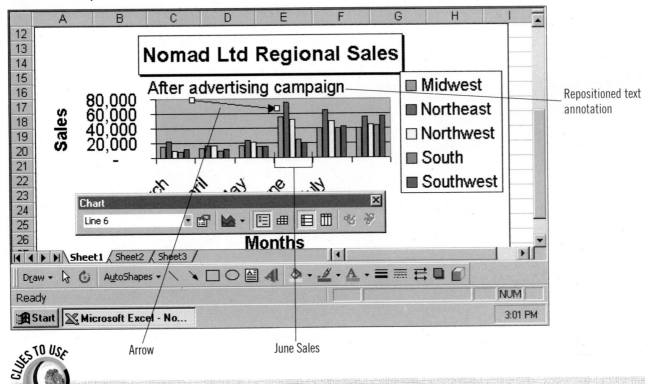

Repositioned text annotation

Arrow

June Sales

CLUES TO USE

Pulling out a pie slice

Just as an arrow can call attention to a data series, you can emphasize a pie slice by exploding it, or pulling it away from, the pie chart. Once the chart is in Edit mode, click the pie to select it, click the desired slice to select only that slice, then drag the slice away from the pie, as shown in Figure D-20.

FIGURE D-20: Exploded pie slice

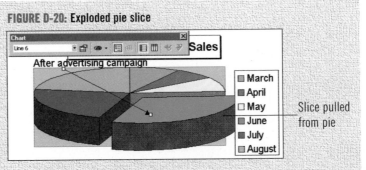

Slice pulled from pie

Previewing and Printing a Chart

After you complete a chart to your satisfaction, you will need to print it. You can print a chart by itself, or as part of the worksheet. ✎ Evan is satisfied with the chart and wants to print it for the annual meeting. He will print the worksheet and the chart together, so that the shareholders can see the actual sales numbers for each tour type.

Steps 1234

1. **Press [Esc] twice to deselect the arrow and the chart**
   If you wanted to print only the chart without the data, you would leave the chart selected.

2. **Click the Print Preview button 🔍 on the Standard toolbar**
   The Print Preview window opens. You decide that the chart and data would look better if they were printed in **landscape** orientation—that is, with the page turned sideways. To change the orientation of the page, you must alter the page setup.

3. **Click the Setup button to display the Page Setup dialog box, then click the Page tab**

4. **Click the Landscape radio button in the Orientation section**
   See Figure D-21.
   Because each page has a left default margin of 0.75", the chart and data will print too far over to the left of the page. You change this using the Margins tab.

5. **Click the Margins tab, click the Horizontal checkbox in the Center on Page section, then click OK**
   The print preview of the worksheet appears again. The data and chart are centered on the page that has a landscape orientation, and no gridlines appear. See Figure D-22. You are satisfied with the way it looks and print it.

6. **Click Print to display the Print dialog box, then click OK**
   Your printed report should look like the image displayed in the Print Preview window.

7. **Save your work**

8. **Close the workbook and exit Excel**

FIGURE D-21: **Page tab of the Page Setup dialog box**

Landscape selected

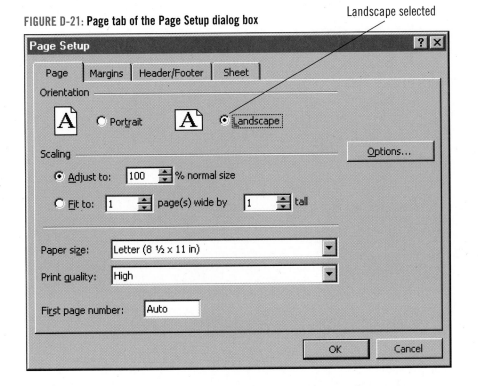

FIGURE D-22: **Chart and data ready to print**

Orientation changed
to landscape

Centered on page

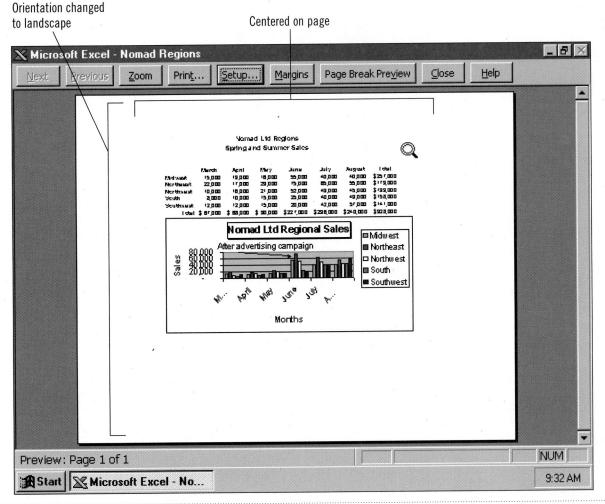

▶ Concepts Review

Label each of the elements of the Excel chart shown in Figure D-23.

FIGURE D-23

1 Area
2 Floating Chart Toolbar
3 Chart Title w/drop shadow
4 Reposition text annotation
5
6 Legend

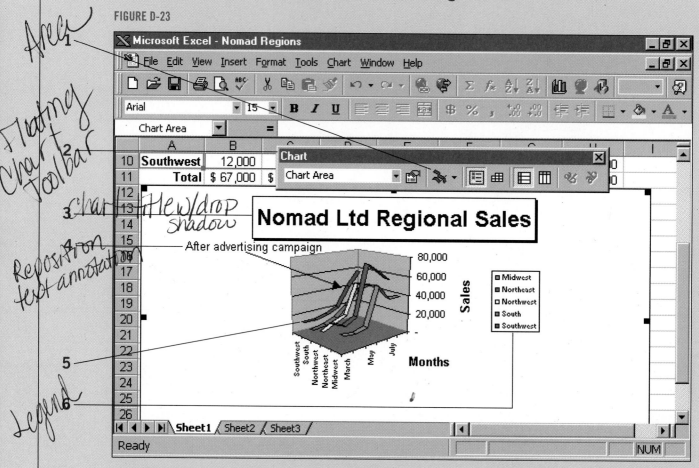

Match each of the statements with its chart type.

7. Column E
8. Area A
9. Pie B
10. Combination C
11. Line D

a. Shows how volume changes over time
b. Compares data as parts of a whole
c. Displays a column and line chart using different scales of measurement
d. Compares trends over even time intervals
e. Compares data over time—the Excel default

Select the best answer from the list of choices.

12. The box that identifies patterns used for each data series is a
 a. Data point   **b.** Plot   **c.** Legend   **d.** Range

13. What is the term for a row or column on a chart?
 a. Range address   **b.** Axis title   **c.** Chart orientation   **d.** Data series

► Skills Review

1. Create a worksheet and plan a chart.
 a. Start Excel, open a new workbook, then save it as Software Used to your Student Disk.
 b. Enter the information from Table D-4 in your worksheet in range A1:E6. Resize columns and rows.
 c. Save your work.
 d. Sketch a chart for a two-dimensional column chart that shows software distribution by department.

TABLE D-4

	Excel	Word	WordPerfect	PageMaker
Accounting	10	1	9	0
Marketing	2	9	0	6
Engineering	12	5	7	1
Personnel	2	2	2	1
Production	6	3	4	0

2. Create a chart.
 a. Select the range you want to chart.
 b. Click the Chart Wizard button.
 c. Complete the Chart Wizard dialog boxes and build a two-dimensional column chart on the same sheet as the data, having a different color bar for each department and with the title "Software Distribution by Department."
 d. Save your work.

3. Move and resize a chart and its objects.
 a. Make sure the chart is still selected.
 b. Move the chart beneath the data.
 c. Drag the chart's selection handles so it fills the range A7:G22.
 d. Click the legend to select it.
 e. Make the legend longer by about ½".
 f. Change the placement of the legend to the bottom right corner of the chart area.
 g. Save your work.

4. Edit a chart.
 a. Change the value in cell B3 to 6.
 b. Click the chart to select it.
 c. Click the Chart Type list arrow on the Chart toolbar.
 d. Click the 3-D Column Chart button in the list.
 e. Rotate the chart to move the data.
 f. Save your work.

5. Change the appearance of a chart.
a. Change the chart type to 2-D column chart.
b. Make sure the chart is still selected.
c. Turn off the displayed gridlines.
d. Change the X- and Y-axis font to Times New Roman.
e. Turn the gridlines back on.
f. Save your work.

6. Enhance a chart.
a. Make sure the chart is still selected, then click Chart on the menu bar, click Chart Options, then click the Titles tab.
b. Click the Category (X) axis text box and type "Department."
c. Click the Value (Y) axis text box, type "Types of Software," and then click OK.
d. Change the size of the X and Y axes font and the legend font to 8 pt.
e. Save your work.

7. Adding a text annotation and arrows to a chart.
a. Select the chart.
b. Create the text annotation "Need More Computers."
c. Drag the text annotation about one inch above any of the Personnel bars.
d. Change the font size of the annotation text to 8 pt.
e. Click the Arrow button on the Drawing toolbar.
f. Click below the text annotation, drag down any one of the Personnel bars, then release the mouse button.
g. Open a second window so you can display the data in the new window and the chart in the original window.
h. Close the second window.
i. Save your work.

8. Preview and print a chart.
a. Deselect the chart, then click the Print Preview button on the Standard toolbar.
b. Center the data and chart on the page and change the paper orientation to landscape.
c. Click Print in the Print Preview window.
d. Save your work, close the workbook, then exit Excel.

Theaters is the file we did on the board.

► Independent Challenges

1. You are the operations manager for the Springfield Recycling Center. The Marketing Department wants you to create charts for a brochure to advertise a new curbside recycling program. The data provided contains percentages of collected recycled goods. You need to create charts that show:

- How much of each type of recycled material Springfield collected in 1995 and what percentage each type represents. The center collects paper, plastics, and glass from business and residential customers.
- The yearly increases in the total amounts of recycled materials the center has collected since its inception three years ago. Springfield has experienced a 30% annual increase in collections.

To complete this independent challenge:

1. Prepare a worksheet plan that states your goal and identifies the formulas for any calculations.
2. Sketch a sample worksheet on a piece of paper describing how you will create the charts. Which type of chart is best suited for the information you need to display? What kind of chart enhancements will be necessary? Will a 3-D effect make your chart easier to understand?
3. Open the workbook XL D-2 on your Student Disk, then save it as Recycling Center.
4. Add a column that calculates the 30% increase in annual collections based on the percentages given.
5. Create at least six different charts to show the distribution of the different types of recycled goods, as well as the distribution by customer type. Use the Chart Wizard to switch the way data is plotted (columns vs. rows and vice versa) and come up with additional charts.
6. After creating the charts, make the appropriate enhancements. Include chart titles, legends, and axes titles.
7. Before printing, preview the file so you know what the charts will look like. Adjust any items as needed.
8. Save your work. Print the charts, then print the entire worksheet. Close the file.
9. Submit your worksheet plan, preliminary sketches, and the final worksheet printouts.

2. One of your responsibilities at the Nuts and Bolts hardware store is to re-create the company's records using Excel. Another is to convince the current staff that Excel can make daily operations easier and more efficient. You've decided to create charts using the previous year's operating expenses. These charts will be used at the next monthly Accounting Department meeting.

Open the workbook XL D-3 on your Student Disk, and save it as Expense Charts.

To complete this independent challenge:

1. Decide which data in the worksheet should be charted. Sketch two sample charts. What type of charts are best suited for the information you need to display? What kind of chart enhancements will be necessary?
2. Create at least six different charts that show the distribution of expenses, either by quarter or expense type.
3. Add annotated text and arrows highlighting data.
4. In one chart, change the colors of the data series, and in another chart, use black-and-white patterns only.
5. Before printing, preview the file so you know what the charts will look like. Adjust any items as needed.
6. Print the charts. Save your work.
7. Submit your sketches and the final worksheet printouts.

Excel 97

3. The Chamber of Commerce is delighted with the way you've organized their membership roster using Excel. The Board of Directors wants to ask the city for additional advertising funds and has asked you to prepare charts that can be used in their presentation.

Open the workbook XL D-4 on your Student Disk, and save it as Chamber Charts. This file contains raw advertising data for the month of January.

To complete this independent challenge:

1. Calculate the annual advertising expenses based on the January summary data.
2. Use the raw data for January shown in the range A16:B24 to create charts.
3. Decide what types of charts would be best suited for this type of data. Sketch two sample charts. What kind of chart enhancements will be necessary?
4. Create at least four different charts that show the distribution of advertising expenses. Show January expenses and projected values in at least two of the charts.
5. Add annotated text and arrows highlighting important data. Change the colors of the data series if you wish.
6. Before printing, preview the file so you know what the charts will look like. Adjust any items as needed.
7. Print the charts. Save your work.
8. Submit your sketches and the final worksheet printouts.

4. Financial information has a greater impact on others if displayed in a chart. Using the World Wide Web you can find out current activity of stocks and create informative charts. Your company has asked you to chart current trading indexes by category.

To complete this independent challenge:

1. Open a new workbook and save it on your Student Disk as Trading Indexes.
2. Log on to the Internet and use your browser to go to http://www.course.com. From there, click the link Student On Line Companions, then click the Microsoft Office 97 Professional Edition - Illustrated: A First Course page, then click the Excel link for Unit D.
3. Use the following site to compile your data, NASDAQ [www.nasdaq.com].
4. Click the Index Activity button on the NASDAQ home page.
5. Locate Index Value data by category and retrieve this information.
6. Create a chart of the Index Values, by category.
7. Save, print, and hand in a print out of your work.

▶ Visual Workshop

Modify a worksheet using the skills you learned in this unit, using Figure D-24 for reference. Open the file XL D-5 on your Student Disk, and save it as Quarterly Advertising Budget. Create the chart, then change the data to reflect Figure D-24. Preview and print your results, and submit your printout.

FIGURE D-24

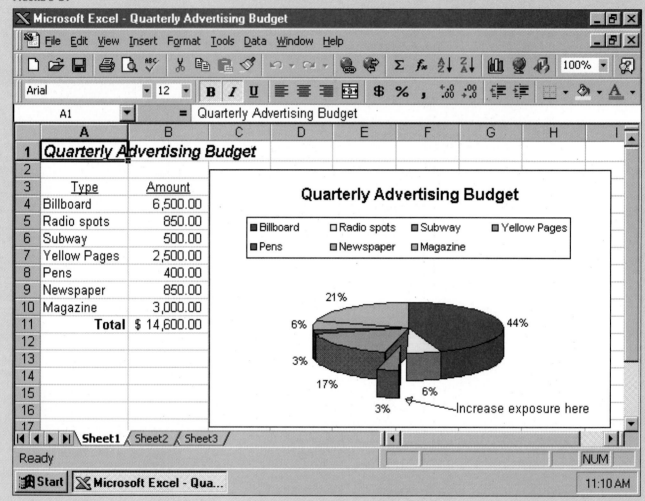

Working
with Formulas and Functions

Objectives

- ► **Create a formula with several operators**
- ► **Use names in a formula**
- ► **Generate multiple totals with AutoSum**
- ► **Use dates in calculations**
- ► **Build a conditional formula with the IF function**
- ► **Use statistical functions**
- ► **Calculate payments with the PMT function**
- ► **Display and print formula contents**

Without formulas, Excel would simply be an electronic grid with text and numbers. Used with formulas, Excel becomes a powerful data analysis software tool. As you learn how to analyze data using different types of formulas, including those that call for functions, you will discover more ways to use Excel. In this unit, you will gain a further understanding of Excel formulas and learn how to build several Excel functions. Top management at Nomad Ltd has asked Evan Brillstein to analyze various company data. To do this, Evan will create several worksheets that require the use of formulas and functions. Because management is considering raising salaries for level-two managers, Evan's first task is to create a report that compares the payroll deductions and net pay for level-two managers before and after a proposed raise.

Creating a Formula with Several Operators

You can create formulas that contain a combination of cell references (for example, Z100 and B2), operators (for example, * [multiplication] and - [subtraction]), and values (for example, 99 or 1.56). You also can create a single formula that performs several calculations. If you enter a formula with more than one operator, Excel performs the calculations in a particular sequence based on algebraic rules called **precedence**; that is, Excel performs the operation(s) within the parentheses first, then performs the other calculations. See Table E-1.  Evan has been given the gross pay and payroll deductions for the first payroll period and needs to complete his analysis. He also has preformatted, with the Comma style, any cells that are to contain values. Evan begins by entering a formula for net pay that subtracts the payroll deductions from gross pay.

1. Start Excel if necessary, open the workbook titled **XL E-1**, then save it as **Pay Info for L2 Mgrs**. Next build the first part of the net pay formula in cell B11

QuickTip

If you make a mistake while building a formula, press [Esc] and begin again.

2. Click cell **B11**, then type **=B6-**
   Remember that you can type cell references in either uppercase or lowercase letters. (Excel automatically converts lowercase cell reference letters to uppercase.) You type the equal sign (=) to tell Excel that a formula follows, B6 to reference the cell containing the gross pay, and the minus sign (-) to indicate that the next entry will be subtracted from cell B6. Now, complete the formula.

Trouble?

If you receive a message box indicating "Parentheses do not match," make sure you have included both a left and a right parenthesis.

3. Type **(B7+B8+B9+B10)** then click the **Enter button** ☑ on the formula bar
   The net pay for Payroll Period 1 appears in cell B11, as shown in Figure E-1. Because Excel performs the operations within parentheses first, you can control the order of calculations on the worksheet. (In this case, Excel sums the values in cells B7 through B10 first.) After the operations within the parentheses are completed, Excel performs the operations outside the parentheses. (In this case, Excel subtracts the total of range B7:B10 from cell B6.) Next, copy the formula across row 11.

4. Copy the formula in cell **B11** into cells **C11:F11**, then return to cell **A1**
   The formula in cell B11 is copied to the range C11:F11 to complete row 11. See Figure E-2.

5. Save the workbook
   Evan is pleased with the formulas that calculate net pay totals. Next, he adds employee names to his worksheet.

TABLE E-1: Example formulas using parentheses and several operators

formula	order of precedence	calculated result
=36+(1+3)	Add 1 to 3; then add the result to 36	40
=(10-20)/10-5	Subtract 20 from 10; divide that by 10; then subtract 5	-6
=(10*2)*(10+2)	Multiply 10 by 2; add 10 to 2; then multiply the results	240

FIGURE E-1: Worksheet showing formula and result

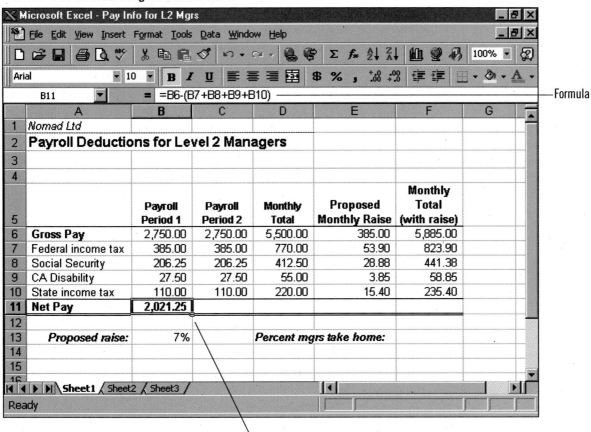

Result in cell B11

FIGURE E-2: Worksheet with copied formulas

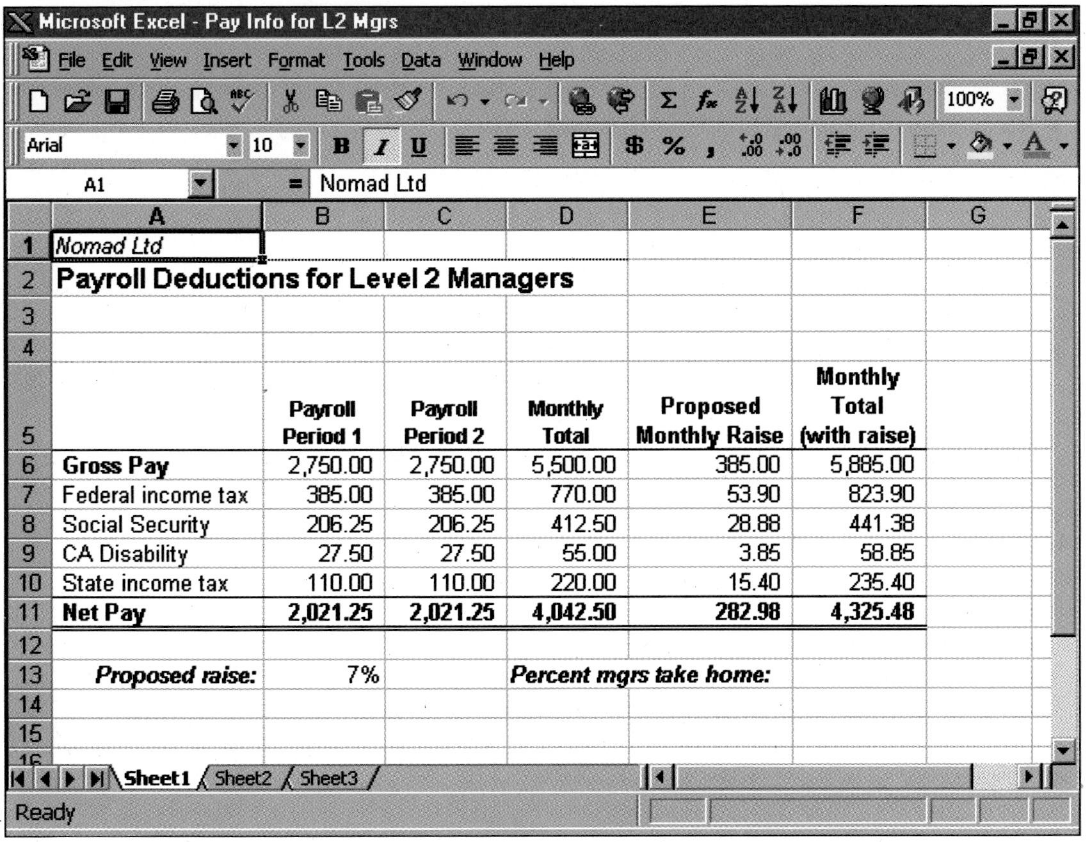

Using Names in a Formula

You can assign names to cells and ranges. Doing so reduces errors and makes a worksheet easier to follow. You also can use names in formulas. Using names in formulas facilitates formula building and provides a frame of reference for formula logic—the names make formulas easy to recognize and maintain. The formula Revenue - Cost, for example, is much easier to comprehend than the formula A2 - D3. You can produce a list of workbook names and their references at any time. ![mark] Evan wants to include a formula that calculates the percentage of monthly gross pay the managers would actually take home (net pay) if a 7% raise is granted.

1. **Click cell F6, click the name box on the formula bar to select the active cell reference, type Gross_with_Raise, then press [Enter]**
   The name assigned to cell F6, Gross_with_Raise, appears in the name box. Note that you must type underscores instead of spaces between words. Cell F6 is now named Gross_with_Raise to refer to the monthly gross pay amount that includes the 7% raise. The name box displays as much of the name as fits (Gross_with_...). Next, name the net pay cell.

2. **Click cell F11, click the name box, type Net_with_Raise, then press [Enter]**
   Now that the two cells are named, you are ready to enter the formula.

3. **Click cell F13, type =Net_with_Raise/Gross_with_Raise, then click the Enter button ☑ on the formula bar (make sure you begin the formula with an equal sign)**
   The formula bar now shows the new formula, and the result 0.735 appears in cell F13. If you add names to a worksheet after all the formulas have been entered, you must click Insert on the menu bar, click Name, click Apply, click the name or names, then click OK. Now format cell F13 as a percent.

4. **Format cell F13 using the Percent Style button % on the Formatting toolbar**
   Notice that the result shown in cell F13 (74%) is rounded to the nearest whole percent as shown in Figure E-3. Save and print the completed worksheet.

5. **Return to cell A1, then save and print the worksheet**

6. **Close the workbook**

QuickTip

To delete a name, click Insert on the menu bar, point to Name, then click Define. Select the name, click Delete, then click OK.

QuickTip

You can use the Label Ranges dialog box (Insert menu, Name submenu, Label command) to specify and name cells using column and row labels in your worksheet.

FIGURE E-3: Worksheet formula that includes cell names

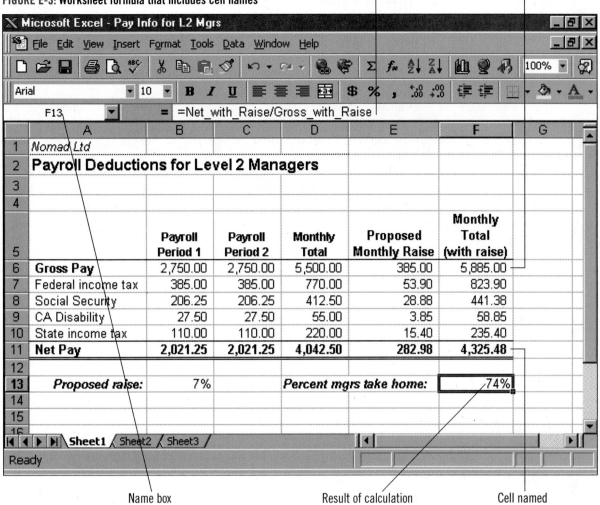

Formula with cell names

Cell named
Gross_with_Raise

Name box

Result of calculation

Cell named
Net_with_Raise

Producing a list of names

You might want to verify the names you have in a workbook and the cells they reference. To paste a list of names in a workbook, select a blank cell that has several blank cells beside and beneath it. Click Insert on the menu bar, point to Name, then click Paste. In the Paste Name dialog box, click Paste List. Excel produces a list that includes the sheet name and the cell or range the name identifies. See Figure E-4.

FIGURE E-4: Worksheet with pasted list of names

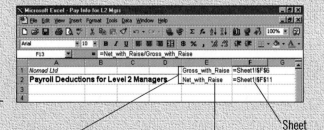

Pasted list of names

List of workbook names

Sheet location

Generating Multiple Totals with AutoSum

In most cases, the result of a function is a value derived from a calculation. Functions also can return results such as text, references, or other information about the worksheet. You enter a function, such as AVERAGE, directly into a cell; you can use the Edit Formula button; or, you can insert it with the Paste Function. You can use cell references, ranges, names, and formulas as arguments between the parentheses. As with other cell entries, you can cut, copy, and paste functions from one area of the worksheet to another and from one workbook to another. The most widely used Excel function, SUM, calculates worksheet totals and can be entered easily using the AutoSum button on the Standard toolbar.　　　　Evan's manager has asked him for a report summarizing annual bicycle sales. She wants the report to compare sales of competitor's brands to sales of Nomad Ltd's bikes. Evan has entered the data for units of bicycles sold. Now he needs to complete the worksheet totals.

Steps

1. Open the workbook titled XL E-2, then save it as Bicycle Sales

You need to generate multiple totals with AutoSum. You can use the [Ctrl] key to select multiple, nonadjacent ranges.

2. Select range B5:E10, press and hold [Ctrl], then select range B12:E14

To select nonadjacent cells, you must press and hold [Ctrl] while selecting the additional cells. Compare your selections with Figure E-5. Now, you are is ready to total the columns in the two selected ranges.

> **Trouble?**
>
> If you select the wrong combination of cells, simply click on a single cell and begin again.

3. Click the AutoSum button ∑ on the Standard toolbar

When the selected range you want to sum (B5:E10 and B12:E14, in this example) includes a blank cell with data values above it, AutoSum enters the total in the blank cell. Next, generate annual totals in column F and grand totals in row 16.

4. Select range B5:F16, then click ∑

Whenever the selected range you want to sum includes a blank cell in the bottom row or right column, AutoSum enters the total in the blank cell. In this case, Excel ignores the data values and totals only the SUM functions. Although Excel generates totals when you click the AutoSum button, it is a good idea to check the results.

5. Click cell B16

The formula bar reads =SUM(B14,B10). See Figure E-6. When generating grand totals, Excel automatically references the cells containing SUM functions with a comma separator between cell references. Excel uses commas to separate multiple arguments in all functions, not just in SUM. You are ready to save and print your work

6. Save and print the worksheet, then close the workbook

FIGURE E-5: Selecting nonadjacent ranges using [Ctrl]

	A	B	C	D	E	F	G	H
1	Nomad Ltd							
2	**Bicycles - Sales Summary in Units Sold**							
3								
4	*Bicycles - Other brands*	Qtr 1	Qtr 2	Qtr 3	Qtr 4	Total		
5	Mountain Climber	33	28	31	34			
6	Rock Roller	25	22	21	24			
7	Tour de Bike	23	16	20	19			
8	Youth Rock Roller	24	23	19	22			
9	Youth Tour de Bike	35	29	25	26			
10	Total							
11	*Nomad Bicycles*							
12	Mountain Master	458	379	299	356			
13	Tour Master	386	325	285	348			
14	Total							
15								
16	Grand Total							
17								
18								

Sheet1 / Sheet2 / Sheet3 /

Ready — Sum=3335

FIGURE E-6: Completed worksheet

B16 = =SUM(B14,B10)

Comma used to separate multiple arguments

	A	B	C	D	E	F	G	H
1	Nomad Ltd							
2	**Bicycles - Sales Summary in Units Sold**							
3								
4	*Bicycles - Other brands*	Qtr 1	Qtr 2	Qtr 3	Qtr 4	Total		
5	Mountain Climber	33	28	31	34	126		
6	Rock Roller	25	22	21	24	92		
7	Tour de Bike	23	16	20	19	78		
8	Youth Rock Roller	24	23	19	22	88		
9	Youth Tour de Bike	35	29	25	26	115		
10	Total	140	118	116	125	499		
11	*Nomad Bicycles*							
12	Mountain Master	458	379	299	356	1,492		
13	Tour Master	386	325	285	348	1,344		
14	Total	844	704	584	704	2,836		
15								
16	Grand Total	984	822	700	829	3,335		
17								
18								

Sheet1 / Sheet2 / Sheet3 /

Ready

CLUES TO USE

Quick calculations with AutoCalculate

To check a total quickly without entering a formula, just select the range you want to sum, and the answer appears in the status bar next to SUM=. You also can perform other quick calculations, such as averaging or finding the minimum value in a selection. To do this, right-click the AutoCalculate area in the status bar and select from the list of options. The option you select remains in effect and in the status bar until you make another selection. See Figure E-7.

FIGURE E-7: Using AutoCalculate

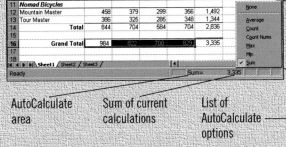

AutoCalculate area — Sum of current calculations — List of AutoCalculate options

Excel 97

Using Dates in Calculations

If you enter dates in a worksheet so that Excel recognizes them as dates, you can sort (arrange) the dates and perform date calculations. For example, you can calculate the number of days between your birth date and today, which is the number of days you have been alive. Commonly used date formats that Excel recognizes are listed in Table E-2. When you enter a date in any of these formats, Excel considers the entry a date function, converts the date to a serial date number, and stores that number in the cell. A date's converted serial date is the number of days to that date. The serial date of January 1, 1900; for example, is 1; the serial date of January 1, 1998 is 35431. ✎ Evan's next task is to complete the Open Accounts Receivable worksheet for Adventure Tours in the Southwest. He remembers to enter the worksheet dates in a format that Excel recognizes, so that he can take advantage of date calculation.

1. **Open the workbook titled XL E-3, then save it as Southwest Tour Receivables to the appropriate folder on your Student Disk**
   Begin by entering the current date, the date that is critical to worksheet calculations.

2. **Click cell C4, type 9/1/98, then press [Enter]**
   The date appears in cell C4 just as you typed it. You want to enter a formula that calculates the invoice due date, which is 30 days from the invoice date. The formula adds 30 days to the invoice date.

3. **Click cell F7, type =, click cell B7, type +30, then click the Enter button ✓ on the formula bar**
   Excel calculates the result by converting the 8/1/98 invoice date to a serial date number, adding 30 to it, then automatically formatting the result as a date. See Figure E-8. Because this same formula will calculate the due date for each invoice, you can copy the formula down the column using the fill handle.

4. **Copy the formula in cell F7 into cells F8:F13**
   Cell referencing causes the copied formula to contain the appropriate cell references. You are pleased at how easily Excel calculated the invoice due dates. Now you are ready to enter the formula that calculates the age of each invoice. You do this by subtracting the invoice date from the current date. Because each invoice age formula must refer to the current date, you must make cell C4, the current date cell, an absolute reference in the formula.

5. **Click cell G7, type =, click cell C4, press [F4] to add the absolute reference symbols ($), type -, click B7, then click ✓**
   The formula bar displays the formula C4-B7. The numerical result, 31, appears in cell G7 because there are 31 days between 8/1/98 and 9/1/98. Again, copy the formula down the column.

6. **Click cell G7, drag the fill handle to select range G7:G13, then press [Ctrl][Home] to deselect the range**
   The age of each invoice appears in column G, as shown in Figure E-9.

7. **Click the Save button 🖫 on the Standard toolbar**

QuickTip

You also can perform time calculations in Excel. For example, you can enter an employee's starting time and ending time, then calculate how many hours and minutes he or she worked. You must enter time in a format that Excel recognizes; for example, 1:35 PM (h:mm AM/PM).

QuickTip

If you perform date calculations and the intended numeric result displays as a date, format the cell(s) using a number format.

FIGURE E-8: Worksheet with formula for invoice due date

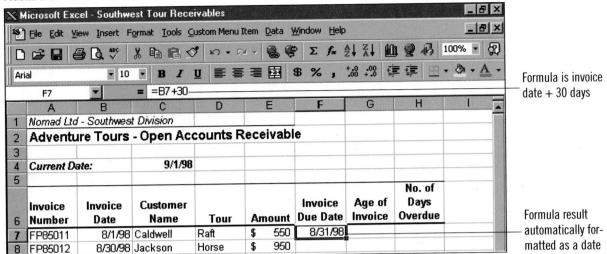

Formula is invoice date + 30 days

Formula result automatically formatted as a date

FIGURE E-9: Worksheet with copied formulas

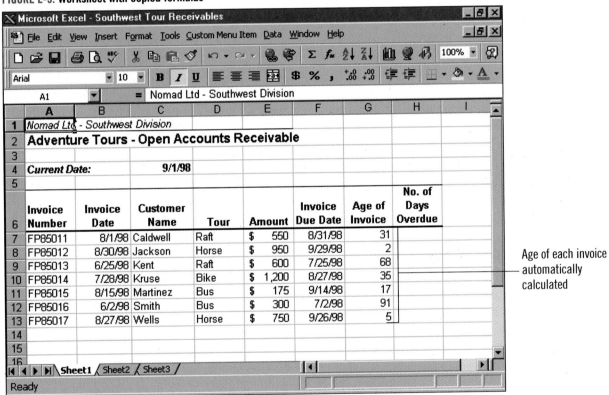

Age of each invoice automatically calculated

TABLE E-2: Commonly used date formats

format	example
M/d/yy	1/1/98
d-mmm-yy	1-Jan-98
d-mmm	1-Jan
Mmm-yy	Jan-98

Building a Conditional Formula with the IF Function

You can build a conditional formula using an IF function. A **conditional formula** is one that makes calculations based on stated conditions. For example, you can build a formula to calculate bonuses based on a person's performance rating. If a person is rated a 5 (the stated condition) on a scale of 1 to 5, with 5 being the highest rating, he or she receives 10% of his or her salary as a bonus; otherwise, there is no bonus. When the condition is a question that can be answered with a true or false response, Excel calls this stated condition a **logical test**. The IF function has three parts, separated by commas: a condition or logical test, an action to take if the logical test or condition is true, then an action to take if the logical test or condition is false. Another way of expressing this is: IF(test_cond,do_this,else_this). Translated into an Excel IF function, the formula to calculate bonuses would look something like: IF(Rating=5,Salary*0.10,0). The translation would be: If the rating equals 5, multiply the salary by 0.10 (the decimal equivalent of 10%), then place the result in the selected cell. If the rating does not equal 5, place a 0 in the cell. When entering the logical test portion of an IF statement, typically you use some combination of the comparison operators listed in Table E-3. Evan is almost finished with the worksheet. To complete it, he needs to use an IF function that calculates the number of days each invoice is overdue.

Steps 1234

1. Click cell **H7**

The cell pointer is now positioned where the result of the function will appear. You want the formula to calculate the number of days overdue as follows: If the age of the invoice is greater than 30, calculate the days overdue (Age of Invoice - 30), and place the result in cell H7; otherwise, place a 0 (zero) in the cell. The formula will include the IF function and cell references.

2. Type =**IF(G7>30,** (make sure to type the comma)

You have entered the first part of the function, the logical test. Notice that you used the symbol for greater than (>). So far, the formula reads: If Age of Invoice is greater than 30 (in other words, if the invoice is overdue). Next, tell Excel the action to take if the invoice is over 30 days old.

3. Type **G7-30,** (make sure to type the comma)

This part of the formula, between the first and second commas, is what you want Excel to do if the logical test is true; that is, if the age of the invoice is over 30. Continuing the translation of the formula, this part means: Take the Age of Invoice value and subtract 30. Finally, tell Excel the action to take if the logical test is false (that is, if the age of the invoice is 30 days or less).

4. Type **0,** then click the Enter button ☑ on the formula bar (you do not have to type The) to complete the formula

The formula is complete and the result, 1 (the number of days overdue), appears in cell H7. See Figure E-10. Next, Copy the formula.

5. Copy the formula in cell H7 into cells **H8:H13**

Compare your results with Figure E-11, then save and print your work.

6. Save, then print the workbook

FIGURE E-10: Worksheet with IF function

Logical test

Action to take if test is true

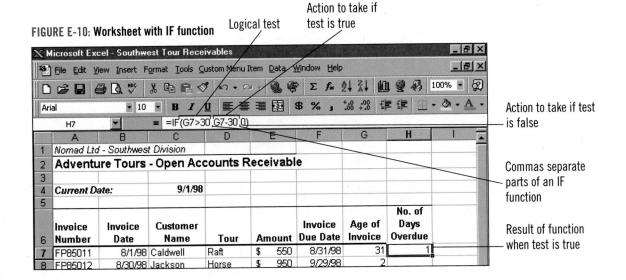

Action to take if test is false

Commas separate parts of an IF function

Result of function when test is true

FIGURE E-11: Completed worksheet

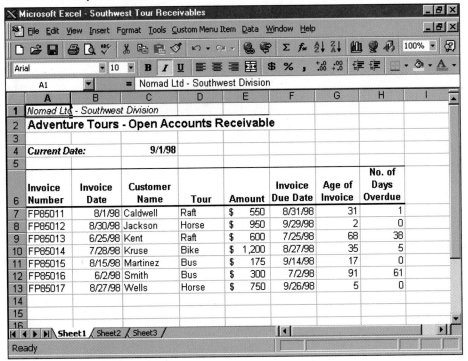

TABLE E-3: Comparison operators

operator	function
<	Less than
>	Greater than
=	Equal to
<=	Less than or equal to
>=	Greater than or equal to
<>	Not equal to

Using Statistical Functions

Excel offers several hundred worksheet functions. A small group of these functions calculates statistics such as averages, minimum values, and maximum values. See Table E-4 for a brief description of these commonly used functions. Evan's manager has asked him to present detailed information about open accounts receivable. To do this, Evan adds some statistical functions to the worksheet. He begins by using the MAX function to calculate the maximum value in a range.

Trouble?

If you have difficulty clicking cells or ranges when you build formulas, try scrolling to reposition the worksheet area until all participating cells are visible.

1. Click cell **D19**, type **=MAX(**, select range **G7:G13**, then press **[Enter]**
Excel automatically adds the right parenthesis upon entering the function. The age of the oldest invoice (or maximum value in range G7:G13) is 91 days, as shown in cell D19. Next, Evan builds a formula to calculate the largest dollar amount among the outstanding invoices.

2. In cell **D20**, type **=MAX(**, select range **E7:E13**, then press **[Enter]**
Note that the largest amount owed is $1,200, as shown in cell D20. Now you can use the MIN function to find the smallest dollar amount and the age of the newest invoice.

3. In cell **D21**, type **=MIN(**, select range **E7:E13**, then press **[Enter]**; in cell **D22**, type **=MIN(**, select range **G7:G13**, then press **[Enter]**
The smallest dollar amount owed is $175, as shown in cell D21, and the newest invoice is two days old. In the next step, you use a function to count the number of invoices by counting the number of entries in column A.

QuickTip

If you don't see the desired function in the Function name list, scroll to display more function names.

4. In cell **D23**, type **=**, then click the **Paste Function button** 𝑓ₓ on the Standard toolbar to open the Paste Function dialog box

5. Under Function category, click **Statistical**, then under Function name click **COUNT**
After selecting the function name, notice that the description of the COUNT function reads, "Counts the number of cells that contain numbers . . ." Because the invoice numbers (for example, FP85011) are considered text entries, not numerical entries, the COUNT function will not work. There is another function, COUNTA, that counts the number of cells that are not empty and therefore can be used to count the number of invoice number entries.

6. Under Function name, click **COUNTA**, then click **OK**
Excel automatically opens the Formula Palette and automatically references the range that is directly above the active cell as the first argument (in this case, range D19:D22, which is not the range you want to count). See Figure E-12. You need to select the correct range of invoice numbers. Because the desired invoice numbers are not visible, you need to collapse the dialog box so that you can select the correct range.

7. With the Value1 argument selected in the Formula Palette, click the Value1 **Collapse Dialog Box button**, 🖼, select range **A7:A13** in the worksheet, click the **Redisplay Dialog Box button** 🖼, then click **OK**
Compare your worksheet with Figure E-13.

8. Save, print, then close the workbook

FIGURE E-12: Formula Palette showing COUNTA function

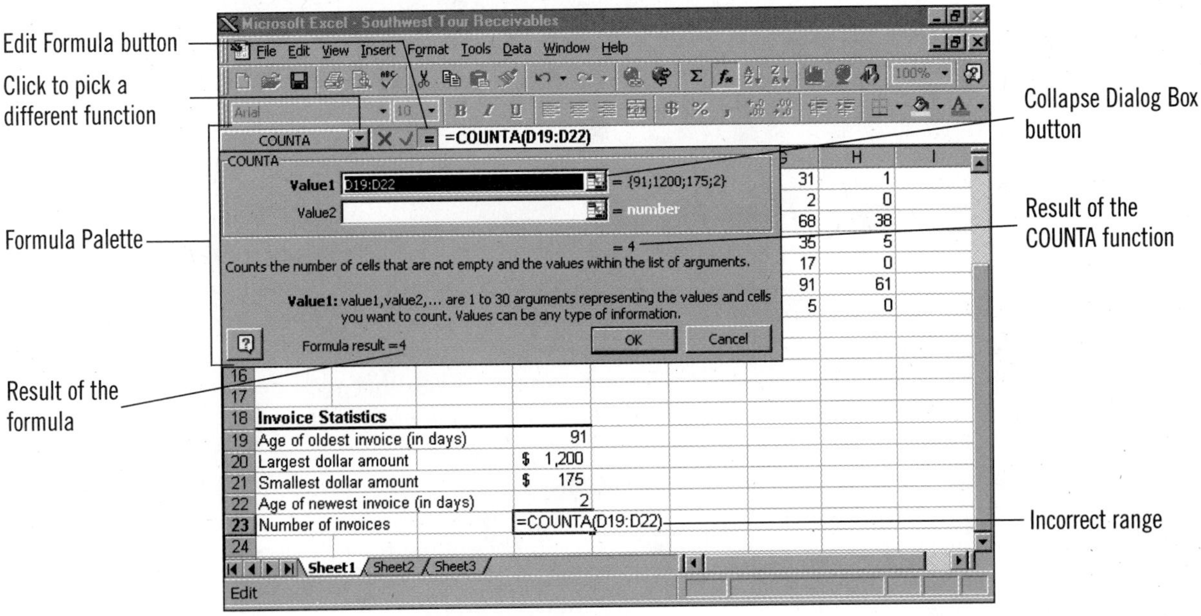

Edit Formula button

Click to pick a different function

Collapse Dialog Box button

Formula Palette

Result of the COUNTA function

Result of the formula

Incorrect range

FIGURE E-13: Worksheet with invoice statistics

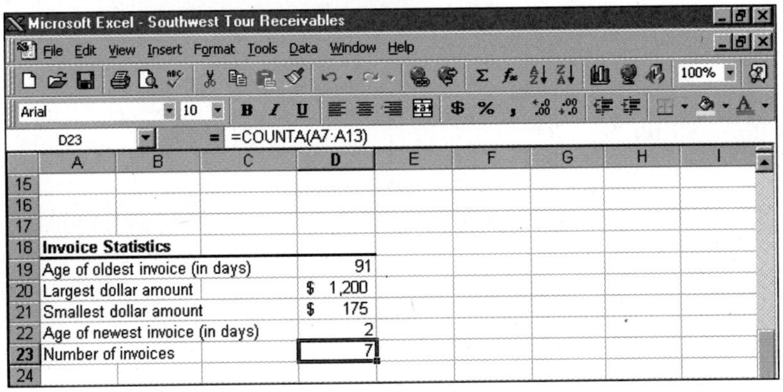

TABLE E-4: Commonly used statistical functions

function	worksheet action
AVERAGE	Calculates an average value
COUNT	Counts the number of values
COUNTA	Counts the number of nonblank entries
MAX	Finds the largest value
MIN	Finds the smallest value
SUM	Calculates a total

Using the Formula Palette to enter and edit formulas

When you use the Paste Function to build a formula, the Formula Palette displays the name and description for the function and each of its arguments, the current result of the function, and the current result of the entire formula. You also can use the Formula Palette to edit functions in formulas. To open the Formula Palette from either a blank cell or one containing a formula, click the Edit Formula button ![=] on the formula bar.

Calculating Payments with the PMT Function

PMT is a financial function that calculates the periodic payment amount for money borrowed. For example, if you want to borrow money to buy a car, the PMT function can calculate your monthly payment on the loan. Let's say you want to borrow $15,000 at 9% interest and pay the loan off in five years. Excel's PMT function can tell you that your monthly payment will be $311.38. The parts of the PMT function are: PMT(rate, nper, pv, fv, type). See Figure E-14 for an illustration of a PMT function that calculates the monthly payment in the car loan example.

 For several months, the management at Nomad Ltd has been planning the development of a new mountain bike. Evan's manager has asked him to obtain quotes from three different lenders on borrowing $25,000 to begin developing the new product. He obtained loan quotes from a commercial bank, a venture capitalist, and an investment banker. Now Evan can summarize the information using Excel's PMT function.

Steps

QuickTip

It is important to be consistent about the units you use for *rate* and *nper*. If, for example, you express *nper* as the number of *monthly* payments, then you must express the interest rate as a *monthly* rate, not an annual rate.

1. Open the workbook titled **XL E-4**, then save it as **Bicycle Loan Summary**
   You have already entered all the data with the lender data already entered; you are ready to calculate the commercial loan monthly payment in cell E5.

2. Click cell **E5**, type **=PMT(C5/12,D5,B5)** (make sure you type the commas); then click the **Enter button** ✓ on the formula bar
   Note that the payment of ($543.56) in cell E5 is a negative amount. (It appears in red on a color monitor.) Excel displays the result of a PMT function as a negative value to reflect the negative cash flow the loan represents to the borrower. You must divide the annual interest by 12 because you are calculating monthly, not annual, payments. Because you want to show the monthly payment value as a positive number, you can convert the loan amount to a negative number by placing a minus sign in front of the cell reference.

3. Edit cell **E5** so it reads **=PMT(C5/12,D5,-B5)**, then click ✓
   A positive value of $543.56 now appears in cell E5. See Figure E-15. Now, copy the formula to generate the monthly payments for the other loans.

4. Click cell **E5**, then drag the fill handle to select range **E5:E7**
   A monthly payment of $818.47 for the venture capitalist loan appears in cell E6. A monthly payment of $1,176.84 for the investment banker loan appears in cell E7. You are surprised that the monthly payments vary so much. You will not know the entire financial picture until you take one more step and calculate the total payments and total interest for each lender.

5. Click cell **F5**, type **=E5*D5**, then press **[Tab]**; in cell G5, type **=F5-B5**, then click ✓

6. Copy the formulas in cells F5:G5 into cells **F6:G7**
   You can experiment with different interest rates, loan amounts, or terms for any one of the lenders; the PMT function generates a new set of values automatically. Compare your results to Figure E-16.

7. Save the workbook, then print the worksheet

FIGURE E-14: Example of PMT function for car loan

PMT(.09/12,60,15000) = $311.38

Interest rate per period | Number of payments | Present value of loan amount | Monthly payment calculated

FIGURE E-15: PMT function calculating monthly loan payment

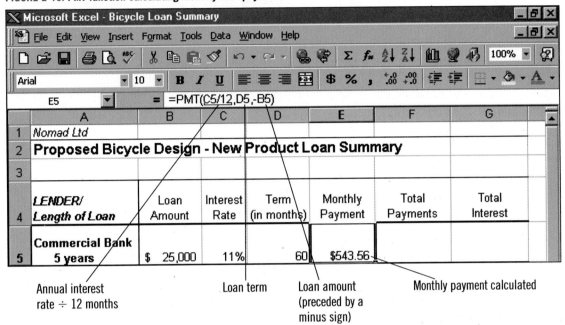

Annual interest rate ÷ 12 months | Loan term | Loan amount (preceded by a minus sign) | Monthly payment calculated

FIGURE E-16: Completed worksheet

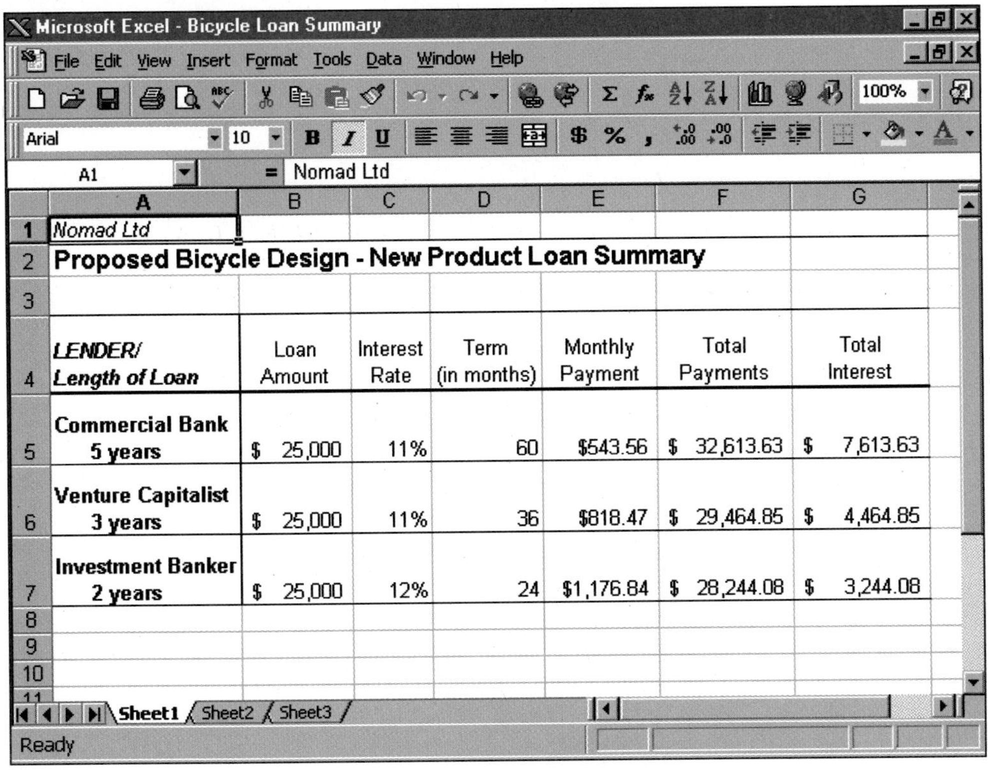

WORKING WITH FORMULAS AND FUNCTIONS EX E-15

Excel 97

Displaying and Printing Formula Contents

Excel usually displays the result of formula calculations in the worksheet area and displays formula contents for the active cell in the formula bar. However, you can instruct Excel to display the formulas directly in the worksheet locations in which they were entered. You can document worksheet formulas in this way: by first displaying the formulas then printing them. These formula printouts are valuable paper-based worksheet documentation. Because formulas are often longer than their corresponding values, landscape orientation is the best choice for printing formulas. Evan is ready to produce a formula printout to submit with the worksheet.

1. Click **Tools** on the menu bar, click **Options**, then click the **View tab**
The View tab of the Options dialog box appears, as shown in Figure E-17.

2. Under Window options, click the **Formulas** check box to select it, then click **OK**
The columns have widened and retain their original formats. You need to scroll horizontally to see that the column widths adjust automatically to accommodate the formulas.

3. Scroll horizontally to bring columns D through G into view
Instead of formula results appearing in the cells, Excel shows the actual formulas. See Figure E-18. In order to see how this worksheet will print, you can preview it.

4. Click the **Print Preview button** 🔍 on the Standard toolbar
The status bar reads Preview: Page 1 of 3, indicating that the worksheet will print on three pages. You want to print it on one page and include the row number and column letter headings. You can do this by selecting several Page Setup options.

5. Click the **Setup button** in the Print Preview window, then click the **Page tab**
Select the Landscape orientation and the Fit to scaling options.

6. Under Orientation, click the **Landscape option button**; then under Scaling, click the **Fit to option button**
Selecting Landscape instructs Excel to print the worksheet sideways on the page. The Fit to option ensures that the document is printed on a single page. Finally, select the Sheet tab to turn on the printing of row number and column letters.

7. Click the **Sheet tab**, under Print click the **Row and Column Headings check box**, click **OK**, then position the Zoom pointer 🔍 over column A and click
The worksheet formulas now appear on a single page, in landscape orientation, with row (number) and column (letter) headings. See Figure E-19. Notice that the contents of cell A2 are slightly hidden.

8. Click the **Print button** in the Print Preview window, then click **OK**
After you retrieve the printout, you want to return the worksheet to display formula results. You can do this by pressing [Ctrl][`] (grave accent mark) to toggle between displaying formula results and displaying formula contents.

9. Press **[Ctrl][`]** to re-display formula results, save and close the workbook, then exit Excel

QuickTip

All Page Setup options—such as landscape orientation, fit to scaling, and printing row and column headings—apply to the active worksheet and are saved with the workbook.

FIGURE E-17: **View tab of the Options dialog box**

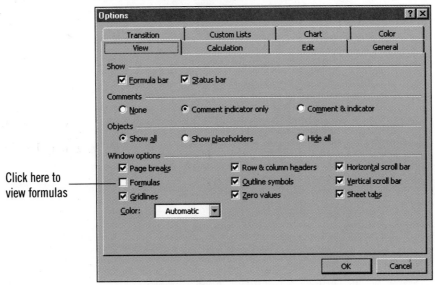

Click here to
view formulas

FIGURE E-18: **Worksheet with formulas visible**

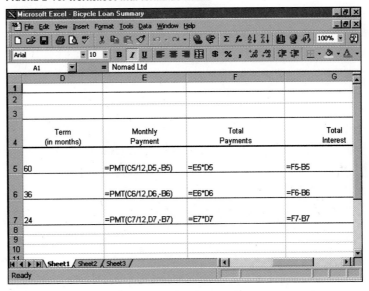

Column headings

FIGURE E-19: **Print Preview window**

Row headings

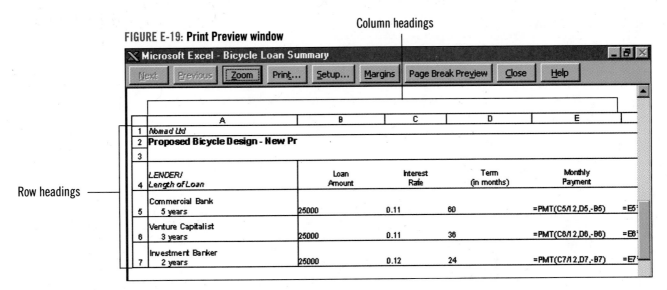

Practice

▶ Concepts Review

Label each of the elements of the Excel screen shown in Figure E-20. *Ryce.) Heading*

FIGURE E-20

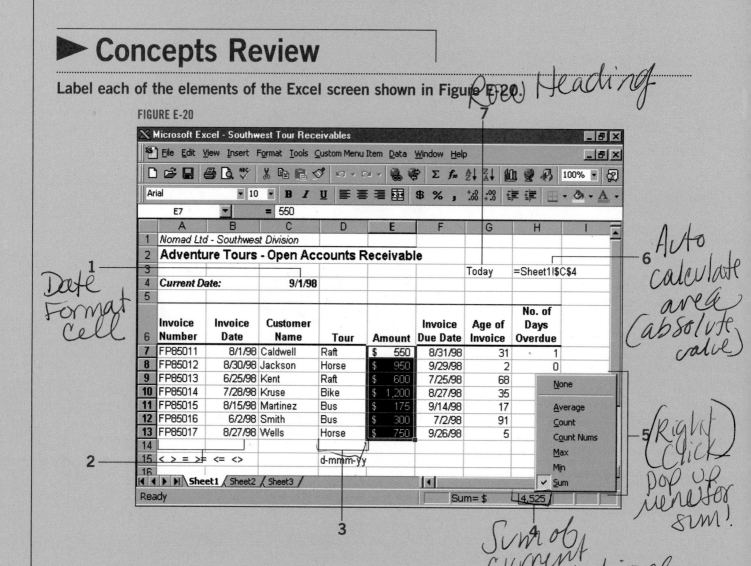

1 — Date Format Cell

2

3

7

6 — Auto calculate area (absolute value)

5 — (Right Click pop up menu for sum!)

4 — Sum of current calculations

Match each of the terms with the statement that best describes its function.

8. Parentheses *A*
9. COUNTA *D*
10. test_cond
11. COUNT *B*
12. pv

a. Part of the IF function in which the conditions are stated
b. Function used to count the number of numerical entries
c. Part of the PMT function that represents the loan amount
d. Function used to count the number of nonblank entries
e. Symbols used in formulas to control formula calculation order

Select the best answer from the list of choices.

13. **To generate a positive payment value when using the PMT function, you must**
    a. Enter the function arguments as positive values.
    b. Enter the function arguments as negative values.
    c. Enter the amount being borrowed as a negative value.
    d. Enter the interest rate divisor as a negative value.

14. **When you enter the rate and nper arguments in a PMT function**
    a. Multiply both units by 12.
    b. Be consistent in the units used.
    c. Divide both values by 12.
    d. Use monthly units instead of annual units.

15. **To express conditions such as less than or equal to, you can use a(n)**
    a. IF function.
    b. Comparison operator.
    c. AutoCalculate formula.
    d. PMT function.

▶ Skills Review

1. **Create a formula with several operators.**
    a. Open workbook XL E-5, and save it as "Annual Bonuses".
    b. In cell C15, enter the formula C13+(C14*7).

2. **Use names in a formula.**
    a. Name cell C13 "Dept_Bonus".
    b. Name cell C14 "Project_Bonus".
    c. In cell E4, enter the formula Dept_Bonus*D4+Project_Bonus.
    d. Copy formula in cell E4 into the range E5:E10.
    e. Format range E4:E10 with the Comma Style button.
    f. In cell F4, enter a formula that sums C4 and E4.
    g. Copy the formula in cell F4 into the range F5:F10.
    h. Return to cell A1, then save your work.

3. **Generate multiple totals with AutoSum.**
    a. Select range E11:F11.
    b. Enter the totals using AutoSum.
    c. Format range E11:F11 using the Currency Style button.
    d. Save your work, preview, then print the worksheet.

4. **Use dates in calculations.**
    a. Make the Merit Pay sheet active.
    b. In cell D6, enter the formula B6+183.
    c. Copy the formula in cell D6 into the range D7:D14.
    d. Save your work.

5. **Build a conditional formula with the IF function.**
   a. In cell F6, enter the formula IF(C6=5,E6*0.05,0).
   b. Copy the formula in cell F6 into the range F7:F14.
   c. Save your work.

6. **Use statistical functions.**
   a. In cell C19, enter a function to calculate the average of range E6:E14.
   b. In cell C20, enter a function to calculate the largest value in range F6:F14.
   c. In cell C21, enter a function to calculate the smallest value in range C6:C14.
   d. In cell C22, enter a function to calculate the number of entries in range A6:A14.
   e. Save, preview, then print this worksheet.

7. **Calculate payments with the PMT function.**
   a. Make the Loan sheet active.
   b. In cell B9, enter the formula PMT(B5/12,B6,-B4).
   c. In cell B10, enter the formula B9*B6.
   d. AutoFit column B, if necessary.
   e. In cell B11, enter the formula B10-B4.
   f. Save, then print the worksheet.

8. **Display and print formula contents.**
   a. Click Tools on the menu bar, click Options, then click the View tab, if necessary.
   b. Turn formulas on, then click OK.
   c. Adjust the column widths as necessary.
   d. Save, preview, and print this worksheet in landscape orientation with the row and column headings.
   e. Close the workbook.

▶ Independent Challenges

1. As the store manager of Heavenly Cones Ice Cream Parlor, you have been asked to create a worksheet that totals the monthly sales of all the stores products. Your monthly report should include the following:

- Sales totals for the current month for each product
- Sales totals for the last month for each product
- The percent change in sales from last month to this month

To document the report further, you decide to include a printout of the worksheet formulas.

To complete this independent challenge:

1. Open the workbook titled XL E-6, then save it as "Heavenly Sales" to the appropriate folder on your Student Disk.
2. Complete the headings for weeks 2 through 4. Enter the weekly totals and the current month's totals, then copy them where appropriate. Calculate the percent change in sales from last month to this month. (*Hint:* The formula in words would be (Current Month-Last Month)/Last Month.) After you enter the percent change formula for regular ice cream, copy the formula down the column.
3. Save, preview, then print the worksheet on a single page. If necessary, print in landscape orientation. If you make any page setup changes, save the worksheet again.
4. Display and print the worksheet formulas with row and column headings. Again, print the formulas on one page.
5. Close the workbook without saving the changes for displaying formulas.
6. Submit your printouts.

2. You are an auditor with a certified public accounting firm. High Rollers, a manufacturer of skating products including roller skates and skateboards, has contacted you to audit its financial records. They have asked you to assist them in preparing their year-end sales summary. Specifically, they want to add expenses and show the percent each expense category represents of annual expenses. They also want to show what percent each expense category represents of annual sales. You should include a formula calculating the difference between sales and expenses and another formula calculating expenses divided by sales. The expense categories and their respective dollar amounts are as follows: Building Lease $36,000; Equipment $235,000; Office $24,000; Salary $350,000; Taxes $315,000. Use these expense amounts to prepare the year-end sales and expenses summary for High Rollers.

To complete this independent challenge:

1. Open the workbook titled XL E-7, then save it as "High Rollers Sales".
2. Name the cell containing the formula for annual expenses "Annual_Expenses". Use the name Annual_Expenses in the first formula calculating percent of annual expenses. Copy this formula as appropriate. Make sure to include a formula that sums all the values for percent of annual expenses, which should equal 1 or 100%.

3. Enter a formula calculating what percent of annual sales each expense category represents. Use the name Annual_Sales in the formula. Enter formulas calculating annual sales minus annual expenses and expenses divided by sales using only the names Annual_Sales and Annual_Expenses. Add formulas for totals as appropriate.

4. Format the cells using the Currency, Percent, or Comma style. Widen the columns as necessary to increase readability.

5. Save, preview, then print the worksheet on a single page. If necessary, use landscape orientation. Save any page setup changes you make.

6. Display and print worksheet formulas on a single page with row and column headings.

7. Close the workbook without saving the changes for displaying formulas.

8. Submit your printouts.

3. As the owner of Build-To-Fit, a general contracting firm specializing in home-storage projects, you are facing yet another business challenge at your firm. Because jobs are taking longer than expected, you decide to take out a loan to purchase some new power tools. According to your estimates, you need a $5,000 loan to purchase the tools. You check three loan sources: the Small Business Administration (SBA), your local bank, and your parents. Each source offers you a loan on its own terms. The local bank offers you the loan at 9.5% interest over four years. The SBA will loan you the money at 9% interest, but you have to pay it off in three years. Your parents offer you an 8% loan, but they require you to pay it back in two years, when they expect to retire. To analyze all three loan options, you decide to build a tool loan summary worksheet. Using the loan terms provided, build a worksheet summarizing your options.

To complete this independent challenge:

1. Open a new workbook, then save it as "Loan Options".

2. Enter labels and worksheet data. You need headings for the loan source, loan amount, interest rate, term or number of payments, monthly payment, total payments, and total interest. Fill in the data provided for the three loan sources.

3. Enter formulas as appropriate: a PMT formula for the monthly payment; a formula calculating the total payments based on the monthly payment and term values; and a formula for total interest based on the total payments and the loan amount.

4. Format the worksheet as desired.

5. Save, preview, then print the worksheet on a single page using landscape orientation. Along with the worksheet, submit a printout of worksheet formulas showing row and column headings. Do not save the worksheet with these settings.

6. Submit your printouts.

4. You can get up-to-date information on nearly any major company on the World Wide Web (WWW). When you get ready to make a major purchase, such as a vehicle, you can search the Web to gather the latest information available on the desired product. You have decided to purchase a new vehicle, and you are excited about logging on to the Web to research your planned purchase. Your self-imposed spending limit is $30,000, including purchase price and total interest on the loan. Create a spreadsheet using vehicle information found on the WWW to support your purchase decision. To complete this independent challenge:

1. Open a new workbook, then save it as "My New Car" to the appropriate folder on your Student Disk.

2. Decide which features you want your ideal vehicle to have, and list these somewhere in your spreadsheet.

3. Log on to the Internet and use your web browser to go to http://www.course.com. From there, click the link Student Online Companions, click the link for this textbook, then click the Excel link for unit E.

4. Use any of the following sites to compile your data: Cadillac, Ford, GM, Honda, Toyota, or any other site with related information.

5. Compare at least three vehicles showing the automaker, the vehicle make and model year, the number of doors, color, and list sales price. Also compare the three vehicles based on the financing available. Specifically, calculate a loan amount (include list sales price, tax, and license fees), a monthly payment based on a five-year loan at 10.25% interest, the total of the payments, and the total interest paid. Make sure the total payments do not exceed your limit of $30,000.

6. Indicate on the worksheet your final purchase decision and the rationale behind that decision.

7. Save, print, then submit your printout.

▶ Visual Workshop

Create the worksheet shown in Figure E-21. (Hint: Enter the items in range C9:C11 as labels by typing an apostrophe before each formula.) Save the workbook as "Mortgage Payment Calculator" to the appropriate folder on your Student Disk. Preview, print, then submit the worksheet.

FIGURE E-21

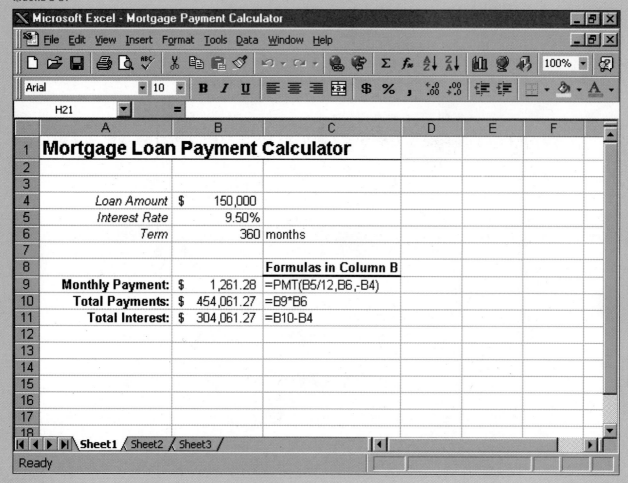

Managing
Workbooks

Objectives

- ► **Freeze columns and rows**
- ► **Insert and delete sheets**
- ► **Reference worksheet data**
- ► **Hide and protect worksheet areas**
- ► **Specify headers and footers**
- ► **Save custom views of a worksheet**
- ► **Control page breaks and page numbering**
- ► **Set margins and alignment**

In this unit, you will learn several Excel features to help you manage and print workbook data. Nomad Ltd has increased the number of its hourly workers by 50% over the past year. Evan Brillstein's manager has designed a timecard summary worksheet to track salary costs for hourly workers. She turned the management of this worksheet over to Evan. In doing so, she has alerted him that she will need several reports generated from the worksheet data.

Freezing Columns and Rows

As rows and columns fill up with data, you might need to scroll through the worksheet to add, delete, modify, and view information. Looking at information without row or column labels can be confusing. In Excel, you can temporarily freeze columns and rows, which enables you to view separate areas of your worksheets at the same time. **Panes** are the columns and rows that **freeze**, or remain in place, while you scroll through your worksheet. The freeze feature is especially useful when you're dealing with large worksheets. Sometimes, though, even freezing is not sufficient. In those cases, you can create as many as four areas, or panes, on the screen at one time and move freely within each of them. ✒ Evan has been asked to verify the hourly pay rate, total hours worked, and total pay for two janitors at Nomad Ltd, Wilbur Collins and Orson Wilks. Because the worksheet is becoming more difficult to read as its size increases, Evan decides to freeze the column and row labels. To gather the requested information, Evan needs to view simultaneously a person's last name, total number of hours, hourly pay rate, and total pay. To do this, he will freeze columns A, B, and C and rows 1 through 5.

Steps

1. Open the workbook titled **XL F-1**, save it as **Timecard Summary**, then scroll through the Monday worksheet to view the data

2. Return to cell A1, then click cell **D6**

Position the pointer in cell A1 to reorient the worksheet, then move to cell D6 because you want to freeze columns A, B, and C. By doing so, you can still view the last name when you scroll to the right. Because you want to be able to scroll down the worksheet and read the column headings, you also freeze the labels in rows 1 through 5. When instructed to do so, Excel freezes the columns to the left and the rows above the cell pointer.

3. Click **Window** on the menu bar, then click **Freeze Panes**

Everything to the left and above the active cell is frozen. A thin line appears along the column border to the left of the active cell, and another line appears along the row above the active cell indicating that columns A through C and rows 1 through 5 are frozen.

4. Scroll to the right until columns A through C and L through P are visible

Because columns A, B, and C are frozen, they remain on the screen; columns D through K are temporarily hidden from view. Notice that the information you are looking for in row 12 (last name, total hours, hourly pay rate, and total pay for Wilbur Collins) is readily available. You jot down Wilbur's data but still need to verify Orson Wilks's information.

5. Scroll down until row 23 is visible

Notice that in addition to columns A through C, rows 1 through 5 remain on the screen as well. See Figure F-1. Evan jots down the information for Orson Wilks. Even though a pane is frozen, you can click in the frozen area of the worksheet and edit the contents of the cells there, if necessary.

6. Press **[Ctrl][Home]**

Because the panes are frozen, the cell pointer moves to cell D6, not A1. Now that you have gathered the requested information, you are ready to unfreeze the panes.

7. Click **Window** on the menu bar, then click **Unfreeze Panes**

The panes are unfrozen. You are satisfied with your ability to navigate and view the worksheet and are ready to save the workbook.

8. Return to cell A1, then save the workbook

Trouble?

If you do not see a thin vertical line in the worksheet area between columns C and D and a thin horizontal black line between rows 5 and 6, click Window on the menu bar, click Unfreeze Panes, then repeat Steps 2 and 3.

QuickTip

When you open an existing workbook, the cell pointer is in the cell it was in when you last saved the workbook. Press [Ctrl][Home] to return to cell A1 prior to saving and closing a workbook.

FIGURE F-1: Scrolled worksheet with frozen rows and columns

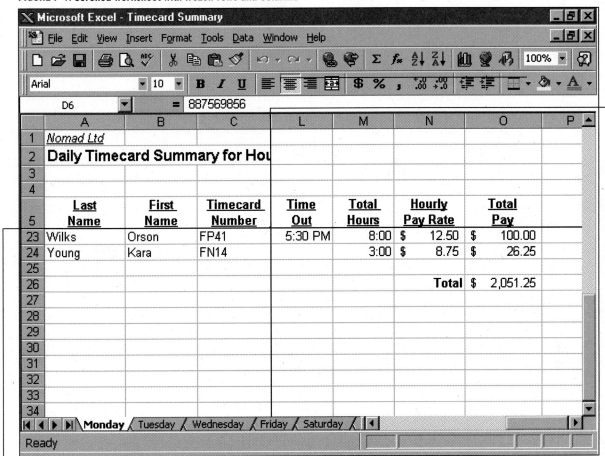

Break in row numbers due to frozen rows 1–5

Break in column letters due to frozen columns A–C

 Splitting the worksheet into multiple panes

Excel provides a way to split the worksheet area into vertical and/or horizontal panes so that you can click inside any one pane and scroll to locate desired information in that pane without any of the other panes moving. See Figure F-2. To split a worksheet area into multiple panes, drag the split box (the small box at the top of the vertical scroll bar or at the right end of the horizontal scroll bar) in the direction you want the split to appear. To remove the split, move the mouse over the split until the pointer changes to ⬌, then double-click.

FIGURE F-2: Worksheet split into two horizontal panes

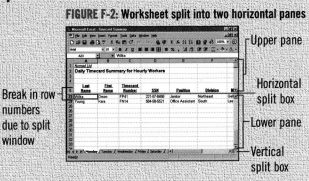

Break in row numbers due to split window

Upper pane

Horizontal split box

Lower pane

Vertical split box

Inserting and Deleting Sheets

You can insert and delete worksheets in a workbook as needed. For example, because new workbooks open with only three sheets available (Sheet1, Sheet2, and Sheet3), you need to insert at least one more sheet if you want to have four quarterly worksheets in an annual financial budget workbook. As for other Excel features, you can do this by using commands on the menu bar or pop-up menu. Evan was in a hurry when he added the sheet tabs to the Timecard Summary workbook. He needs to insert a sheet for Thursday and delete the sheet for Sunday because hourly workers do not work on Sunday.

Steps 1234

QuickTip

You also can copy the active worksheet by clicking Edit on the menu bar, then clicking Move or Copy Sheet. You choose the sheet the copy will precede, then select the Create a copy check box.

1. Click the **Friday sheet tab**, click **Insert** on the menu bar, then click **Worksheet**
Excel automatically inserts a new sheet tab labeled Sheet1 to the left of the selected sheet. See Figure F-3. Next, rename the inserted sheet to something more meaningful.

2. Rename the Sheet1 tab **Thursday**
Now the tabs read Monday, Tuesday, Wednesday, Thursday, Friday, and Saturday. The tabs for Sunday and Weekly Summary are not visible, but you still need to delete the Sunday worksheet.

3. Scroll until the Sunday sheet tab is visible, move the pointer over the **Sunday tab**, then click the **right mouse button**
A pop-up menu appears. See Figure F-4. The pop-up menu allows you to insert, delete, rename, move, or copy sheets, select all the sheets, or view the code in a workbook.

4. Click **Delete** on the pop-up menu
A message box warns that the selected sheet will be deleted permanently. You must acknowledge the message before proceeding.

5. Click **OK**
The Sunday sheet is deleted. Next, to check your work, you view a menu of sheets in the workbook.

QuickTip

You can scroll several tabs at once by pressing [Shift] while clicking one of the middle tab scrolling buttons.

6. Move the mouse pointer over any tab scrolling button, then **right-click**
When you right-click a tab scrolling button, Excel automatically opens a menu of the sheets in the active workbook. Compare your list with Figure F-5.

7. Click **Monday**, return to cell A1, then save the workbook

FIGURE F-3: Workbook with inserted sheet

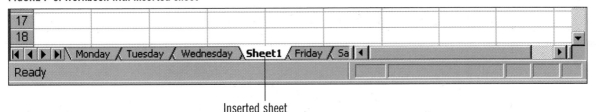

Inserted sheet

FIGURE F-4: Sheet pop-up menu

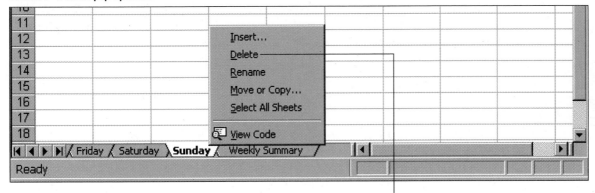

Click to delete
selected sheet

FIGURE F-5: Workbook with menu of sheets

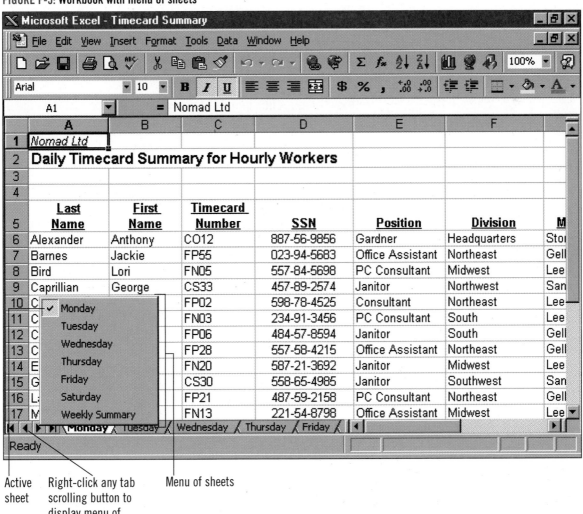

Active sheet

Right-click any tab
scrolling button to
display menu of
sheets

Menu of sheets

Referencing Worksheet Data

You can reference data within a worksheet, between sheets, and between workbooks. For example, you can reference data within a worksheet if you want to reference a calculated total elsewhere in the sheet. Retyping the calculated result in another cell is not recommended because the data values on which the calculated total depend might change. Referencing data between sheets might be necessary if you have quarterly worksheets and an annual summary worksheet in the same workbook. ✎ Although Evan does not have timecard data for the remaining days of the week, he wants to try out the Weekly Summary sheet. He does this by creating a reference from the total pay data in the Monday sheet to the Weekly Summary sheet. First, he freezes panes to improve the view of the worksheets prior to initiating the reference between them.

1. Click cell **D6**, click **Window** on the menu bar, click **Freeze Panes**, then scroll horizontally to bring columns L through O into view
Next, you right-click a tab scrolling button to access the pop-up menu for moving between sheets.

2. Right-click a **tab scrolling button**, then click **Weekly Summary**
Because the Weekly Summary sheet will contain the reference, the cell pointer must reside there when the reference is initiated. A simple **reference** within the same sheet or between sheets is made by positioning the cell pointer in the cell to contain the reference, typing = (equal sign), positioning the cell pointer in the cell containing the contents to be referenced, and then completing the entry. You complete the entry either by pressing [Enter] or clicking the Enter button on the formula bar.

Trouble?

If you have difficulty referencing cells between sheets, press [Esc] and begin again.

3. While in the Weekly Summary sheet, click cell **C6**, type **=**, activate the Monday sheet, click cell **O6**, then click the **Enter button** ✓ on the formula bar
The formula bar reads =Monday!O6. See Figure F-6. *Monday* references the Monday sheet. The ! (exclamation point) is an **external reference indicator** meaning that the cell referenced is outside the active sheet; O6 is the actual cell reference in the external sheet. The result $41.00 appears in cell C6 of the Weekly Summary sheet showing the reference to the value displayed in cell O6 of the Monday sheet. You are ready to copy the formula reference down the column.

4. While in the Weekly Summary sheet, copy cell C6 into cells C7:C24
Excel copies the contents of cell C6 with its relative reference down the column. Test the reference for Anthony Alexander in cell C6 by correcting the time he clocked out for the day.

5. Make the Monday sheet active, edit cell L6 to read **3:30 PM**, then activate the Weekly Summary sheet
Cell C6 now shows $20.50. By changing Anthony's time-out to two hours earlier, his pay dropped from $41.00 to $20.50. This makes sense because Anthony's hours went from four to two and his hourly salary is $10.25. Additionally, the reference to Monday's total pay was automatically updated in the Weekly Summary sheet. See Figure F-7.

6. Preview, then print the Weekly Summary sheet

7. Activate the Monday sheet, then unfreeze the panes
You are ready to save the workbook.

8. Save the workbook

FIGURE F-6: Worksheet showing referenced cell

Cell referenced

Sheet referenced —

Formula referencing cell

External reference indicator

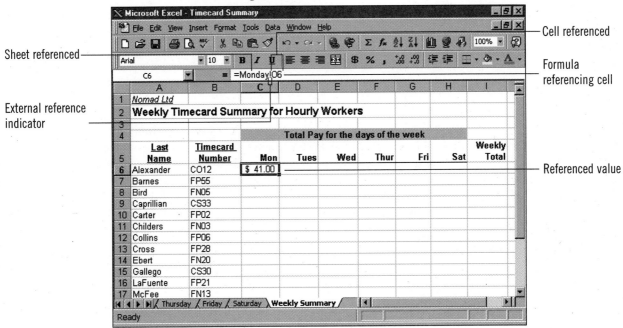

Referenced value

FIGURE F-7: Weekly Summary worksheet with updated reference

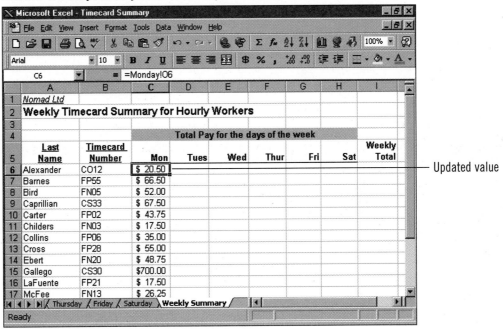

Updated value

Linking workbooks

Just as you can reference data between cells in a worksheet and between sheets, you can reference data between workbooks dynamically so that any changes made in one workbook are reflected immediately in the other workbook. This dynamic referencing is called linking. To link a single cell between workbooks, simply open both workbooks, select the cell to receive the linked data, press = (equal sign), select the cell containing the data to be linked, then press [Enter]. If you are linking more than one cell, you can copy the linked data to the Clipboard, select the upper-left cell to receive the link, click Edit on the menu bar, click Paste Special, then click Paste Link.

Hiding and Protecting Worksheet Areas

Worksheets can contain sensitive information that is not intended to be altered or even viewed by all users. In Excel, you can hide individual formulas, rows, columns, or entire sheets. In addition, you can **protect** selected cells so they cannot be changed while allowing other cells in the worksheet to be altered. See Table F-1 for a list of options you can use to hide and protect a worksheet. Cells that are protected so that their contents cannot be altered are called **locked cells**. You lock and unlock cells by clicking the Locked check box in the Format Cells dialog box. A common worksheet protection strategy is to unlock cells that will be changed, sometimes referred to as the **data entry area**, and to leave the remaining cells locked. ▰▰▰ Because Evan will assign someone to enter the sensitive timecard information into the worksheet, he plans to hide and protect selected areas of the worksheet.

Steps 1234

1. **Make sure the Monday sheet is active, select range I6:L25; click Format on the menu bar, click Cells, then click the Protection tab**
   You include row 25, even though it does not contain data, in the event that new data is added to the row later. Notice that the Locked box in the Protection tab is checked, as shown in Figure F-8. By default, the Locked check box is selected, which indicates that all the cells in a new workbook start out locked.

2. **Click the Locked check box to deselect it, then click OK**
   Excel stores time as a fraction of a 24-hour day. In the formula for total pay, hours must be multiplied by 24. This concept might be confusing to the data entry person, so you hide the formulas before you protect the worksheet.

3. **Select range O6:O25; click Format on the menu bar, click Cells, click the Protection tab, click the Hidden check box to select it, then click OK**
   The screen data remains the same (unhidden and unlocked) until you set the protection in the next step.

4. **Click Tools on the menu bar, point to Protection, then click Protect Sheet**
   The Protect Sheet dialog box opens. You choose not to use a password.

5. **Click OK**
   You are ready to put the new worksheet protection status to the test.

6. **Click cell O6**
   Notice that the formula bar is empty because of the hidden formula setting. Now you attempt to change the cell contents of O6, which is a locked cell.

7. **In cell O6, type T to confirm that locked cells cannot be changed, then click OK**
   When you attempt to change a locked cell, a message box reminds you of the protected cell's read-only status. See Figure F-9. Next, you attempt to make an entry in the Time In column to make sure it is unlocked.

8. **Click cell I6, type 9, and notice that Excel allows you to begin the entry; press [Esc] to cancel the entry, then save the workbook**
   Evan is satisfied that the Time In and Time Out data can be changed as needed.

QuickTip
To turn off worksheet protection, click Tools on the menu bar, point to Protection, then click Unprotect Sheet. If prompted for a password, type the password, then click OK. Keep in mind that passwords are case sensitive.

FIGURE F-8: Protection tab in Format Cells dialog box

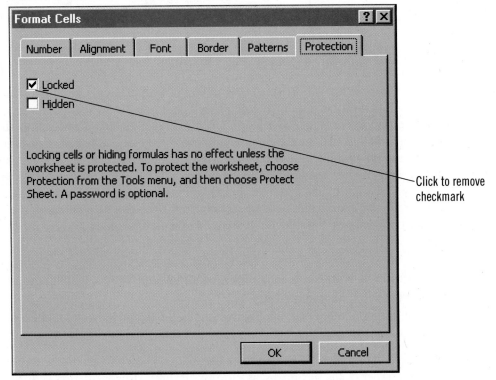

Click to remove checkmark

FIGURE F-9: Message box reminder of protected cell's read-only status

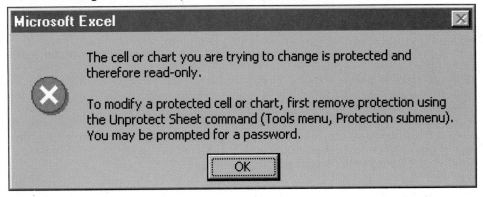

TABLE F-1: Options for hiding and protecting worksheet elements

task	menu commands
Hide/Unhide a column	Format, Column, Hide, or Unhide
Hide/Unhide a formula	Format, Cells, Protection tab, select/deselect Hidden check box
Hide/Unhide a row	Format, Row, Hide, or Unhide
Hide/Unhide a sheet	Format, Sheet, Hide, or Unhide
Protect workbook	Tools, Protection, Protect Workbook, assign optional password
Protect worksheet	Tools, Protection, Protect Sheet, assign optional password
Unlock/Relock cells	Format, Cells, Protection tab, deselect/select Locked check box

Note: Some of the hide and protect options do not take effect until protection is enabled.

Specifying Headers and Footers

A **header** is information that appears at the top of each printed page, and a **footer** is information that appears at the bottom of each printed page. You do not see headers and footers on the screen, except in the Print Preview window. By default, in Microsoft Excel 97 the header and footer are set to "none" in new worksheets. You can override the default of no headers and footers by creating your own. Excel provides a group of buttons that you can use to print specific information in your headers and footers. See Table F-2 for a description of these buttons. Evan remembers that his manager will use the Timecard Summary sheet as part of a report to upper management. He wants to include the date and filename in the footer, and he thinks it will improve the report to make the header text larger and more descriptive.

Steps

1. **With the Monday sheet active, click File on the menu bar, click Page Setup, then click the Header/Footer tab**
   The Header/Footer tab of the Page Setup dialog box opens. Notice that Excel automatically sets the header and footer to none. First, you customize the header.

2. **Click Custom Header**
   The Header dialog box opens, as shown in Figure F-10. By entering your header information in the Center section box, Excel automatically centers this information on the printout.

3. **Click the Center section box, then type Monday – 8/4**
   In the case of a long header, header text might wrap to the next line in the box but will appear on one line in the printout. Next, you change the font size and style.

4. **Drag to select the header text Monday – 8/4, then click the Font button A in the Header dialog box; in the Size box click 12, in the Font style box click Bold, click OK, then click OK to return to the Header/Footer tab**
   The new header appears in the Header box. You are ready to customize the footer.

5. **In the Header/Footer tab, click Custom Footer**
   The Footer dialog box opens. The information you enter in the Left section box is left-aligned on the printout. The text you enter in the Right section box is right-aligned on the printout.

6. **Click the Right section box, type Workbook: and press [Spacebar], then click the File Name button 🔳 in the Footer dialog box to insert the filename code &[File], then click OK**
   You return to the Page Setup dialog box, and the revised footer appears in the Footer box. See Figure F-11.

7. **Preview, print, then save the worksheet**
   Evan is ready to submit the report to his manager.

QuickTip
You can easily turn off the header and/or footer in a worksheet by clicking the header or footer list arrow on the Header/Footer tab, scrolling to the top of the list, then choosing (none).

FIGURE F-10: Header dialog box

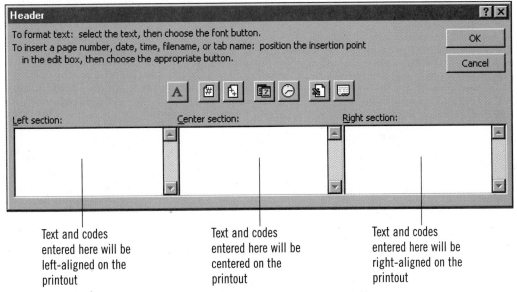

Text and codes
entered here will be
left-aligned on the
printout

Text and codes
entered here will be
centered on the
printout

Text and codes
entered here will be
right-aligned on the
printout

FIGURE F-11: Header/Footer tab with revised header and footer information

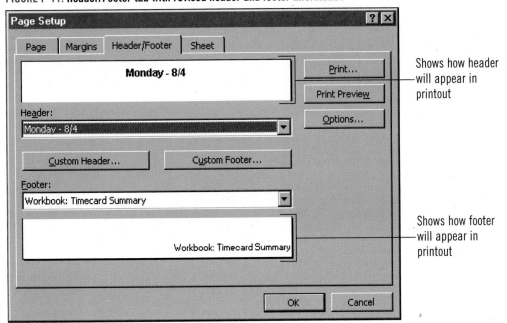

Shows how header
will appear in
printout

Shows how footer
will appear in
printout

TABLE F-2: Buttons for customizing headers and footers

button	button name	code	result
A	Font	None	Displays the Font dialog box in which you choose attributes for the header or footer
#	Page Number	&[Page]	Inserts current page number
	Total Pages	&[Pages]	Inserts total number of printed pages
	Date	&[Date]	Inserts the current date as it is stored in your computer
	Time	&[Time]	Inserts the current time as it is stored in your computer
	File Name	&[File]	Inserts the name of the workbook file
	Sheet Name	&[Tab]	Inserts the name of the worksheet

Saving Custom Views of a Worksheet

A **view** is a set of display and/or print settings that you can name and save, then access at a later time. By using Excel's Custom Views feature, you can create several different views of a worksheet without having to save separate sheets under separate filenames. For example, if you often switch between portrait and landscape orientations when printing different parts of a worksheet, you can create two views with the appropriate print settings for each view. You define the display and/or print settings first, then name the view. 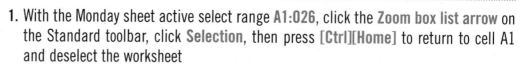 Because Evan will be generating several reports from this data, he will save the current print and display settings as a custom view. In order to better view the data to be printed, Evan decides to use the Zoom box to display the entire worksheet on one screen. The Zoom box has a default setting of 100% magnification and appears on the Standard toolbar.

Steps 1 2 3 4

QuickTip

With **Report Manager add-in**, you can group worksheets and their views to be printed in sequence as one large report.

1. With the Monday sheet active select range A1:O26, click the Zoom box list arrow on the Standard toolbar, click Selection, then press [Ctrl][Home] to return to cell A1 and deselect the worksheet

Excel automatically adjusts the display magnification so that the data selected fit on one screen. See Figure F-12. After selecting the **Zoom box**, you also can pick a magnification percentage from the list or type the desired percentage. Now that you have set up the desired view of the data, you are ready to save the current print and display settings as a custom view.

2. Click View, then click Custom Views

The Custom Views dialog box opens. Any previously defined views for the active worksheet appear in the Views box. In this case, Evan's manager had created a custom view named Generic containing default print and display settings. See Figure F-13. Next, you choose Add to create a new view.

3. Click Add

The Add View dialog box opens, as shown in Figure F-14. Here, you enter a name for the view and decide whether to include print settings and hidden rows, columns and filter settings. Leave these two options checked.

QuickTip

To delete views from the active worksheet, select the view in the Views list box, then click Delete.

4. In the Name box, type Complete Daily Worksheet, then click OK

After creating a custom view of the worksheet, you return to the worksheet area. You are ready to test the two custom views. First, you turn off worksheet protection in case the views require a change to the worksheet.

5. Click Tools on the menu bar, point to Protection, then click Unprotect Sheet

With the worksheet protection turned off, you are ready to show your custom views.

6. Click View on the menu bar, then click Custom Views

The Custom Views dialog box opens, listing both the Complete Daily Worksheet and Generic views.

Trouble?

If you receive the message, "Some view settings could not be applied," repeat Step 5 to ensure worksheet protection is turned off.

7. Click Generic in the Views list box, click Show, then preview the worksheet

The Generic custom view returns the worksheet to Excel's default print and display settings. Now, you are ready to test the new custom view.

8. Click View on the menu bar, click Custom Views, click Complete Daily Worksheet in the Views list box, click Show, then save the workbook

Evan is satisfied with the custom view of the worksheet he created.

FIGURE F-12: Worksheet at 48% magnification

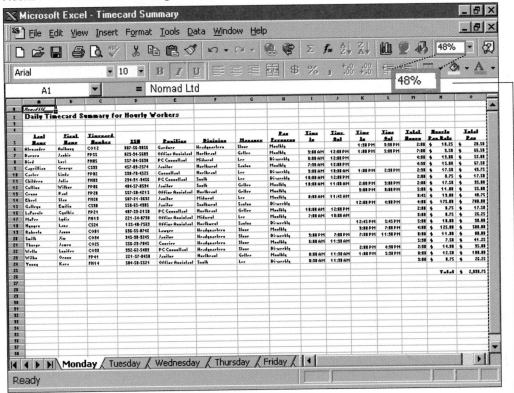

Zoom box showing
current magnification

FIGURE F-13: Custom Views dialog box

List of views in
workbook

Click to create
new view

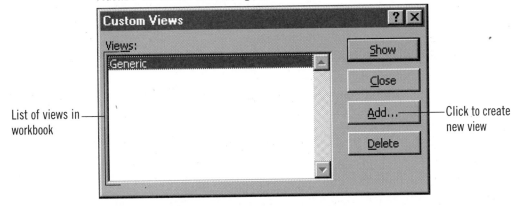

FIGURE F-14: Add View dialog box

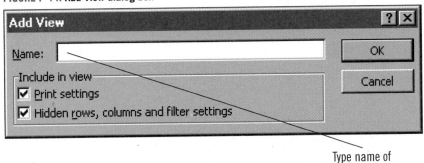

Type name of
view here

Controlling Page Breaks and Page Numbering

The vertical and horizontal dashed lines in your worksheets indicate page breaks. Excel automatically inserts a page break when your worksheet data doesn't fit on one page. These page breaks are **dynamic**, which means they adjust automatically when you insert or delete rows and columns and when you change column widths or row heights. Everything to the left of the first vertical dashed line and above the first horizontal dashed line is printed on the first page. You can override the automatic breaks by choosing the Page Break command on the Insert menu. Table F-3 describes the different types of page breaks you can use.  Evan's manager wants another report displaying no more than half the hourly workers on each page. To accomplish this, Evan must insert a manual page break. He begins by returning the screen display to 100% magnification.

1. Click the Zoom box list arrow on the Standard toolbar, then click 100%
   The screen display returns to 100% magnification. Because there are 19 hourly employees, you insert the page break above the name Cynthia LaFuente.

2. Click cell A16, click Insert on the menu bar, then click Page Break
   A dashed line appears between rows 15 and 16 indicating a horizontal page break. See Figure F-15. Next, you preview the worksheet.

3. Preview the worksheet, then click Zoom
   Notice that the status bar reads "Page 1 of 2" and that the data for the employees up through Emilio Gallego appear on the first page. Evan decides to reinstate the page number in the footer because the report now spans two pages.

4. While in the Print Preview window, click Setup, click the Header/Footer tab, click Custom Footer, click the Center section box, click the Page Number button 🔢, then click OK
   Check your footer, then print the worksheet.

5. In the Header/Footer tab, click OK, check to make sure both pages show page numbers, click Print, then click OK
   Next, you save a custom view with the current display and print settings.

6. Click View on the menu bar, click Custom Views, click Add, type Half N Half, then click OK

7. Save the workbook

Trouble?
If you don't see the page breaks inserted by Excel, click Tools on the menu bar, click Options, then click the View tab. Make sure the Page breaks check box is selected.

QuickTip
To remove a manual page break, select any cell directly below or to the right of the page break, click Insert on the menu bar, then click Remove Page Break.

TABLE F-3: Page break options

type of page break	where to position cell pointer
Both horizontal and vertical page breaks	Select the cell below and to the right of the gridline where you want the breaks to occur
Only a horizontal page break	Select the cell in column A that is directly below the gridline where you want the page to break
Only a vertical page break	Select a cell in row 1 that is to the right of the gridline where you want the page to break

FIGURE F-15: Worksheet with horizontal page break

Microsoft Excel - Timecard Summary

File Edit View Insert Format Tools Data Window Help

Arial   10   **B** *I* U

A16   =   LaFuente

	A	B	C	D	E	F	M
1	*Nomad Ltd*						
2	**Daily Timecard Summary for Hourly Workers**						
3							
4							
5	**Last Name**	**First Name**	**Timecard Number**	**SSN**	**Position**	**Division**	**M**
6	Alexander	Anthony	CO12	887-56-9856	Gardner	Headquarters	Stor
7	Barnes	Jackie	FP55	023-94-5683	Office Assistant	Northeast	Gell
8	Bird	Lori	FN05	557-84-5698	PC Consultant	Midwest	Lee
9	Caprillian	George	CS33	457-89-2574	Janitor	Northwest	San
10	Carter	Linda	FP02	598-78-4525	Consultant	Northeast	Lee
11	Childers	Julia	FN03	234-91-3456	PC Consultant	South	Lee
12	Collins	Wilbur	FP06	484-57-8594	Janitor	South	Gell
13	Cross	Paul	FP28	557-58-4215	Office Assistant	Northeast	Gell
14	Ebert	Stan	FN20	587-21-3692	Janitor	Midwest	Lee
15	Gallego	Emilio	CS30	558-65-4985	Janitor	Southwest	San
16	LaFuente	Cynthia	FP21	487-59-2158	PC Consultant	Northeast	Gell
17	McFee	Lydia	FN13	221-54-8798	Office Assistant	Midwest	Lee

Monday / Tuesday / Wednesday / Thursday / Friday /

Ready

Dashed line indicates horizontal break after row 15

Using Page Break Preview

By clicking View on the menu bar, then clicking Page Break Preview, or clicking Page Break Preview in the Print Preview window, you can view and change page breaks manually. Simply drag the dashed page break lines to the desired location. See Figure F-16.

FIGURE F-16: Page Break Preview window

	Last Name	First Name	Timecard Number	SSN	Position	Division	Manager	Pay Frequenc	Time In	Time Out	Time In	Time Out
5											1:30 PM	3:30 F
6	Alexander	Anthony	CO12	887-56-9856	Gardner	Headquarters	Stone	Monthly	9:00 AM	######	1:00 PM	5:00 F
7	Barnes	Jackie	FP55	023-94-5683	Office Assistant	Northeast	Geller	Monthly	8:00 AM	######		
8	Bird	Lori	FN05	557-84-5698	PC Consultant	Midwest	Lee	Bi-weekly	7:30 AM	######		
9	Caprillian	George	CS33	457-89-2574	Janitor	Northwest	Santos	Monthly	9:00 AM	######	1:00 PM	2:30 F
10	Carter	Linda	FP02	598-78-4525	Consultant	Northeast	Lee	Bi-weekly	######	######		
11	Childers	Julia	FN03	234-91-3456	PC Consultant	South	Lee	Bi-weekly	######	######	2:00 PM	3:00 F
12	Collins	Wilbur	FP06	484-57-8594	Janitor	South	Geller	Monthly	######	######	3:00 PM	8:00 F
13	Cross	Paul	FP28	557-58-4215	Office Assistant	Northeast	Geller	Monthly	8:00 AM	######		
14	Ebert	Stan	FN20	587-21-3692	Janitor	Midwest	Lee	Monthly			######	4:00 F
15	Gallego	Emilio	CS30	558-65-4985	Janitor	Southwest	Santos	Bi-weekly				
16	LaFuente	Cynthia	FP21	487-59-2158	PC Consultant	Northeast	Geller	Monthly	######	######		
17	McFee	Lydia	FN13	221-54-8798	Office Assistant	Midwest	Lee	Monthly	7:00 AM	######		
18	Nguyen	Lana	CS24	125-48-7569	Office Assistant	Northwest	Santos	Monthly			######	5:45 F
19	Roberts	Jason	CO01	696-55-8742	Lawyer	Headquarters	Stone	Monthly			3:00 PM	7:00 F
20	Smith	Jim	CO34	345-98-3245	Janitor	Headquarters	Stone	Bi-weekly	3:00 PM	7:00 PM	7:30 PM	#####
21	Thorpe	James	CO25	556-23-7845	Courier	Headquarters	Stone	Monthly	6:00 AM	######		
22	Wells	Lucifer	CO99	332-62-5489	PC Consultant	Headquarters	Stone	Monthly			2:00 PM	4:30 F
23	Wilks	Orson	FP41	221-57-8458	Janitor	Northeast	Geller	Bi-weekly	8:00 AM	######	1:00 PM	5:30 F
24	Young	Kara	FN14	584-58-5521	Office Assistant	South	Lee	Bi-weekly	8:30 AM	######		
25												
26												

Cell pointer in cell A16

Dashed page break line

Setting Margins and Alignment

You can set top, bottom, left, and right margins for a worksheet printout and determine the distance you want headers and footers to print from the edge of a page. Also, you can align data on a page by centering it horizontally and/or vertically between the margins. 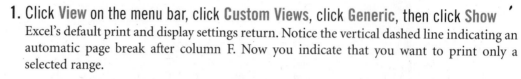 Evan has been asked to print selected information from the Timecard Summary. His manager wants an additional report showing last name, first name, timecard number, social security number, position, and division. First, Evan returns to the Generic custom view of the worksheet.

1. Click **View** on the menu bar, click **Custom Views**, click **Generic**, then click **Show**
Excel's default print and display settings return. Notice the vertical dashed line indicating an automatic page break after column F. Now you indicate that you want to print only a selected range.

2. Select range **A1:F24**, click **File** on the menu bar, click **Print**, under Print what click **Selection**, then click **Preview**
The Print Preview window displays only the selected cells. Next, center the data horizontally and start printing farther down the page.

3. From the Print Preview window, click **Setup**, click the **Margins tab**, double-click the **Top text box** to select the 1, then type **3**
Notice that the top margin line darkens in the Preview section of the dialog box. The Preview section reflects your activity in the Margins tab. Next, change the header so it prints 1.5" from the top edge of the page.

4. Double-click the **Header text box**, then type **1.5**
Finally, center the report horizontally on the page.

5. In the Center on page section, click the **Horizontally check box** to select it
You have completed the changes in the Margins tab. See Figure F-17. Because all the data fits nicely on one page, you decide to set the footer to "none".

6. Click the **Header/Footer tab**, click the **Footer list arrow**, scroll to the top of the list, then click **(none)**
Check the report to ensure that it begins farther down from the top of the page, is centered horizontally, and does not include a page number. Because the report is complete, preview and print the worksheet.

7. Click **OK** to preview the worksheet, then print the worksheet
Compare your screen with Figure F-18. Because Evan will be switching between reports, he first prints this latest report, and then creates a custom view called Employee Info.

8. Click **View** on the menu bar, click **Custom Views**, click **Add**, type **Employee Info**, then click **OK**

9. Save the workbook

FIGURE F-17: Margins tab with changed settings

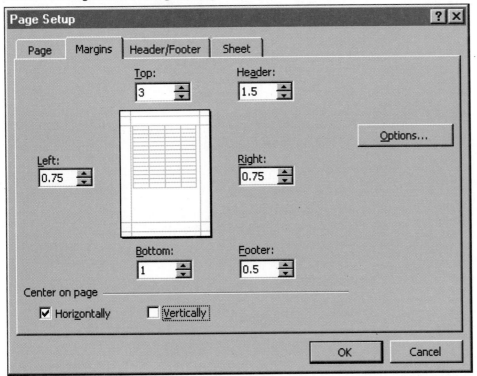

FIGURE F-18: Print Preview window showing employee information

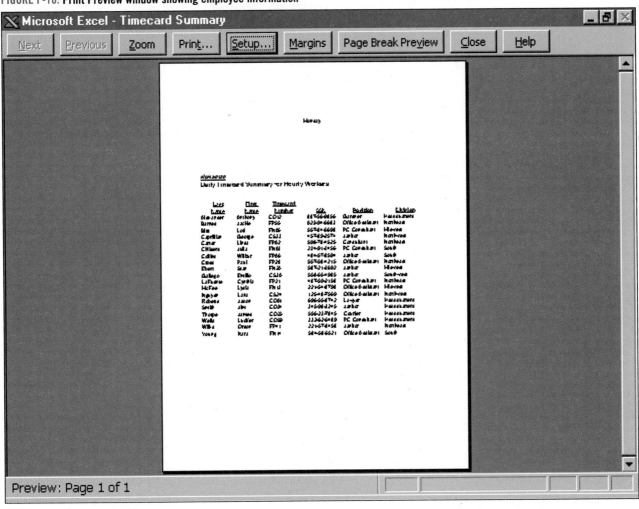

Practice

► Concepts Review

Label each of the elements of the Excel screen shown in Figure F-19.

FIGURE F-19

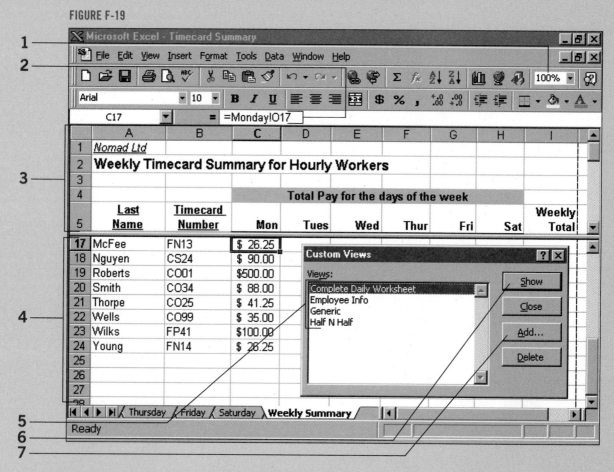

Match each of the terms with the statement that describes its function.

8. Inserts a code to print the total number of pages
9. Indicates how far down the page to start printing worksheet data
10. Indicates a page break
11. Inserts a code to print the sheet tab name in a header or footer
12. Indicates a selection to be printed

a. Dashed line
b.
c. Top margin
d.
e. Print what

Select the best answer from the list of choices.

13. You can save frequently used display and print settings by using the _____ feature.

   a. Report Manager   **b.** View menu   **c.** Custom Views   **d.** Save command

14. You freeze areas of the worksheet to_____.

   a. Freeze data and unlock formulas.

   b. Lock open windows in place.

   c. Freeze all data in place so that you can see it.

   d. Lock column and row headings in place while you scroll through the worksheet.

15. To protect a worksheet, you must first unlock those cells that _____, and then issue the Protect Sheet command.

   a. never change   **c.** have hidden formulas

   b. the user will be allowed to change   **d.** are locked

► Skills Review

1. Freeze columns and rows.

   a. Open the workbook titled XL F-2, then save it as "Quarterly Household Budget".

   b. Freeze columns A through B and rows 1 through 4 for improved viewing. (*Hint:* Click cell C4 prior to issuing the Freeze Panes command.)

   c. Scroll until columns A through B and F through H are visible.

   d. Press [Ctrl][Home] to return to cell C4.

   e. Unfreeze the panes.

2. Insert and delete sheets.

   a. With the 1997 sheet active, use the sheet pop-up menu to insert a new Sheet1.

   b. Activate Sheet1.

   c. Delete Sheet1.

3. Reference worksheet data.

   a. In the 1997 sheet, click cell C22.

   b. Type =, click cell G7, then press [Enter].

   c. In cell C23, type =, click cell G18, then press [Enter].

   d. To link data between the two worksheets, first activate the 1998 worksheet.

   e. Click cell C4.

   f. Type =.

   g. Activate the 1997 worksheet.

   h. Click cell F4, then press [Enter].

   i. In the 1998 worksheet, copy the contents of cell C4 into cells C5:C6.

   j. Preview, then print the 1998 worksheet.

   k. Save the workbook.

4. Hide and protect worksheet areas.

a. In the 1997 worksheet, select row 16.

b. Issue the Hide Row command.

c. To unlock the expense data so you can make changes, first select range C10:F17.

d. Using the Protection tab of the Format Cells dialog box, turn off the locked status.

e. Using the Tools, Protection menu options, protect the sheet.

f. To make sure the other cells are locked, click cell D4.

g. Type 3.

h. Confirm the message box warning.

i. To change the first-quarter mortgage expense to $3,400, click cell C10, then type 3400.

j. Save the workbook.

5. Specify headers and footers.

a. Activate the 1997 worksheet. Using the File, Page Setup menu options, customize the Center Section of the Header to read "Lowe Family".

b. Further customize the header by changing it to appear in 12 pt bold type.

c. Set the footer to (none).

d. Preview, then print the 1997 worksheet.

e. Save the workbook.

6. Save custom views of a worksheet.

a. In the 1997 worksheet, select the range A1:H23.

b. Using the Zoom box, set the magnification so that the entire selection appears on the screen.

c. Using the View, Custom Views menu options, add a new view called "Entire Budget".

d. Save the workbook.

7. Control page breaks and page numbering.

a. Click cell A9.

b. Using the Insert, Page Break menu options, insert a page break.

c. Customize the footer to include a page number.

d. Preview and print the worksheet.

e. Save the workbook.

8. Set margins and alignment.

a. Activate the Generic custom view.

b. Select range A1:C20.

c. Using the Print menu option, under Print what, click Selection.

d. Preview the worksheet.

e. From the Print Preview window, click Setup; using the Margins tab, change the left margin to 2", and center the worksheet vertically on the page.

f. Preview, then print the worksheet.

g. Save the workbook.

▶ Independent Challenges

1. You own PC Assist, a software training company. You have added several new entries to the August check register and are ready to enter September's check activity. Because the sheet for August will include much of the same information you need for September, you decide to copy it. Then you will edit the new sheet to fit your needs for September check activity. You will use sheet referencing to enter the beginning balance and beginning check number. Using your own data, you will complete five checks for the September register.

To complete this independent challenge:

1. Open the workbook entitled XL F-3, then save it as "Update to Check Register".
2. Delete Sheet2 and Sheet3, then create a worksheet for September by copying the August sheet.
3. With the September sheet active, delete the data in range A6:E24.
4. To update the balance at the beginning of the month, use sheet referencing from the last balance entry in the August sheet.
5. Generate the first check number. (*Hint:* Use a formula that references the last check number in August and adds one.)
6. Enter data for five checks.
7. Add a footer that includes your name left-aligned on the printout and the system date right-aligned on the printout. Add a header that displays the sheet name centered on the printout.
8. Save the workbook. Preview the September worksheet, then print it in landscape orientation on a single page.
9. Submit your printout.

2. You are a new employee for a computer software manufacturer. Your responsibility is to track the sales of different product lines and determine which computer operating system generates the most software sales each month. Although sales figures vary from month to month, the format in which data is entered does not. Use Table F-4 as a guide to create a worksheet tracking sales across personal computer (PC) platforms. Use your own data for the number of software packages sold in the DOS, Windows, and Macintosh columns. Create a summary report with all the sales summary information, then create three detailed reports for each software category: Games Software, Business Software, and Utilities Products.

To complete this independent challenge:

1. Create a new workbook, then save it as "Software Sales Summary".
2. Enter row and column labels, your own data, and formulas for the totals.

TABLE F-4

	DOS	Windows	Macintosh	Total
Games Software				
Space Wars 99				
Safari				
Flight School				
Total				
Business Software				
Word Processing				
Spreadsheet				
Presentation				
Graphics				
Page Layout				
Total				
Utilities Products				
Antivirus				
File recovery				
Total				

3. Create a summary report that includes the entire worksheet. Customize the header to include your name and the date. Set the footer to (none). Center the page both horizontally and vertically. Save the workbook. Preview and print the report.

4. Create three detailed report pages. Insert page breaks so that each software category is printed on a separate page. Number the report pages consecutively as follows: Games Software, page 1; Business Software, page 2; Utilities Products, page 3. Include your name and the date in the header of each page and the page number in the footer of each page. Save the workbook. Preview and print the report.

5. Submit your printouts.

3. You are a college student with two roommates. Each month you receive your long-distance telephone bill. Because no one wants to figure out who owes what, you split the bill three ways. You are sure that one of your roommates makes two-thirds of the long-distance calls. In order to make the situation more equitable, you decide to create a spreadsheet to track the long-distance phone calls each month. By doing so, you hope to determine who is responsible for each call. Create a spreadsheet with a separate area for each roommate. Track the following information for each month's long-distance calls: date of call, time of call, (AM or PM), call minutes, location called, state called, area code, phone number, and call charge. Total the charges for each roommate. Print a summary report of all three roommates' charges, and print a report for each roommate totaling his or her charges for the month.

To complete this independent challenge:

1. Create a new workbook, then save it as "Monthly Long Distance" to the appropriate folder on your Student Disk.

2. Enter column headings and row labels to track each call.

3. Use your own data, entering at least three long-distance calls for each roommate.

4. Create a report that prints all the call information for the month. Use the filename as the header. Format the header to make it stand out from the rest of the text. Enter your name and the date in the footer.

5. Create a report page for each roommate. Insert appropriate page breaks to print out a report for each roommate. Use the roommate's name as the header, formatted in 14-point italic type. Enter your name and the date in the footer. Center the reports on the page both horizontally and vertically. Save the workbook.

6. Preview, print, then submit the reports.

4. The World Wide Web can be used as a research tool to locate information on just about every topic imaginable, including careers. You have decided to conduct a job search using the Web. Currently, you are taking classes on computer programming, specializing in the C++ language and the Internet tool called Java. You plan to perform a search for jobs requiring these skills tracking the following information: position title, company name, city and state where company is located, whether experience is required, and salary. Your goal is to locate and list in a worksheet at least five jobs requiring C++ knowledge, and, in a separate worksheet, at least five jobs requiring Java knowledge.

To complete this independent challenge:

1. Open the workbook titled XL F-4, then save it as "Job Research – PC Programming".
2. Log on to the Internet and use your Web browser to go to http://www.course.com. From there, click Student Online Companions, click the link for this textbook, then click the Excel link for Unit F.
3. Use any combination of the following sites to search for and compile your data: Online Career Center, America's Job Bank, or The Monster Board.
4. Fill in information on at least five positions in each of the two above-mentioned worksheets.
5. Name the two sheets based on their content and copy sheets where appropriate.
6. Using your own judgment, customize the header, footer, margins, and alignment of each sheet.
7. Save the workbook, print both worksheets, then submit your printouts.

▶ Visual Workshop

Create the worksheet shown in Figure F-20. Save the workbook as "Generations of PCs". Preview, print, then submit the worksheet.

FIGURE F-20

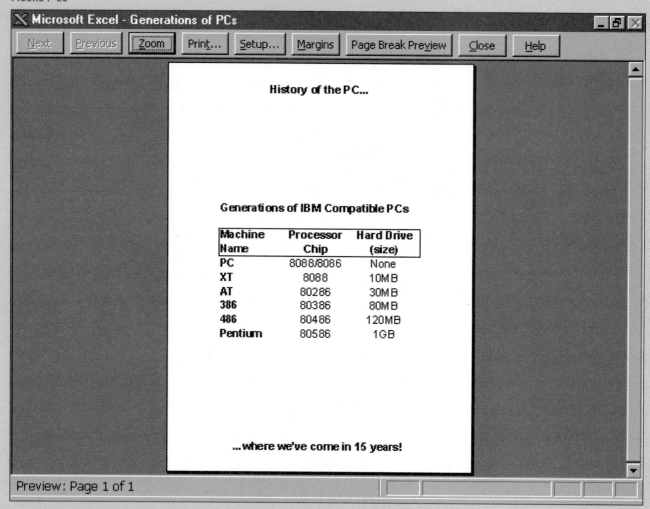

Automating
Worksheet Tasks

Objectives

► **Plan a macro**
► **Record a macro**
► **Run a macro**
► **Edit a macro**
► **Use shortcut keys with macros**
► **Use the Personal Macro Workbook**
► **Add a macro as a menu item**
► **Create a toolbar for macros**

A **macro** is a set of instructions that performs tasks in the order you specify. You create macros to automate frequently performed Excel tasks that require a series of steps. For example, if you usually type your name and date in a worksheet footer, Excel can record the keystrokes in a macro that types the text and insert the current date automatically. In this unit, you will plan and design a simple macro, then record and run the macro. Then you will edit the macro. You will also create a macro to run using shortcut keys, store a macro in the Personal Macro Workbook, add a macro option to the Tools menu, and create a new toolbar for macros. ✐ First, Evan Brillstein wants to create a macro that adds a stamp to his worksheets to identify them as originating in the accounting department.

Planning a Macro

As mentioned earlier, you create macros for tasks that you perform on a regular basis. For example, you can create a macro to enter and format text or to save and print a worksheet. To create a macro, you record the series of actions or write the instructions in a special format. Because the sequence of actions is important, you need to plan the macro carefully before you record it. Commands used to record, run, and modify macros are located on the Tools menu. Make sure to view the CourseHelp, "Using Macros," for more information before completing this lesson. Evan wants to put a stamp on all his worksheets that identifies them as originating in the accounting department. He records a macro to automate this process. Evan plans the macro using the following guidelines:

CourseHelp

To view the CourseHelp for this lesson, click the Start button, point to Programs, point to CourseHelp, then click Microsoft Excel 97 Illustrated. Choose the Using Macros CourseHelp.

1. Assign the macro a descriptive name, and write out the steps the macro will perform
This preplanning helps eliminate careless errors. Evan decides to name the macro DeptStamp. He writes a description of the macro, as shown in Figure G-1. See Table G-1 for a list of macros Evan might create.

2. Decide how you will perform the actions you want to record
You can use the mouse, the keyboard, or a combination of the two methods. Evan decides to use a combination of the mouse and the keyboard.

3. Practice the steps you want Excel to record and write them down
Evan wrote down the sequence of actions as he performed them and he is now ready to record and test the macro.

4. Decide where to locate the description of the macro and the macro itself
Macros can be stored in an unused area of the active workbook, in a new workbook, or in the Personal Macro Workbook. Evan stores the macro in a new workbook.

TABLE G-1: Possible macros and their descriptive names

description of macro	descriptive name
Enter a frequently used proper name, such as Evan Brillstein	EvanBrillstein
Enter a frequently used company name, such as Nomad Ltd	CompanyName
Print the active worksheet on a single page, in landscape orientation	FitToLand
Turn off the header and footer in the active worksheet	HeadFootOff
Show a frequently used custom view, such as a generic view of the worksheet, setting the print and display settings back to Excel's defaults	GenericView

Macro to create stamp with the department name

Name:	DeptStamp
Description:	Adds a stamp to the top-left of worksheet identifying it as an accounting department worksheet
Steps:	1. Position the cell pointer in cell A1
	2. Type Accounting Department, then click the Enter button
	3. Click Format on the menu bar, click Cells
	4. Click Font tab, under Font style click Bold, under Underline click Single, and under Color click Red, then click OK

Viewing CourseHelp

The camera icon on the opposite page indicates there is a CourseHelp available for this lesson. CourseHelps are on-screen "movies" that bring difficult concepts to life, to help you understand the material in this book. Your instructor received a CourseHelp disk and should have installed it on the machine you are using. To start CourseHelp, click the Start button, point to Programs, point to CourseHelp, then click Microsoft Excel 97 Illustrated. In the main CourseHelp window, click the topic that corresponds to this lesson. Because CourseHelp runs in a separate window, you can start and view a movie even if you're in the middle of completing a lesson. Once the movie is finished, you can click the Excel program button on the taskbar and continue with the lesson, right where you left off.

Recording a Macro

The easiest way to create a macro is to record it using Excel's Macro Recorder. You simply turn the Macro Recorder on, enter the keystrokes, select the commands you want the macro to perform, then stop the recorder. As you record the macro, each action is translated into programming code that you can later view and modify. ✎ Evan wants to create a macro that enters a department stamp in cell A1 of the active worksheet. He creates this macro by recording his actions.

Steps 1 2 3 4

1. **If necessary, click the New button 🗋 on the Standard toolbar, then save the blank workbook as My Excel Macros**
   Now you are ready to start the macro recording process.

2. **Click Tools on the menu bar, point to Macro, then click Record New Macro**
   The Record Macro dialog box opens. See Figure G-2. Notice the default name Macro1 is selected. You can either assign this name or type a new name. The first character of a macro name must be a letter; the remaining characters can be letters, numbers, or underscores; spaces are not allowed in macro names; use underscores in place of spaces. This dialog box also allows you to assign a shortcut key for running the macro and to instruct Excel where to store the macro. Enter the name of the macro, then accept the remaining dialog box settings.

3. **In the Macro name box, type DeptStamp, then click OK**
   The dialog box closes. Excel displays the small Stop Recording toolbar containing the Stop Recording button ▪, and the word "Recording" appears on the status bar. Take your time performing the steps because Excel records every keystroke, menu option, and mouse action that you make. Next, execute the steps that create the department stamp.

4. **Press [Ctrl][Home]**
   The cell pointer moves to cell A1. When you begin an Excel session, macros record absolute cell references. By beginning the recording in cell A1, you ensure that the macro includes the instruction to select cell A1 as the first step.

5. **In cell A1, type Accounting Department, then click the Enter button ✓ on the formula bar**

6. **Click Format on the menu bar, then click Cells**
   Now, you change the font style and attributes of the text.

7. **Click the Font tab, in the Font style list box click Bold, click the Underline list arrow and click Single, then click the Color list arrow and click red (third row, first color on left)**
   See Figure G-3. Confirm the changes in the dialog box, then stop the macro recording.

8. **Click OK, click the Stop Recording button ▪ on the Stop Recording toolbar, click cell D1 to deselect cell A1, then save the workbook**
   Compare your results with Figure G-4.

FIGURE G-2: Record Macro dialog box

Type macro name here —

Reflects your name and system date —

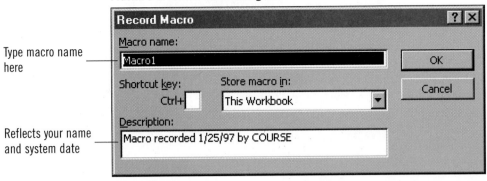

FIGURE G-3: Font tab of the Format Cells dialog box

Changes for macro —

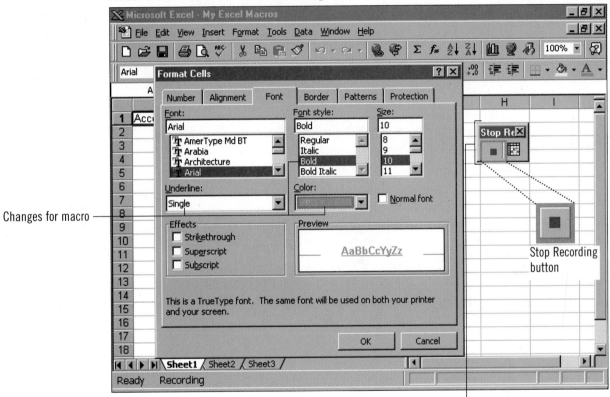

Stop Recording button

Stop Recording toolbar

FIGURE G-4: Personalized department stamp

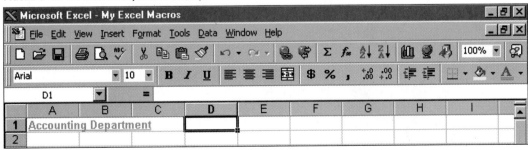

Excel 97

Running a Macro

Once you record a macro, you should test it to make sure that the actions performed are correct. To test a macro, you **run** or execute it. One method of running a macro is to select the macro in the Macros dialog box, then click Run. 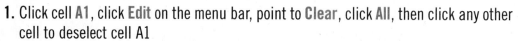 Evan clears the contents of cell A1 and then tests the DeptStamp macro. After he runs the macro from the My Excel Macros workbook, he decides to test the macro once more from a newly opened workbook.

1. **Click cell A1, click Edit on the menu bar, point to Clear, click All, then click any other cell to deselect cell A1**
   When you delete the contents of a cell, any formatting still remains in the cell. By using the Clear All option on the Edit menu, you can be sure that the cell is free of contents and formatting.

QuickTip

To delete a macro, select the macro name in the Macro dialog box, click Delete, then click OK to confirm.

2. **Click Tools on the menu bar, point to Macro, then click Macros**
   The Macro dialog box, shown in Figure G-5, lists all the macros contained in the open workbooks.

3. **Make sure DeptStamp is selected, click Run, then deselect cell A1**
   Watch your screen as the macro quickly plays back the steps you recorded in the previous lesson. When the macro is finished, your screen should look like Figure G-6. As long as the workbook containing the macro remains open, you can run the macro from any open workbook. Now you test this.

4. **Click the New button ▯ on the Standard toolbar**
   Because the new workbook automatically fills the screen, it is difficult to be sure that the My Excel Macros workbook is still open. Use the Window menu to display a list of open workbooks before you run the macro.

5. **Click Window on the menu bar**
   A list of open workbooks displays underneath the menu options. The active workbook name (in this case, Book2) appears with a checkmark to its left. See Figure G-7. Confirming that My Excel Macros is still open, you run the macro from this new workbook.

QuickTip

To stop a macro while it is running, press **[Esc]**.

6. **Deselect cell A1 if necessary, click Tools on the menu bar, point to Macro, click Macros, make sure 'My Excel Macros.xls'!DeptStamp is selected, click Run, then deselect cell A1**
   Cell A1 should look like Figure G-6. Notice that when multiple workbooks are open, the macro name includes the workbook name between single quotation marks, followed by an exclamation point indicating that the macro is outside the active workbook. Because you do not need to save the new workbook in which you tested the macro, you close the file without saving it.

7. **Close Book2 without saving changes, then return to the My Excel Macros workbook**

FIGURE G-5: Macro dialog box

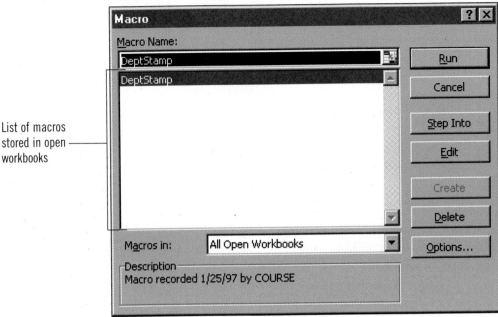

List of macros stored in open workbooks

FIGURE G-6: Result of running the DeptStamp macro

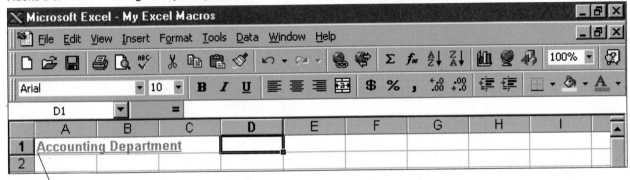

First macro instruction positions pointer in cell A1

FIGURE G-7: Window menu showing list of open workbooks

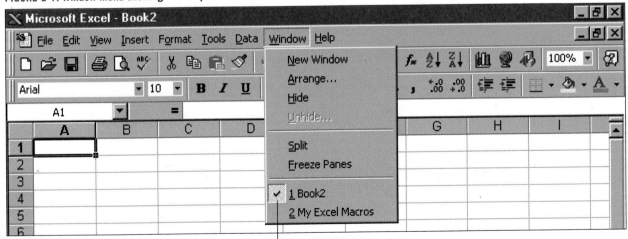

Check mark indicates active workbook

Editing a Macro

When you use the Macro Recorder to create a macro, the instructions are recorded automatically in Visual Basic for Applications programming language. Each macro is stored as a **module**, or program code container, attached to the workbook. Once you record a macro, you might need to change it. If you have a lot of changes to make, it might be best to re-record the macro. If you need to make only minor adjustments, you can edit the macro code, or program instructions, directly using the Visual Basic Editor. ✍ Evan wants to modify his macro to change the point size of the department stamp to 12.

QuickTip

You can also start the Visual Basic Editor by clicking Tools on the menu bar, pointing to Macro, then clicking Visual Basic Editor or by pressing [Alt][F11].

1. Make sure the My Excel Macros workbook is open, click Tools on the menu bar, point to Macro, click Macros, make sure DeptStamp is selected, then click Edit

The Visual Basic Editor starts showing the DeptStamp macro steps in a numbered module window (in this case, Module1). You can maximize the module window to get a better look at the macro code.

2. Maximize the window titled My Excel Macros.xls – [Module1 (Code)], then examine the steps in the macro

See Figure G-8. The name of the macro and the date it was recorded appear at the top of the module window. Notice that Excel translates your keystrokes and commands into words, known as macro **code**. For example, the line .FontStyle = "Bold" was generated when you clicked Bold in the Format Cells dialog box. When you make changes in a dialog box during macro recording, Excel automatically stores all the dialog box settings in the macro code. You also see lines of code that you didn't generate directly while recording the DeptStamp macro; for example, .Name = "Arial".

3. In the line .Size = 10, double-click 10 to select it, then type 12

Because Module1 is attached to the workbook and not stored as a separate file, any changes to the module are saved automatically when the workbook is saved. Next, print the change to Module1.

4. In the Visual Basic Editor, click File on the menu bar, click Print, then click OK to print the module

Review the printout of Module1, then return to Excel.

5. Click File on the menu bar, then click Close and Return to Microsoft Excel

You want to rerun the DeptStamp macro to view the point size edit you made using the Visual Basic Editor.

6. Click cell A1, click Edit on the menu bar, point to Clear, click All, deselect cell A1, click Tools on the menu bar, point to Macro, click Macros, make sure DeptStamp is selected, click Run, then deselect cell A1

Compare your results with Figure G-9.

7. Save the workbook

FIGURE G-8: **Visual Basic Editor showing Module1**

Name of the macro

Code window

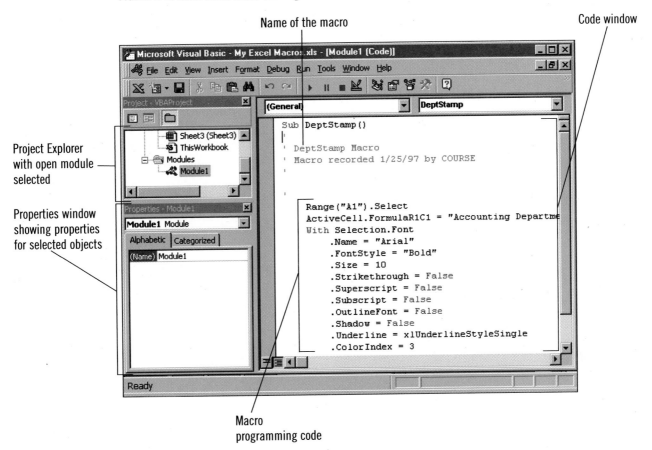

Project Explorer with open module selected

Properties window showing properties for selected objects

Macro programming code

FIGURE G-9: **Result of running the edited DeptStamp macro**

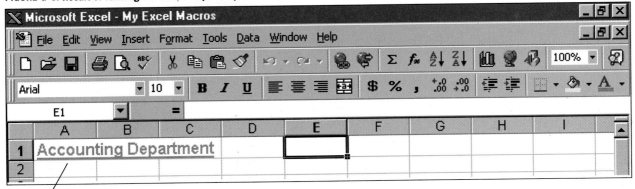

Font size enlarged to 12pt

Adding comments to code

With practice, you will be able to interpret the lines of code within your macro. Others who use your macro, however, might want to know the function of a particular line. You can explain the code by adding comments to the macro. Comments are explanatory text added to the lines of code. When you enter a comment, you must type an apostrophe (') before the comment text. Otherwise, Excel thinks you have entered a command. On a color monitor, comments appear in green after you press [Enter]. See Figure G-8. You also can insert blank lines in the macro code to make the code more readable. To do this, type an apostrophe, then press [Enter].

Using Shortcut Keys with Macros

In addition to running a macro from the Macro dialog box, you can run a macro by assigning a shortcut key combination. Using shortcut keys to run macros reduces the number of keystrokes required to begin macro play back. You assign shortcut key combinations in the Record Macro dialog box. ◢▬▬ Evan also wants to create a macro called CompanyName to enter the company name into a worksheet. He assigns a shortcut key combination to run the macro.

1. Click cell **B2**

You will record the macro in cell B2. You want to be able to enter the company name anywhere in a worksheet. Therefore, you will not begin the macro with an instruction to position the cell pointer as you did in the DeptStamp macro.

2. Click **Tools** on the menu bar, point to **Macro**, then click **Record New Macro**

The Record Macro dialog box opens. You notice the option Shortcut key: Ctrl+ followed by a blank box. You can type a letter (A–Z) in the Shortcut key box to assign the key combination of [Ctrl] plus a letter to run the macro. Use the key combination [Ctrl][Shift] plus a letter. Doing this avoids overriding any of Excel's previously assigned [Ctrl]+[letter] shortcut keys, such as [Ctrl]+[C] for Copy.

3. With the default macro name selected, type **CompanyName**, click the **Shortcut key box**, press and hold **[Shift]**, then type **C**

Compare your screen with Figure G-10. You are ready to record the CompanyName macro.

4. Click **OK** to close the dialog box, then start recording the macro

By default, Excel records absolute cell references in macros. Beginning the macro in cell B2 causes the macro code to begin with a statement to select cell B2. Because you want to be able to run this macro in any active cell, you need to instruct Excel to record relative cell references while recording the macro. You can do this before recording the macro keystrokes by selecting the Relative Reference button ▦ on the Stop Recording toolbar.

5. Click the **Relative Reference button** ▦ on the Stop Recording toolbar

The Relative Reference button appears indented to indicate that it is selected. See Figure G-11. This button is a toggle and retains the relative reference setting until it is clicked off.

6. In cell B2, type **Nomad Ltd**, click the **Enter button** ☑ on the formula bar, press **[Ctrl][i]** to italicize the text, click the **Stop Recording button** ■ on the Stop Recording toolbar, then deselect cell B2

Nomad Ltd appears in italics in cell B2. You are ready to run the macro in cell A5 using the shortcut key combination.

7. Click cell **A5**, press and hold **[Ctrl][Shift]**, type **C**, deselect the cell

The result appears in cell A5. See Figure G-12. Because the macro played back in selected cell (A5) instead of the cell where it was recorded (B2), Evan is convinced that the macro recorded relative cell references.

8. Save the workbook

> **QuickTip**
>
> When you begin an Excel session, the Relative Reference button is toggled off, indicating that Excel is recording absolute cell references in macros. Once selected, and until it is toggled back off, the Relative Reference setting remains in effect during the current Excel session.

FIGURE G-10: Record Macro dialog box with shortcut key assigned

Record Macro

Macro name:

CompanyName

Shortcut key: Store macro in:
Ctrl+Shift+ C   This Workbook

Description:
Macro recorded 1/25/97 by COURSE

OK

Cancel

Shortcut to run
macro

FIGURE G-11: Stop Recording toolbar with Relative Reference button selected

Stop Re X

Relative Reference
button instructs
Excel to record
relative references

FIGURE G-12: Result of running CompanyName macro

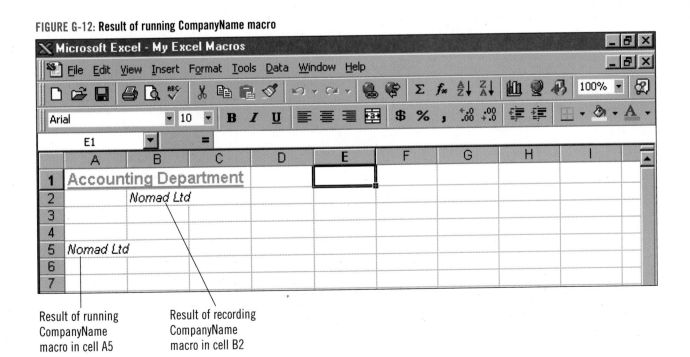

Microsoft Excel - My Excel Macros

File   Edit   View   Insert   Format   Tools   Data   Window   Help

Arial   10   **B** *I* U

E1   =

	A	B	C	D	E	F	G	H	I
1	Accounting Department								
2		Nomad Ltd							
3									
4									
5	Nomad Ltd								
6									
7									

Result of running
CompanyName
macro in cell A5

Result of recording
CompanyName
macro in cell B2

Excel 97

Using the Personal Macro Workbook

You can store commonly used macros in a **Personal Macro Workbook**. The Personal Macro Workbook is always available, unless you specify otherwise, and gives you access to all the macros it contains, regardless of which workbooks are open. The Personal Macro Workbook file is created automatically the first time you choose to store a macro in it. Additional macros are added to the Personal Macro Workbook when you store them there. ✐ Evan often finds himself adding a footer to his worksheets identifying his department, the workbook name, the sheet name, the page number, and current date. He saves time by creating a macro that automatically inserts this footer. Because he wants this macro to be available whenever he uses Excel, Evan decides to store this macro in the Personal Macro Workbook.

Steps

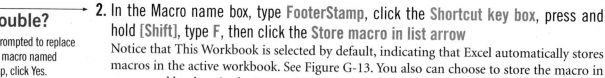

1. From any cell in the active worksheet, click Tools on the menu bar, point to Macro, then click Record New Macro
The Record Macro dialog box opens. Name the macro FooterStamp. You also want to assign a shortcut key.

Trouble?

If you are prompted to replace an existing macro named FooterStamp, click Yes.

2. In the Macro name box, type FooterStamp, click the Shortcut key box, press and hold [Shift], type F, then click the Store macro in list arrow
Notice that This Workbook is selected by default, indicating that Excel automatically stores macros in the active workbook. See Figure G-13. You also can choose to store the macro in a new workbook or in the Personal Macro Workbook.

QuickTip

Once created, the Personal Macro Workbook file is usually stored in the XLSTART folder under the name "Personal".

3. Click Personal Macro Workbook, then click OK
The recorder is on, and you are ready to record the macro keystrokes.

4. Click File on the menu bar, click Page Setup, click the Header/Footer tab (make sure to do this even if it is already active), click Custom Footer, in the Left section box, type Accounting, click the Center section box, click the File Name button 🗐, press [Spacebar], type /, press [Spacebar], click the Sheet Name button 🗐, click the Right section box, click the Date button 🗐, click OK to return to the Header/Footer tab
The footer stamp is set up, as shown in Figure G-14.

QuickTip

You can copy or move macros stored in other workbooks to the Personal Macro Workbook using the Visual Basic Editor.

5. Click OK to return to the worksheet, then click the Stop Recording button ■ on the Stop Recording toolbar
You want to ensure that the macro will set the footer stamp in any active worksheet. To test this, you activate Sheet2, type some sample text, run the FooterStamp macro, then preview the worksheet.

6. Activate Sheet2, in cell A1 type Testing the FooterStamp macro, press [Enter], press and hold [Ctrl][Shift], then type F
The FooterStamp macro plays back the sequence of commands. Preview the worksheet to ensure the macro worked.

7. Preview, then save the worksheet
Evan is satisfied that the FooterStamp macro works on any active worksheet. Next, Evan adds the macro as a menu item on the Tools menu.

FIGURE G-13: Record Macro dialog box showing Store macro in options

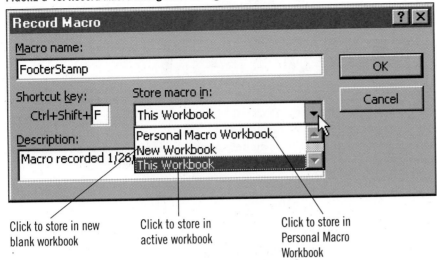

Click to store in new blank workbook

Click to store in active workbook

Click to store in Personal Macro Workbook

FIGURE G-14: Header/Footer tab showing custom footer settings

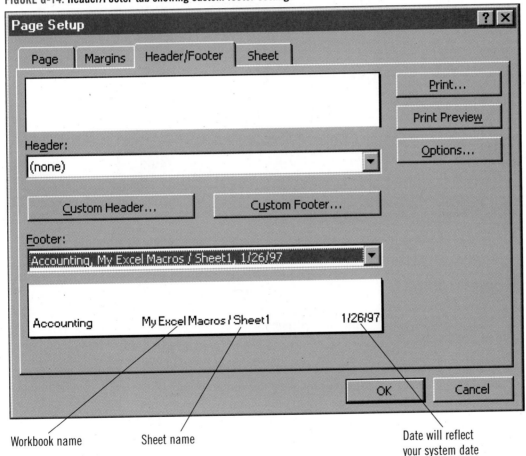

Workbook name

Sheet name

Date will reflect your system date

Working with the Personal Macro Workbook

Once created, the Personal Macro Workbook automatically opens each time you start Excel. By default, the Personal Macro Workbook is hidden as a precautionary measure. You can add macros to the Personal Macro Workbook when it is hidden, but you cannot delete macros from it.

Adding a Macro as a Menu Item

The **Worksheet menu bar** is a special toolbar at the top of the Excel screen that you can customize. In addition to storing macros in the Personal Macro Workbook so that they are always available, you can add macros as items on a menu. ➤ To increase the macro's availability, Evan decides to add the FooterStamp macro as an item on the Tools menu. First, he adds a custom menu item to the Tools menu, then he assigns the macro to that menu item.

QuickTip

If you want to add a command to a menu bar, the first step is to display the toolbar containing the menu to which you want to add the command.

1. Click **Tools** on the menu bar, click **Customize**, click the **Commands tab**, then under Categories, click **Macros**
   See Figure G-15.

2. Under Commands, click **Custom Menu Item**, drag the selection to Tools on the menu bar (the menu opens), then point just under the Wizard option, *but do not release the mouse button*
   Compare your screen to Figure G-16.

3. Release the mouse button
   Now, Custom Menu Item is the last item on the Tools menu. Next, edit the name of the menu item and assign the macro to it.

Trouble?

If you don't see 'PERSONAL.XLS'!FooterStamp under Macro name, try repositioning the Assign Macro dialog box.

4. With the Tools menu still open, right-click **Custom Menu Item**, select the text in the Name box (&Custom Menu Item), type **Footer Stamp**, then click **Assign Macro**
   The Assign Macro dialog box opens behind the Tools menu. You need to select the FooterStamp macro from the list.

5. Under Macro name, click **PERSONAL.XLS!FooterStamp**, click **OK**, then click **Close**
   Return to the worksheet, and test the new menu item in Sheet3.

6. Click the **Sheet3 tab**, in cell A1 type **Testing macro menu item**, press [Enter], then click **Tools** on the menu bar
   The Tools menu appears with the new menu option at the bottom. See Figure G-17. You can now test this menu option.

7. Click **Footer Stamp**, preview the worksheet, then close the Print Preview window
   The Print Preview window appears with the footer stamp. Now, you'll reset the menu options.

8. Click **Tools** on the menu bar, click **Customize**, click the **Toolbars tab**, click **Worksheet Menu Bar** to select it, click **Reset**, click **OK** to confirm, click **Close**, then click **Tools** on the menu bar to ensure the custom item has been deleted
   Because you did not make any changes to your workbook, you don't need to save it. Next, you create a toolbar for macros and add macros to it.

FIGURE G-15: Commands tab of the Customize dialog box showing macro options

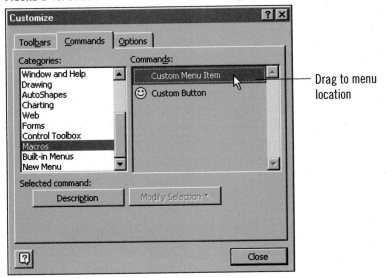

Drag to menu location

FIGURE G-16: Tools menu showing placement of Custom Menu Item

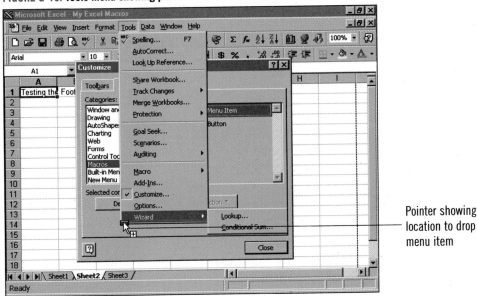

Pointer showing location to drop menu item

FIGURE G-17: Tools menu with new Footer Stamp item

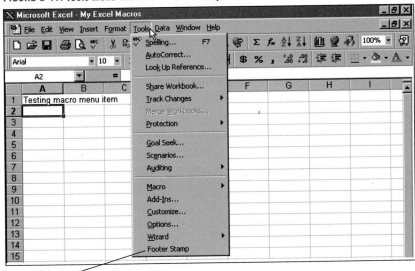

Added menu item

Excel 97

Creating a Toolbar for Macros

Toolbars contain buttons that allow you to access commonly used commands. You can create your own custom toolbars to organize commands so that you can find and use them quickly. Once you create a toolbar, you then add buttons to access Excel commands such as macros. Evan has decided to create a custom toolbar called Macros that will contain buttons to run two of his macros.

Steps

QuickTip

Toolbars you create or customize are available to all workbooks on your own PC. You also can ensure that a custom toolbar is available with a specific workbook by attaching the toolbar to the workbook using the Toolbar tab in the Customize dialog box.

1. **With Sheet3 active, click Tools on the menu bar, click Customize, click the Toolbars tab if necessary, then click New**
   The New Toolbar dialog box opens, as shown in Figure G-18. Under Toolbar name, a default name of Custom1 is selected. You name the toolbar Macros.

2. **Type Macros, then click OK**
   Excel adds the new toolbar named Macros to the bottom of the list and a small, empty toolbar named Macros opens. See Figure G-19. Notice that you cannot see the entire toolbar name. A toolbar starts small and automatically expands to fit the buttons assigned to it. Now you are ready to add buttons to the toolbar.

3. **If necessary, drag the Macros toolbar off the Customize dialog box and into the worksheet area; in the Customize dialog box, click the Commands tab, under Categories click Macros, then drag the ☺ Custom Button over the new Macros toolbar**
   The Macros toolbar now contains one button. Because you want the toolbar to contain two macros, you add an additional Custom Button to the toolbar.

4. **Drag the ☺ Custom Button over the Macros toolbar again**
   With the two buttons in place, you customize the buttons and assign macros to them.

5. **Right-click the leftmost ☺ on the Macros toolbar, in the Name box select &Custom Button, type Department Stamp, click Assign Macro, click DeptStamp, then click OK**
   With the first toolbar button customized, you are ready to customize the second button.

6. **With the Customize dialog box open, right-click the rightmost ☺ on the Macros toolbar, edit the name to read Company Name, click Change Button Image, click 🏃 (bottom row, third from the left) in the Macros dialog box, right-click 🏃, click Assign Macro, click Company Name to select it, click OK, then close the Customize dialog box**
   The Macros toolbar appears with the two customized macro buttons. Next, you test the buttons.

7. **Move the mouse pointer over ☺ on the Macros toolbar to display the macro name (Department Stamp), then click to run the macro; click cell B2, move the mouse pointer over 🏃 on the Macros toolbar to display the macro name (Company Name), click 🏃, then deselect the cell**
   Compare your screen with Figure G-20. Notice that the DeptStamp macro automatically replaces the contents of cell A1. Now remove the toolbar.

8. **Click Tools on the menu bar, click Customize, click the Toolbars tab if necessary, under Toolbars click Macros to select it, click Delete, click OK to confirm the deletion, then click Close**

9. **Save, then close the workbook**

Trouble?

If you are prompted to save the changes to the Personal Macro Workbook, click Yes.

FIGURE G-18: New Toolbar dialog box

Type toolbar
name here

FIGURE G-19: Customize dialog box with new Macros toolbar

New Macros toolbar

Check mark
indicates toolbar
is in view

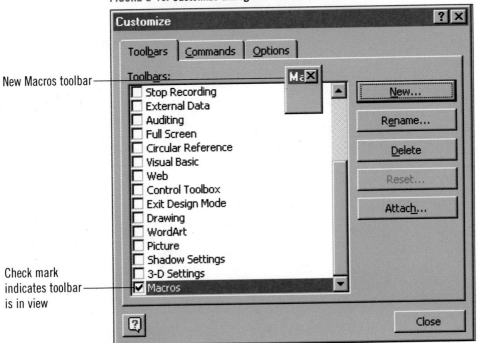

FIGURE G-20: Worksheet showing Macros toolbar with two customized buttons

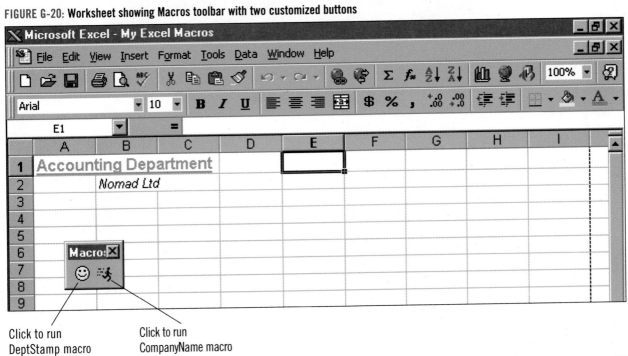

Click to run
DeptStamp macro

Click to run
CompanyName macro

Practice

▶ Concepts Review

Label each of the elements of the Excel screen shown in Figure G-21.

FIGURE G-21

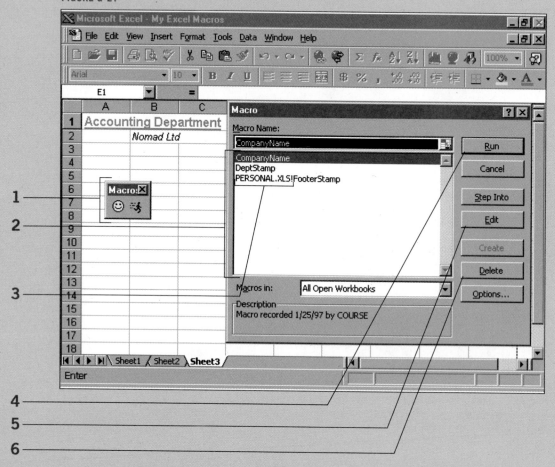

Select the best answer from the list of choices.

7. Which of the following is the best candidate for a macro?
   a. One-button or one-keystroke commands
   b. Often-used sequences of commands or actions
   c. Seldom-used commands or tasks
   d. Nonsequential tasks

8. When you are recording a macro, you can execute commands by using
   a. Only the keyboard.
   b. Only the mouse.
   c. Any combination of the keyboard and the mouse.
   d. Only menu commands.

9. **A macro is stored in**
   a. The body of a worksheet used for data.
   b. An unused area to the far right or well below the worksheet contents.
   c. A module attached to a workbook.
   d. A Custom Menu Item.

10. **Which of the following is *not* true about editing a macro?**
   a. You edit macros using the Visual Basic Editor.
   b. A macro cannot be edited and must be recorded again.
   c. You can type changes directly in the existing macro code.
   d. You can make more than one editing change in a macro.

11. **Why is it important to preplan a macro?**
   a. Macros won't be stored if they contain errors.
   b. Planning helps prevent careless errors from being introduced into the macro.
   c. It is very difficult to correct errors you make in a macro.
   d. Planning ensures that your macro will not contain errors.

12. **Macros are recorded with relative references**
   a. Only if the Relative Reference button is selected.
   b. In all cases.
   c. Only if relative references are chosen while recording the macro.
   d. Only if the Absolute Reference button is not selected.

13. **You can run macros**
   a. From the Macro dialog box.
   b. From shortcut key combinations.
   c. As items on menus.
   d. Using all of the above.

► Skills Review

1. **Record a macro.**
   a. Create a new workbook, then save it as "Macros".
   b. You will record a macro to enter and format your name, address, and telephone number in a worksheet. Click Tools on the menu bar, point to Macro, then click Record New Macro.
   c. In the Macro name box, type "MyAddress", click the Store macro in list arrow and click This Workbook, then click OK to begin recording.
   d. Ensure that the Relative Reference button on the Stop Recording toolbar is toggled off.
   e. Enter your personal information as follows: Type your name in cell A1; type your street address in cell A2; type your city, state, and ZIP code in cell A3; then type your telephone number in cell A4.
   f. Select range A1:D4, then format it to be 14-point Arial bold.
   g. Add a border and color of your choice to the selected range.
   h. Click the Stop Recording button on the Stop Recording toolbar.
   i. Save the workbook.

2. Run a macro.

    a. Make sure range A1:D4 is selected. Using the menu commands Edit, Clear, All, clear the cell entries.

    b. Click Tools on the menu bar, point to Macro, click Macros, in the list box click MyAddress, then click Run.

    c. Clear the cell entries generated by running the MyAddress macro.

    d. Save the workbook.

3. Edit a macro.

    a. Click Tools on the menu bar, point to Macro, click Macros, click MyAddress, then click Edit.

    b. Locate the line of code that defines the font size, then change the size to 18 points.

    c. Edit the selected range to A1:E4 (increasing it by one column to accommodate the changed label size).

    d. Add a comment line that describes this macro.

    e. Print the module, then return to Excel.

    f. Test the macro in Sheet1.

    g. Save the workbook.

4. Use shortcut keys with macros.

    a. While in Sheet1, using the Tools menu, open the Record Macro dialog box.

    b. In the Macro name box, type MyName.

    c. In the Shortcut key box, press and hold [Shift], then type N.

    d. Click OK to begin recording.

    e. Enter your full name in cell G1. Format as desired.

    f. Click the Stop Recording button on the Stop Recording toolbar.

    g. Clear cell G1.

    h. Use the shortcut key to run the MyName macro.

    i. Save the workbook.

5. Use the Personal Macro Workbook.

    a. Open the Record Macro dialog box.

    b. Name the macro FitToLand.

    c. Choose to store the macro in the Personal Macro Workbook, then click OK. If you are prompted to replace the existing FitToLand macro, click Yes.

    d. Record a macro that sets print orientation to landscape, scaled to fit on a page.

    e. Stop the macro recording.

    f. Activate Sheet2, and enter some test data in cell A1.

    g. Run the FitToLand macro.

    h. Preview Sheet2.

6. Add a macro as a menu item.

    a. Click Tools on the menu bar, click Customize, click the Commands tab, under Categories click Macros, then under Commands click Custom Menu Item.

    b. Drag the Custom Menu Item to the Tools menu, point to Macro, then release the mouse button.

    c. Right-click Custom Menu Item on the Tools menu, then rename the item "Fit to Landscape".

    d. Click Assign Macro, click PERSONAL.XLS!FitToLand, then click OK.

    e. Close the Customize dialog box.

    f. Activate Sheet3, then enter some test data in cell A1.

    g. Run the Fit to Landscape macro from the Tools menu.

    h. Preview the worksheet.

    i. Using the Tools, Customize menu options, reset the toolbar titled Worksheet menu bar.

    j. Save the workbook.

7. Create a toolbar for macros.

a. Make sure the Macros workbook is activated, click Tools on the menu bar, click Customize, click the Toolbars tab, then click New.

b. Name the toolbar "My Info", then click OK.

c. Click the Commands tab, click Macros, then drag the new toolbar onto the worksheet.

d. Drag the Custom Button to the My Info toolbar.

e. Again, drag the Custom Button to the My Info toolbar.

f. Right-click the first button, rename it My Address, click Assign Macro, click MyAddress, then click OK.

g. Right-click the second button, edit the name to read My Name, click Change Button Image, click the button image of your choice; right-click the new button, click Assign Macro, change the store option to This Workbook, click MyName, then click OK.

h. Close the dialog box.

i. Clear the cell data, then test both macro buttons on the My Info toolbar.

j. Use the Toolbars tab of the Customize dialog box to delete the toolbar named My Info.

k. Save, then close the workbook.

► Independent Challenges

1. As a computer-support employee of an accounting firm, you are required to develop ways to help your fellow employees work more efficiently. Employees have asked for Excel macros that will do the following:

- Delete the current row and insert a blank row
- Delete the current column and insert a blank column
- Format a selected group of cells with a red pattern, in 12-point Times bold italic

To complete this independent challenge:

1. Plan and write the steps necessary for each macro.
2. Create a new workbook, then save it as "Excel Utility Macros".
3. Create a new toolbar called Helpers.
4. Create a macro for each employee request described above.
5. Add descriptive comment lines to each module.
6. Add each macro to the Tools menu.
7. On the Helpers toolbar, install buttons to run the macros.
8. Test each macro by using the Run command, the menu command, and the new buttons.
9. Save, then print the module for each macro.
10. Delete the new toolbar, reset the Worksheet menu bar, then submit your printouts.

2. You are an analyst in the finance department of a large bank. Every quarter, you produce a number of single-page quarterly budget worksheets. Your manager has informed you that certain worksheets need to contain a footer stamp indicating that the worksheet was produced in the finance department. The footer also should show the date, the current page number of the total pages, and the worksheet filename. You decide that the stamp should not include a header. It's tedious to add the footer stamp and to clear the existing header and footer for the numerous worksheets you produce. You will record a macro to do this.

To complete this independent challenge:

1. Plan and write the steps to create the macro.
2. Create a new workbook, then save it as "Header and Footer Stamp".
3. Create the macro described above. Make sure it adds the footer with the department name, and so forth and also clears the header.
4. Add descriptive comment lines to the macro code.
5. Add the macro to the Tools menu.
6. Create a toolbar titled Stamp, then install a button on the toolbar to run the macro.
7. Test the macro to make sure it works from the Run command, menu command, and new button.
8. Save and print the module for the macro.
9. Delete the new toolbar, reset the Worksheet menu bar, then submit your printout.

3. You are an administrative assistant to the marketing vice-president at Sweaters, Inc. A major part of your job is to create spreadsheets that project sales results in different markets. It seems that you are constantly changing the print settings so that workbooks print in landscape orientation and are scaled to fit on one page. You have decided that it is time to create a macro to streamline this process.

To complete this independent challenge:

1. Plan and write the steps necessary for the macro.
2. Create a new workbook, then save it as "Sweaters Inc Macro".
3. Create a macro that changes the page orientation to landscape and scales the worksheet to fit on a page.
4. Test the macro.
5. Save and print the module sheet.
6. Delete any toolbars you created, reset the Worksheet menu bar, then submit your printout.

4. Research conducted using the World Wide Web (WWW) usually yields vast amounts of information and can generate up-to-the-minute data in every field imaginable. Because macros are often shared among PC users, they are prone to develop viruses. Think of a virus as software that is intended to harm computers or files. Using the WWW, you can gather up-to-date information about computer viruses, particularly those known to appear as macros in Excel workbooks. You have decided to collect information on Excel macro viruses. Using a selection of Web search engines, you will gather detailed data on at least five viruses associated with Excel macros.

To complete this independent challenge:

1. Open a new workbook, then save it as "Excel Macro Viruses".
2. Log on to the Internet and use your browser to go to http://www.course.com. From there, click Student Online Companions, click the link for this textbook, then click the Excel link for Unit G.
3. Use any combination of the following sites to search for and compile your data: Yahoo!, WebCrawler, or Alta Vista.
4. Fill in information on at least five viruses known to exist in Excel macros. Possible column headings are Name of Virus, Date Discovered, Name of Macro, Who Discovered, Where Discovered, How it Gets Transmitted, Damage it Causes, and Recovery Tips.
5. Format the worksheet as desired to increase readability. (*Hint*: To word wrap text in cells, you can use the wrap text feature located in the Alignment tab of the Format Cells dialog box.)
6. Save the workbook, print the worksheet, then submit your printout.

▶ Visual Workshop

Create the macro shown in Figure G-22. (*Hint:* Save a blank workbook as "File Utility Macros", then create a macro called SaveClose that saves a previously named workbook. Finally, include the line ActiveWorkbook.Close in the module, as shown in the figure.) Print the module. Test the macro. Submit your module printout. (The line "Macro recorded...by ..." will reflect your system date and name.)

FIGURE G-22

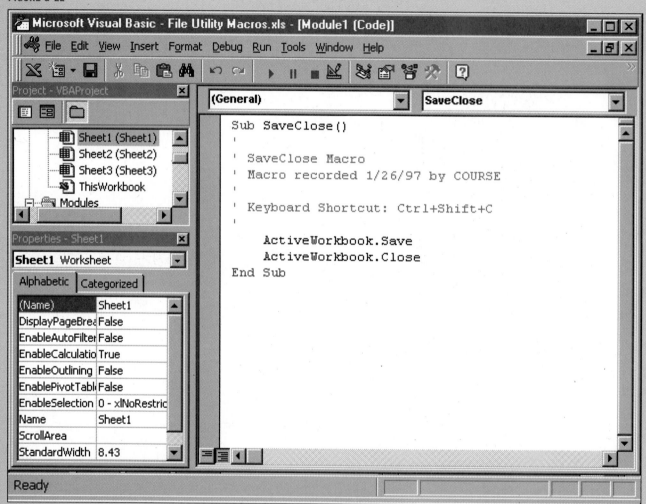

Using

Lists

Objectives

▶ **Plan a list**

▶ **Create a list**

▶ **Add records with the data form**

▶ **Find records**

▶ **Delete records**

▶ **Sort a list by one field**

▶ **Sort a list by multiple fields**

▶ **Print a list**

A **database** is an organized collection of related information. Examples
of databases include a telephone book, a card catalog, and a roster of
company employees. Excel refers to a database as a **list**. Using an Excel
list, you can organize and manage worksheet information so that you
can quickly find needed data for projects, reports, and charts. In this
unit, you'll learn how to plan and create a list; add, change, find, and
delete information in a list; and then sort and print a list.
Nomad Ltd uses lists for analyzing new customer information. Evan's
manager has asked him to build and manage a list of new customers as
part of the ongoing strategy to focus the company's advertising dollars.

Planning a List

When planning a list, consider the information the list will contain and how you will work with the data now and in the future. Lists are organized into records. A **record** contains data about an object or person. Records, in turn, are divided into fields. **Fields** are columns in the list; each field describes a characteristic about the record, such as a customer's last name or street address. Each field has a **field name**, a column label that describes the field. See Table H-1 for additional planning guidelines. Also, make sure to view CourseHelp "Using Databases" before completing this lesson. ✐ At his manager's request, Evan will compile a list of new customers. Before entering the data into an Excel worksheet, he uses the following guidelines to plan the list:

CourseHelp

The camera icon indicates there is a CourseHelp available with this lesson. Click the Start button, point to Programs, point to CourseHelp, then click Excel 97 Illustrated. Choose the CourseHelp entitled Using Databases.

1. Identify the purpose of the list.

Determine the kind of information the list should contain. Evan will use the list to identify areas of the country in which new customers live.

2. Plan the structure of the list.

Determine the fields that make up a record. Evan has customer cards that contain information about each new customer. A typical card is shown in Figure H-1. Each customer in the list will have a record. The fields in the record correspond to the information on the cards.

3. Write down the names of the fields.

Field names can be up to 255 characters in length (the maximum column width), although shorter names are easier to see in the cells. Field names appear in the first row of a list. Evan writes down field names that describe each piece of information shown in Figure H-1.

4. Determine any special number formatting required in the list.

Most lists contain both text and numbers. When planning a list, consider whether any fields require specific number formatting or prefixes. Evan notes that some Zip codes begin with zero. Because Excel automatically drops a leading zero, Evan must type an apostrophe (') when he enters a Zip code that begins with 0 (zero). The apostrophe tells Excel that the cell contains a label rather than a value. If a column contains both numbers and numbers that contain a text character, such as an apostrophe ('), you should format all the numbers as text. Otherwise, the numbers are sorted first, and the numbers that contain text characters are sorted after that; for example, 11542, 60614, 87105, '01810, '02115. To instruct Excel to sort the Zip codes properly, Evan enters all Zip codes with a leading apostrophe.

Lists versus databases

If your list contains more records than can fit on one worksheet (that is, more than 65,536), you should consider using database software rather than spreadsheet software.

FIGURE H-1: Customer record and corresponding field names

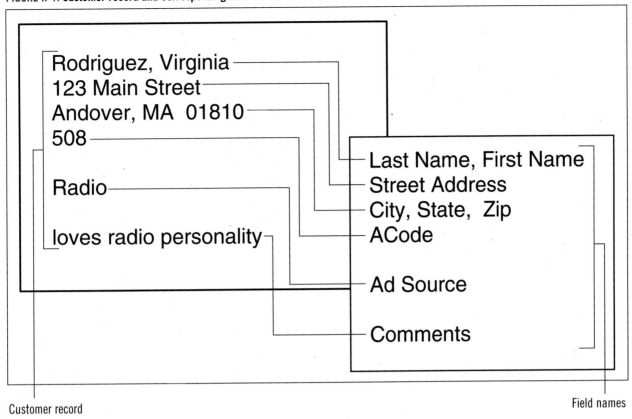

Rodriguez, Virginia — Last Name, First Name
123 Main Street — Street Address
Andover, MA 01810 — City, State, Zip
508 — ACode

Radio — Ad Source

loves radio personality — Comments

Customer record

Field names

TABLE H-1: Guidelines for planning a list

size and location guidelines	row and column content guidelines
Devote an entire worksheet to your list and list summary informationbecause some list management features can be used on only one listat a time.	Plan and design your list so that all rows have similar items in the same column.
Leave at least one blank column and one blank row between your list and list summary data. Doing this helps Excel select your list when it performs list management tasks such as sorting.	Do not insert extra spaces at the beginning of a cell because that can affect sorting and searching.
Avoid placing critical data to the left or right of the list.	Use the same format for all cells in a column.

Creating a List

Once you have planned the list structure, the sequence of fields, and any appropriate formatting, you need to create field names. Table H-2 provides guidelines for naming fields.  Evan is ready to create the list using the field names he wrote down earlier.

Steps

1. **Open the workbook titled XL H-1, save it as New Customer List, then rename Sheet1 as Practice List**
   It is a good idea to devote an entire worksheet to your list.

2. **Beginning in cell A1 and moving horizontally, type each field name in a separate cell, as shown in Figure H-2**
   Always put field names in the first row of the list. Don't worry if your field names are wider than the cells; you will fix this later. Next, format the field names.

3. **Select the field headings in range A1:I1, then click the Bold button** $\boxed{B}$ **on the Formatting toolbar; with range A1:I1 still selected, click the Borders list arrow, then click the thick bottom border (second item from left in the second row)**
   Next, enter three of the records in the customer list.

4. **Enter the information from Figure H-3 in the rows immediately below the field names, using a leading apostrophe (') for all Zip codes; do not leave any blank rows**
   If you don't type an apostrophe, Excel deletes the leading zero (0) in the Zip code. The data appears in columns organized by field name. Next, adjust the column widths so that each column is as wide as its longest entry.

5. **Select range A1:I4, click Format on the menu bar, point to Column, click AutoFit Selection, click anywhere in the worksheet to deselect the range, then save the workbook**
   Automatically resizing the column widths this way is faster than double-clicking the column divider lines between each pair of columns. Compare your screen with Figure H-4.

QuickTip

If the field name you plan to use is wider than the data in the column, you can turn on Wrap Text to stack the heading in the cell. Doing this allows you to use descriptive field names and still keep the columns from being unnecessarily wide. If you prefer a keyboard shortcut, you can press **[Alt][Enter]** to force a line break while entering field names.

TABLE H-2: Guidelines for naming fields

guideline	explanation
Use labels to name fields.	Numbers can be interpreted as parts of formulas.
Do not use duplicate field names.	Duplicate field names can cause information to be incorrectly entered and sorted.
Format the field names to stand out from the list data.	Use a font, alignment, format, pattern, border, or capitalization style for the column labels that is different from the format of your list data.
Use descriptive names.	Avoid names that might be confused with cell addresses, such as Q4.

FIGURE H-2: Field names entered and formatted in row 1

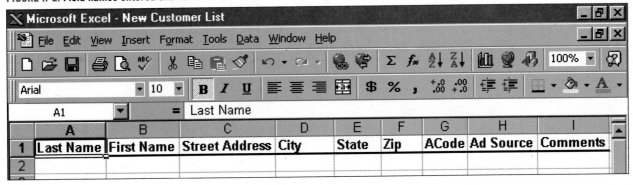

FIGURE H-3: Cards with customer information

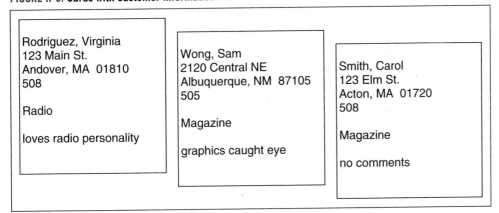

FIGURE H-4: List with three records

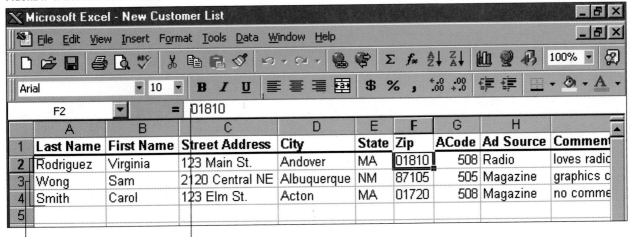

New records   Leading apostrophe

Maintaining the quality of information in a list

To protect the list information, make sure the data is entered in the correct field. Stress care and consistency to all those who enter the list data. Haphazardly entered data can yield invalid results later when it is manipulated.

Adding Records with the Data Form

You can add records to a list by typing data directly into the cells within the list range. Once the field names are created, you also can use the data form as a quick, easy method of data entry. By naming a list range in the name box, you can select the list at any time, and all new records added to the list will be included in the list range. 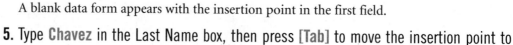 Evan has entered all the customer records he had on his cards, but he received the names of two more customers. He decides to use Excel's data form to add the new customer information.

1. **Make sure the New Customer List is open, then rename Sheet2 as Working List**
   Working List contains the nearly complete customer list. Before using the data form to enter the new data, define the list range.

2. **Select range A1:I45, click the name box to select A1, type Database, then press [Enter]**
   The Database list range name appears in the name box. When you assign the name Database to the list, the commands on Excel's Data menu default to the list named "Database". Next, enter a new record using the data form.

3. **While the list is still selected, click Data on the menu bar, then click Form**
   A data form containing the first record appears, as shown in Figure H-5.

4. **Click New**
   A blank data form appears with the insertion point in the first field.

5. **Type Chavez in the Last Name box, then press [Tab] to move the insertion point to the next field**

6. **Enter the rest of the information for Jeffrey Chavez, as shown in Figure H-6**
   Press [Tab] to move the insertion point to the next field, or click in the next field's box to move the insertion point there.

7. **Click New to add Jeffrey Chavez's record and open another blank data form, enter the record for Cathy Relman as shown in Figure H-6, then click Close**
   The list records that you add with the data form are placed at the end of the list and are formatted like the previous records. Verify that the new records were added.

8. **Scroll down the worksheet to bring rows 46 and 47 into view, confirm both records, return to cell A1, then save the workbook**

FIGURE H-5: Data form showing first record in list

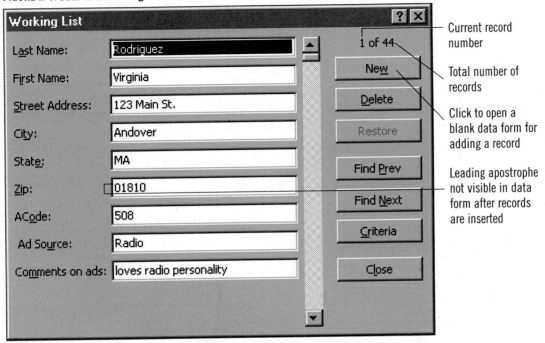

Current record number

Total number of records

Click to open a blank data form for adding a record

Leading apostrophe not visible in data form after records are inserted

FIGURE H-6: Two data forms with information for two new records

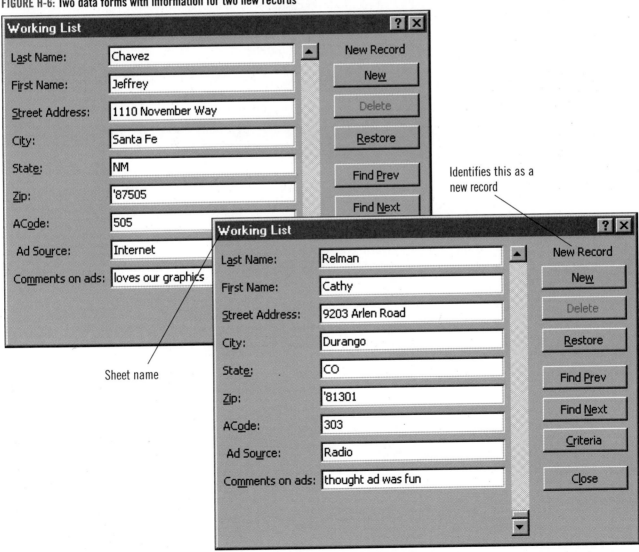

Identifies this as a new record

Sheet name

Finding Records

From time to time, you need to locate specific records in your list. You can use Excel's Find command on the Edit menu or the data form to perform searches in your list. Also, you can use the Replace command on the Edit menu to locate and replace existing entries or portions of entries with specified information. ◢ Evan's manager has asked him to list the specific Ad Source for each new customer rather than list the general ad category. She also wants to know how many of the new customers originated from the company's Internet site. Evan begins by searching for those records with the Ad Source "Internet".

Steps

Trouble?

If you receive the message, "No list found", simply select any cell within the list, then repeat Step 1.

1. From any cell within the list, click **Data** on the menu bar, click **Form**, then click **Criteria**

The data form changes so that all fields are blank and "Criteria" appears in the upper-right corner. See Figure H-7. You want to search for records whose Ad Source field contains the label "Internet".

2. Press **[Alt][U]** to move to the Ad Source box, type **Internet**, then click **Find Next**

Excel displays the first record for a customer who learned about the company through the Internet site. See Figure H-8.

QuickTip

You also can use comparison operators when performing a search using the data form. For example, you could specify >50,000 in a Salary field box to return those records whose value in the Salary field is greater than 50,000.

3. Click **Find Next** until there are no more matching records, then click **Close**

There are six customers whose Ad Source is the Internet. Next, change the Ad Source entries that currently read "Radio" to "KWIN Radio".

4. Return to cell A1, click **Edit** on the menu bar, then click **Replace**

The Replace dialog box opens with the insertion point located in the Find what box. See Figure H-9.

5. In the Find what box, type **Radio**, then click the **Replace with box**

Next, instruct Excel to search for entries containing "Radio" and replace them with "KWIN Radio".

6. In the Replace with box, type **KWIN Radio**

You are about to perform the search and replace option specified. Because you notice that there are other list entries containing the word "radio" with a lowercase "r", you choose the option "Match case" in the dialog box.

7. Click the **Match case box** to select it, then click **Find Next**

Excel moves the cell pointer to the first occurrence of "Radio". Next, instruct Excel to replace all existing entries with the information specified.

8. Click **Replace All**

The dialog box closes, and you complete the replacement and check to make sure all references to radio in the Ad Source column now read "KWIN Radio".

9. Make sure there are no entries in the Ad Source column that read "Radio", then save the workbook

FIGURE H-7: **Criteria data form**

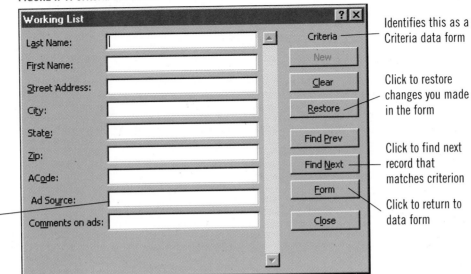

Type Internet here

Identifies this as a Criteria data form

Click to restore changes you made in the form

Click to find next record that matches criterion

Click to return to data form

FIGURE H-8: **Finding a record using the data form**

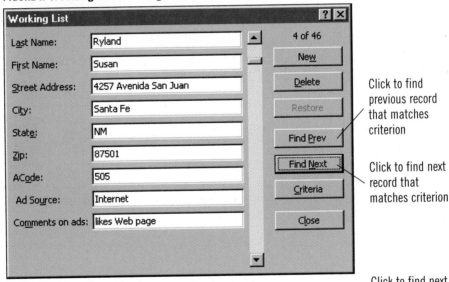

Click to find previous record that matches criterion

Click to find next record that matches criterion

FIGURE H-9: **Replace dialog box**

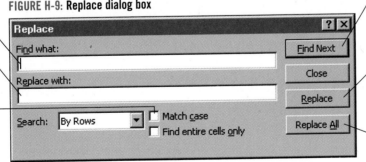

Type Radio here

Type KWIN Radio here

Click to find exact case matches

Click to find next occurrence of item in Find what box

Click to replace current item that matches Find what box

Click to replace all occurrences of item in Find what box

CLUES TO USE

Using wildcards to fine-tune your search

You can use special symbols called **wildcards** when defining search criteria in the data form or Find dialog box. The question mark (?) wildcard stands for any single character. For example, if you do not know whether a customer's last name is Paulsen or Paulson, you can specify Pauls?n as the search criteria to locate

both options. The asterisk (*) wildcard stands for any group of characters. For example, if you specify Jan* as the search criteria in the First Name field, Excel locates all records with first names beginning with Jan (for instance, Jan, Janet, Janice, and so forth).

Deleting Records

You need to keep your list up to date by removing obsolete records. One way to remove records is to use the Delete button on the data form. You also can delete all records that meet certain criteria—that is, records that have something in common. For example, you can specify a criterion for Excel to find the next record containing Zip code 01879, then remove the record using the Delete button. If specifying one criterion does not meet your needs, you can set multiple criteria.  After she noticed two entries for Carolyn Smith, Evan's manager asked him to check the database for additional duplicate entries. Evan uses the data form to delete the duplicate record.

Steps

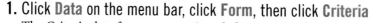

QuickTip

Besides using the data form to add, search for, and delete records, you also can use the data form to edit records. Just find the desired record and edit the data directly in the appropriate box.

1. Click **Data** on the menu bar, click **Form**, then click **Criteria**

The Criteria data form appears. Search for records whose Last Name field contains the label "Smith" and whose First Name field contains the label "Carolyn".

2. In the **Last Name box**, type **Smith**, click the **First Name box**, type **Carolyn**, then click **Find Next**

Excel displays the first record for a customer whose name is Carolyn Smith. You decide to leave the initial entry for Carolyn Smith (record 5 of 46) and delete the second one once you confirm it is a duplicate.

3. Click **Find Next**

The duplicate record for Carolyn Smith, record number 40, appears as shown in Figure H-10. You are ready to delete the duplicate entry.

QuickTip

Clicking Restore on the data form will not restore deleted record(s).

4. Click **Delete**, then click **OK** to confirm the deletion

The duplicate record for Carolyn Smith is deleted, and all the other records move up one row. The new record, Manuel Julio, is shown in the data form. Next, view the worksheet to confirm deletion of the duplicate entry.

5. Click **Close** to return to the worksheet, scroll down until rows 40–46 are visible, then read the entry in row 40

Notice that the duplicate entry for Carolyn Smith is gone and that Manuel Julio moved up a row and is now in row 41. You also notice a record for K. C. Splint in row 43, which is a duplicate entry.

6. Return to cell A1, and read the record information for K. C. Splint in row 8

After confirming another duplicate entry, you decide to delete the row.

7. Click cell **A8**, click **Edit** on the menu bar, then click **Delete**

The Delete dialog box opens as shown in Figure H-11. Choose the option to delete the entire row.

8. Click the **Entire row option button**, then click **OK**

You are pleased that the duplicate record for K. C. Splint is deleted and that the other records move up to fill in the gap.

9. Save the workbook

FIGURE H-10: Data form showing duplicate record for Carolyn Smith

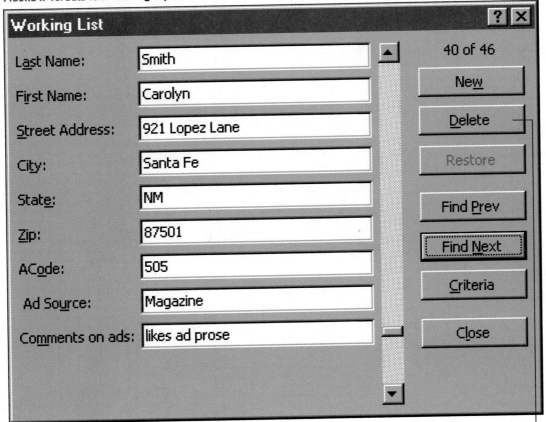

Click to delete
current record
from list

FIGURE H-11: Delete dialog box

Click to shift
remaining cells to
fill gap created by
deleting cells

Click to delete
current row

Click to delete
current column

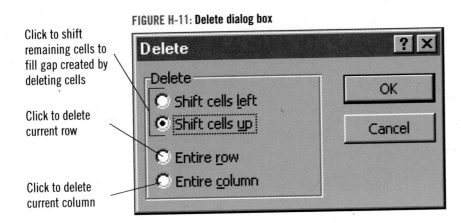

Deleting records using the data form versus deleting rows from the worksheet area

When you delete a record using the data form, you cannot undo your deletion. When you delete a record by deleting the row in which it resides inside the worksheet area, however, you can immediately restore the record by using the Undo command on the Edit menu, the Undo button, or by pressing [Ctrl][Z].

Sorting a List by One Field

Usually, you enter records in the order in which they are received, rather than in alphabetical or numerical order. When you add records to a list using the data form, the records are added to the end of the list. Using Excel's sorting feature, you can rearrange the order in which the records appear. You can use the sort buttons on the Standard toolbar to sort records by one field, or you can use the Sort command on the Data menu to perform more complicated sorts. Alternatively, you can sort an entire list or any portion of a list, or you can arrange sorted information in ascending or descending order. In ascending order, the lowest value (the beginning of the alphabet, or the earliest date) appears at the top of the list. In a field containing labels and numbers, numbers come first. In descending order, the highest value (the end of the alphabet, or the latest date) appears at the top of the list. In a field containing labels and numbers, labels come first. Table H-3 provides examples of ascending and descending sorts. Because Evan wants to be able to return the records to their original order following any sorts, he begins by creating a new field called Entry Order. Then he will perform several single field sorts on the list.

QuickTip

Before you sort records, it is a good idea to make a backup copy of your list or create a field that numbers the records so you can return them to their original order, if necessary.

1. In cell J1, enter the text and format for cell J1 as shown in Figure H-12, then AutoFit column J

Next, fill in the entry order numbers for all records.

2. In cell J2 type 1, press [Enter], in cell J3 type 2, press [Enter], select cells J2:J3, drag the fill handle to cell J45, then return to cell A1

With the Entry Order column complete as shown in Figure H-12, you are ready to sort the list in ascending order by last name. You must position the cell pointer within the column you want to sort prior to issuing the sort command.

QuickTip

If your sort does not perform as intended, press [Ctrl][Z] immediately to undo the sort and repeat the step.

3. While in cell A1, click the Sort Ascending button on the Standard toolbar

Excel instantly rearranges the records in ascending order by last name, as shown in Figure H-13. Next, sort the list in descending order by area code.

4. Click cell G1, then click the Sort Descending button on the Standard toolbar

Excel sorts the list, placing those records with higher-digit area codes at the top. Next, update the list range to include original entry order.

5. Select range A1:J45, click the name box, type Database, then press [Enter]

You are now ready to return the list to original entry order.

6. Click cell J1, click the Sort Ascending button on the Standard toolbar, then save the workbook

The list is back to its original order, and the workbook is saved.

TABLE H-3: Sort order options and examples

option	alphabetic	numeric	date	alphanumeric
Ascending	A, B, C	7, 8, 9	1/1, 2/1, 3/1	12A, 99B, DX8, QT7
Descending	C, B, A	9, 8, 7	3/1, 2/1, 1/1	QT7, DX8, 99B, 12A

FIGURE H-12: List with Entry Order field added

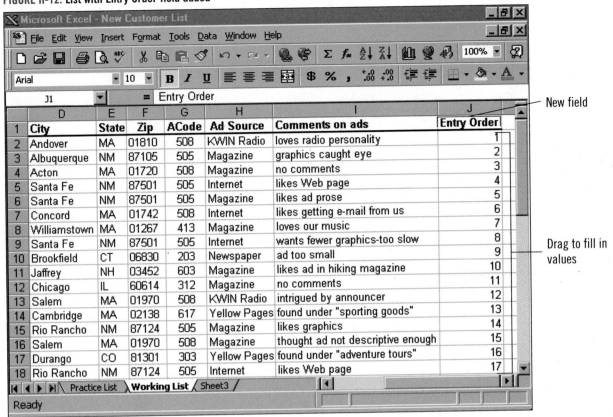

New field

Drag to fill in values

	D	E	F	G	H	I	J
1	City	State	Zip	ACode	Ad Source	Comments on ads	Entry Order
2	Andover	MA	01810	508	KWIN Radio	loves radio personality	1
3	Albuquerque	NM	87105	505	Magazine	graphics caught eye	2
4	Acton	MA	01720	508	Magazine	no comments	3
5	Santa Fe	NM	87501	505	Internet	likes Web page	4
6	Santa Fe	NM	87501	505	Magazine	likes ad prose	5
7	Concord	MA	01742	508	Internet	likes getting e-mail from us	6
8	Williamstown	MA	01267	413	Magazine	loves our music	7
9	Santa Fe	NM	87501	505	Internet	wants fewer graphics-too slow	8
10	Brookfield	CT	06830	203	Newspaper	ad too small	9
11	Jaffrey	NH	03452	603	Magazine	likes ad in hiking magazine	10
12	Chicago	IL	60614	312	Magazine	no comments	11
13	Salem	MA	01970	508	KWIN Radio	intrigued by announcer	12
14	Cambridge	MA	02138	617	Yellow Pages	found under "sporting goods"	13
15	Rio Rancho	NM	87124	505	Magazine	likes graphics	14
16	Salem	MA	01970	508	Magazine	thought ad not descriptive enough	15
17	Durango	CO	81301	303	Yellow Pages	found under "adventure tours"	16
18	Rio Rancho	NM	87124	505	Internet	likes Web page	17

Practice List / **Working List** / Sheet3

Ready

FIGURE H-13: List sorted alphabetically by last name

List sorted in ascending order by Last Name

	A	B	C	D	E	F	G	H
1	Last Name	First Name	Street Address	City	State	Zip	ACode	Ad Source
2	Alderson	Bert	12 East Shore Blvd.	Albany	NY	12201	518	Magazine
3	Ballard	Adelia	3 Hall Rd.	Williamstown	MA	01267	413	Magazine
4	Black	John	11 River Rd.	Brookfield	CT	06830	203	Newspaper
5	Carter	Yvonne	900 Cam. del Monte Sol	Santa Fe	NM	87501	505	Magazine
6	Chavez	Jeffrey	1110 November Way	Santa Fe	NM	87505	505	Internet
7	Dewey	Evan	823 Northside Heights	Albuquerque	NM	87105	505	Magazine
8	Dickenson	Tonia	92 Main Avenue	Durango	CO	81301	303	Yellow Pages
9	Dobbins	Camilla	486 Intel Circuit	Rio Rancho	NM	87124	505	Internet
10	Duran	Maria	Galvin Hghwy East	Chicago	IL	60614	312	Magazine
11	Fried	Martha	Hyde Park Estates	Santa Fe	NM	87501	505	Magazine
12	Gonzales	Fred	Purgatory Ski Area	Durango	CO	81301	303	Yellow Pages
13	Graham	Shelley	989 26th Street	Durango	CO	81301	303	Yellow Pages
14	Green	Latrell	343 3rd Avenue	Brooklyn	NY	11201	718	Internet
15	Hesh	Gayle	1192 Don Diego	Santa Fe	NM	87501	505	Magazine
16	Ichikawa	Pam	232 Shore Rd	Woburn	MA	01801	508	Magazine
17	Janis	Steve	402 9th Street	Durango	CO	81301	303	Magazine
18	Julio	Manuel	544 Cameo Place	Lenox	MA	02140	413	Magazine

Practice List / **Working List** / Sheet3

Ready

Sorting a List by Multiple Fields

You can sort lists by as many as three fields by specifying **sort keys,** the criteria upon which the sort is based. To perform sorts on multiple fields, you must use the Sort dialog box, which you access through the Sort command on the Data menu. ⟋⟋⟋ Evan wants to sort the records alphabetically by state first, then within the state by Zip code.

1. Click the name box list arrow, then click Database

The list is selected. Because you want to sort the list by more than one field, use the Sort command on the Data menu.

2. Click Data on the menu bar, then click Sort

The Sort dialog box opens, as shown in Figure H-14. You want to sort the list by state and then by Zip code.

3. Click the Sort by list arrow, click State, then click the Ascending option button, if necessary

The list will be sorted alphabetically in ascending order (A–Z) by the State field. Next, define a second sort field for the Zip code.

4. Click the top Then by list arrow, click Zip, then click the Descending option button

You also could sort by a third key by selecting a field in the bottom Then by list box.

5. Click OK to execute the sort, press [Ctrl][Home], then scroll through the list to see the result of the sort

The list is sorted alphabetically by state in ascending order, then within each state by Zip code in descending order. Compare your results with Figure H-15. Notice that Massachusetts, New Mexico, and New York have multiple Zip codes.

6. Return to cell A1, then save the workbook

FIGURE H-14: Sort dialog box

Fields on which the sort will be based → Sort by

First sort field

Second sort field

Third sort field

Indicates field name labels will not be included in sort

FIGURE H-15: List sorted by multiple fields

First sort by state →

	Last Name	First Name	Street Address	City	State	Zip	ACode	Ad Source
1	**Last Name**	**First Name**	**Street Address**	**City**	**State**	**Zip**	**ACode**	**Ad Source**
2	Dickenson	Tonia	92 Main Avenue	Durango	CO	81301	303	Yellow Pages
3	Gonzales	Fred	Purgatory Ski Area	Durango	CO	81301	303	Yellow Pages
4	Graham	Shelley	989 26th Street	Durango	CO	81301	303	Yellow Pages
5	Janis	Steve	402 9th Street	Durango	CO	81301	303	Magazine
6	Nelson	Michael	229 Route 55	Durango	CO	81301	303	Yellow Pages
7	Relman	Cathy	9203 Arlen Road	Durango	CO	81301	303	KWIN Radio
8	Black	John	11 River Rd.	Brookfield	CT	06830	203	Newspaper
9	Owen	Scott	72 Yankee Way	Brookfield	CT	06830	203	Newspaper
10	Duran	Maria	Galvin Hghwy East	Chicago	IL	60614	312	Magazine
11	Roberts	Bob	56 Water St.	Chicago	IL	60614	312	Magazine
12	Wallace	Salvatore	100 Westside Avenue	Chicago	IL	60614	312	Magazine
13	Ballard	Adelia	3 Hall Rd.	Williamstown	MA	01267	413	Magazine
14	Smith	Carol	123 Elm St.	Acton	MA	01720	508	Magazine
15	Kane	Peter	67 Main St.	Concord	MA	01742	508	Internet
16	Spencer	Robin	293 Serenity Drive	Concord	MA	01742	508	KWIN Radio
17	Ichikawa	Pam	232 Shore Rd	Woburn	MA	01801	508	Magazine
18	Paxton	Gail	100 Main Street	Woburn	MA	01801	508	Magazine

Second sort by Zip code within state

Specifying a custom sort order

You can identify a custom sort order for the field selected in the Sort by box. To do this, click Options in the Sort dialog box, click the First key sort order list arrow, then click the desired custom order.

Commonly used custom sort orders are days of the week (Mon, Tues, Wed, and so forth) and months (Jan, Feb, Mar, and so forth), where alphabetic sorts do not sort these items properly.

Excel 97

Printing a List

If a list is small enough to fit on one page, you can print it as you would any other Excel work-sheet. However, if you have more columns than can fit on a portrait-oriented page, try setting the page orientation to landscape. Because lists often have more rows than can fit on a page, you can define the first row of the list (containing the field names) as the **print title**. Most lists do not have any descriptive information above the field names on the worksheet. To augment the information contained in the field names, you can use headers and footers to add identifying text, such as the list title or report date. If you want to exclude any fields from your list report, you can hide the desired columns from view so that they do not print. ✐➤ Evan has finished updating his list and is ready to print it. He begins by previewing the list.

QuickTip

You can print multiple ranges in your worksheets at the same time by clicking the Print area box in the Sheet tab of the Page Setup dialog box. Then simply drag to select areas in the worksheet you wish to print.

1. Click the **Print Preview button** 🔍 on the Standard toolbar

Notice that the status bar reads Page 1 of 2. You want all the fields in the list to fit on a single page, but you'll need two pages to fit all the data. So you set the page orientation to landscape and adjust the Fit to options.

2. From the Print Preview window, click **Setup**, click the **Page tab**, under Orientation click the **Landscape option button**, under Scaling click the **Fit to option button**, double-click the **tall box** and type **2**, then click **OK**

The list still does not fit on a single page. Check to see what is on page 2.

3. Click **Next**

Because the records on page 2 appear without column headings, you can set up the first row of the list, containing the field names, as a repeating print title.

4. Click **Close** to exit the Print Preview window, click **File** on the menu bar, click **Page Setup**, click the **Sheet tab**, under Print titles click the **Rows to repeat at top box**, then click any cell in row 1

When you select row 1 as a print title, Excel automatically inserts an absolute reference to a beginning and ending row to repeat at the top of each page—in this case, the print title to repeat beginning and ending with row 1. See Figure H-16.

5. Click **Print Preview**, click **Next** to view the second page, then click **Zoom** to get a closer look

Setting up a print title to repeat row 1 causes the field names to appear at the top of each printed page. Next, change the header to reflect the contents of the list.

6. Click **Setup**, click the **Header/Footer tab**, click **Custom Header**, click the **Center section box**, type **Nomad Ltd—New Customer List**

7. Select the header text in the Center section box, click the **Font button** **A**, change the font size to **14** and the style to **Bold**, click **OK**, click **OK** again to return to the Header/Footer tab, then click **OK** to preview the list

Page 2 of the report appears as shown in Figure H-17.

8. Save, print, then close the workbook

FIGURE H-16: Sheet tab of the Page Setup dialog box

Indicates row 1 will appear at top of each printed page

Indicates which columns will appear at left of each printed page

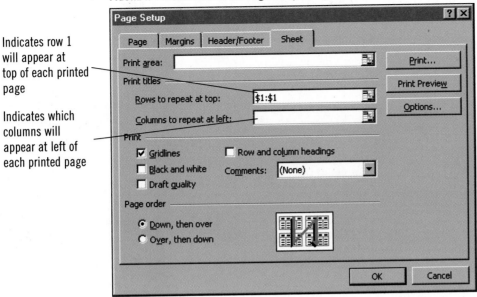

FIGURE H-17: Print Preview window showing page 2 of completed report

List header

Row 1 of list repeated as a print title

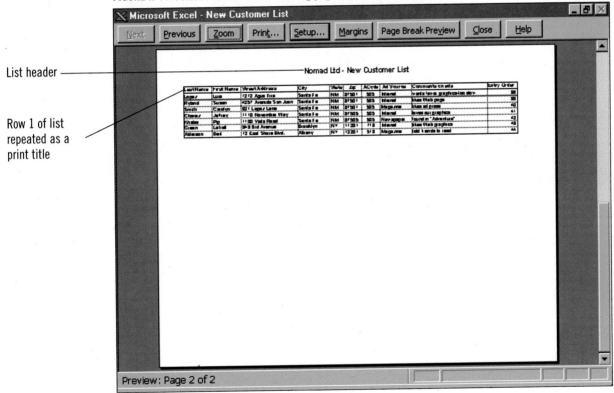

Setting page printing order

You can control the order Excel creates pages from your worksheet in the Sheet tab of the Page Setup dialog box. See the Page order option in Figure H-16. Normally, Excel prints pages by selecting a pageful of data going down the rows first, then across columns. You also can print by first filling pages going across the columns and then down the rows.

Practice

▶ Concepts Review

Label each of the elements of the Excel screen shown in Figure H-18.

FIGURE H-18

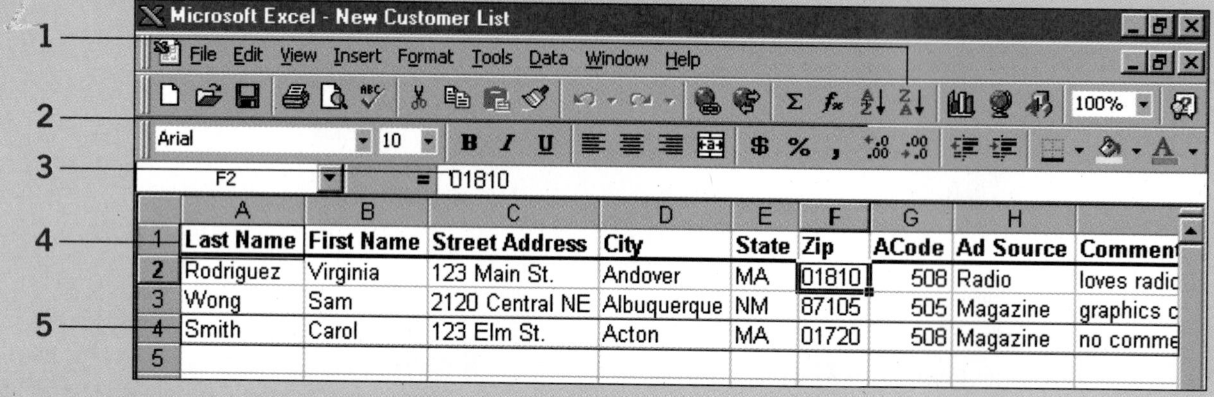

Match each statement with the term it describes.

6. Arrange records in a particular sequence
7. Organized collection of related information in Excel
8. Row in an Excel list
9. Type of software used for lists containing more than 65,536 records
10. Label positioned at the top of the column identifying data for that field

a. List
b. Record
c. Database
d. Sort
e. Field name

Select the best answer from the list of choices.

11. Which of the following Excel sorting options do you use to sort a list of employee names in A-to-Z order?
   a. Ascending
   b. Absolute
   c. Alphabetic
   d. Descending

12. Which of the following series is in descending order?
   a. 4, 5, 6, A, B, C
   b. C, B, A, 6, 5, 4
   c. 8, 7, 6, 5, 6, 7
   d. 8, 6, 4, C, B, A

13. Once the _____ is defined, any new records added to the list using the data form are included in the _____.
    a. Database, database
    b. Data form, data form
    c. Worksheet, worksheet
    d. List range, list range

14. When printing a list on multiple pages, you can define a print title containing repeating row(s) to
    a. Include appropriate fields in the printout.
    b. Include field names at the top of each printed page.
    c. Include the header in list reports.
    d. Exclude from the printout all rows under the first row.

▶ Skills Review

1. **Create a list.**
    a. Create a new workbook, then save it as "M.K. Electric Employee List".
    b. In cell A1, type the title "M.K. Electric Employees".
    c. Enter the field names and records using the information in Table H-4.
    d. Apply bold formatting to the field names.

TABLE H-4

Last name	First name	Years	Position	Pension	Union
Smith-Hill	Janice	8	Office Manager	Y	N
Doolan	Mark	3	Customer Service	N	N
Coleman	Steve	4	Senior Installer	N	Y
Quinn	Jamie	7	Junior Installer	N	Y
Rabinowicz	Sarah	11	Field Manager	Y	Y

    e. Center the entries in the Years, Pension, and Union fields.
    f. Adjust the column widths to make the data readable.
    g. Save, then print the list.

2. Add records with the data form.

a. Select all the records in the list, including the field names, then define the range as "Database".

b. Open the data form and add a new record for David Gitano, a newly hired junior installer at M.K. Electric. David is not eligible for the employee pension, but he is a member of the union.

c. Add a new record for George Worley, the company's new office assistant. George is not eligible for the employee pension, and he is not a union member.

d. Save the list.

3. Find and delete records.

a. Find the record for Jamie Quinn.

b. Delete the record.

c. Save the list.

4. Sort a list by one field.

a. Select the Database list range.

b. Sort the list alphabetically in ascending order by last name.

c. Save the list.

5. Sort a list by multiple fields.

a. Select the Database list range.

b. Sort the list alphabetically in ascending order first by union membership and then by last name.

c. Save the list.

6. Print a list.

a. Add a header that reads, "Employee Information".

b. Print the list, then save and close the workbook.

c. Exit Excel.

1. Your advertising firm, Personalize IT, specializes in selling specialty items imprinted with the customer's name and/or logo such as hats, pens, and T-shirts. Plan and build a list of information with a minimum of 10 records using the three items sold. Your list should contain at least five different customers. (Some customers will place more than one order.) Each record should contain the customer's name, item sold, and its individual and extended cost. Enter your own data and make sure you include at least the following list fields:

- Item—Describe the item.
- Cost-Ea.—What is the item's individual cost?
- Quantity—How many items did the customer purchase?
- Ext. Cost—What is the total purchase price?
- Customer—Who purchased the item?

To complete this independent challenge:

1. Prepare a list plan that states your goal, outlines the data you'll need, and identifies the list elements.
2. Sketch a sample list on a piece of paper, indicating how the list should be built. What information should go in the columns? In the rows? Which of the data fields will be formatted as labels? As values?
3. Build the list first by entering the field names, then by entering the records. Remember you will invent your own data. Save the workbook as "Personalize IT".
4. Reformat the list, as needed. For example, you might need to adjust the column widths to make the data more readable. Also, remember to check your spelling.
5. Sort the list in ascending order by Item, then by Customer, then by Quantity
6. Preview the worksheet; adjust any items as needed; then print a copy.
7. Save your work before closing.
8. Submit your list plan, preliminary sketches, and final printouts.

2. You are taking a class titled "Television Shows: Past and Present" at a local community college. The instructor has provided you with an Excel list of television programs from the '60s and '70s. She has included fields tracking the following information: the number of years the show was a favorite, favorite character, least favorite character, the show's length in minutes, the show's biggest star, and comments about the show. The instructor has included data for each show in the list. She has asked you to add a field (column label) and two records (shows of your choosing) to the list. Because the list should cover only 30-minute shows, you need to delete any records for shows longer than 30 minutes. Also, your instructor wants you to sort the list by show name and format the list as needed prior to printing. Feel free to change any of the list data to suit your tastes and opinions.

To complete this independent challenge:

1. Open the workbook titled XL H-2, then save it as "Television Shows of the Past".
2. Using your own data, add a field, then use the data form to add two records to the list. Make sure to enter information in every field.
3. Delete any records having show lengths other than 30. (*Hint*: Use the Criteria data form to set the criteria, then find and delete any matching records.)

4. Make any formatting changes to the list as needed.

5. Save the list prior to sorting.

6. Sort the list in ascending order by show name.

7. Preview, then print the list. Adjust any items as needed so that the list can be printed on a single page.

8. Sort the list again, this time in descending order by number of years the show was a favorite.

9. Change the header to read "Television Shows of the Past: '60s and '70s".

10. Preview, then print the list.

11. Save the workbook.

3. You work as a sales clerk at Nite Owl Video. Your roommate and co-worker, Albert Lee, has put together a list of his favorite movie actors and actresses. He has asked you to add several names to the list so he can determine which artists and what kinds of films you enjoy most. He has recorded information in the following fields: artist's first and last names, life span, birthplace, the genre or type of roles the artist plays most (for example, dramatic or comedic), the name of a film for which the artist has received or been nominated for an Academy Award, and finally, two additional films featuring the artist. Using your own data, add at least two artists known for dramatic roles and two artists known for comedic roles.

To complete this independent challenge:

1. Open the workbook titled XL H-3, then add at least four records using the criteria mentioned above. Remember, you are creating and entering your own movie data for all relevant fields.

2. Save the workbook as "Film Star Favorites". Make formatting changes to the list as needed. Remember to check your spelling.

3. Sort the list alphabetically by Genre. Perform a second sort by Last Name.

4. Preview the list, adjust any items as needed, then print a copy of the list sorted by Genre and Last Name.

5. Sort the list again, this time in descending order by the Life Span field, then by Last Name.

6. Print a copy of the list sorted by Life Span and Last Name.

7. Save your work, then submit your printouts.

4. Because Web users are located all over the world, you can use the World Wide Web (WWW) to locate almost any type of information, in just about any country around the globe. Travel information is especially helpful when you are planning vacations. You have decided to travel to Hawaii for one month over the summer. Your choice of accommodations includes a condominium close to the beach with full kitchen facilities. Use your choice of search engines on the WWW to locate information on condo rentals in Hawaii, and then build an Excel list with the information you gather.

To complete this independent challenge:

1. Open a new workbook, then save it as "Hawaiian Vacation".
2. Create a list with the following field names: Complex Name, Island, Ocean View?, Peak Season Rate, Off-Season Rate (rates per night), Max # of Bedrooms, On-Site Pool?, On-Site Golf?, Air Conditioning?, and Web Site Address.
3. Log on to the Internet and use your Web browser to go to http://www.course.com. From there, click the link Student Online Companions, then click the Excel link for Unit H.
4. Use any combination of the following sites to search for and compile your data: Yahoo!, WebCrawler, or Alta Vista. (*Hint:* When using Web search engines, the + (plus sign) before a word means that the word must appear in the Web document. Therefore, a suggested search string would be +Hawaii +Condo +Rentals.) Be sure to gather information on 10 different possible vacation sites (minimum 10 records). While on the Web, print at least two graphics of sites chosen to accompany your worksheet data.
5. Add the Web data as records in your list.
6. Format the worksheet as desired to increase readability.
7. Save and print the workbook, then submit your printouts.

Visual Workshop

Create the worksheet shown in Figure H-19. Save the workbook as "Famous Jazz Performers". Once you've entered the field names and records, sort the list by Contribution to Jazz and then by Last Name. Change the page setup so that the list is centered on the page horizontally and the header reads "Famous Jazz Performers". Preview and print the list, then save the workbook. Submit your printouts.

FIGURE H-19

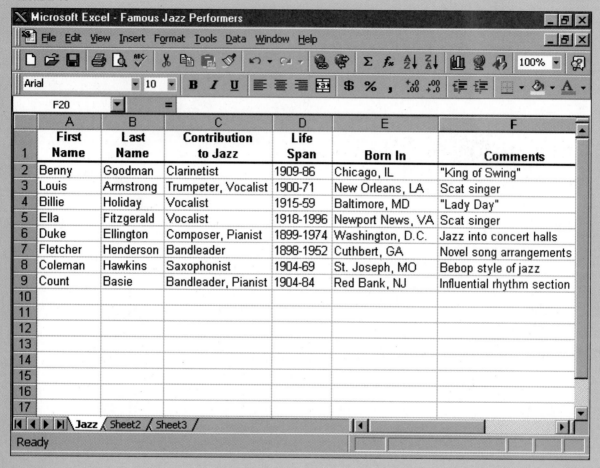

Glossary

Add-in An additional utility program that comes with Excel but is not automatically installed during a standard installation.

Alignment The horizontal position of cell contents; for example, left, center, or right.

Argument A value, range of cells, or text used in a macro or function. An argument is enclosed in parentheses; for example, =SUM(A1..B1).

Ascending Order Data organized from A to Z or 0 to 9.

Attribute A styling feature such as bold, italics, and underlining that can be applied to cell contents.

AutoCalculate area The area in the status bar that displays the sum (or function of your choice) of the values in the selected range.

AutoSum A feature that automatically calculates worksheet totals accessed by a button on the Standard toolbar.

Border Edges of a selected cell or area of cells in a worksheet. Lines and color can be applied to borders.

Cell The intersection of a column and row.

Cell address Unique location identified by intersecting column and row coordinates.

Cell pointer A highlighted rectangle around a cell that indicates the active cell.

Cell reference The address or name of a specific cell; cell references can be used in formulas and are relative or absolute.

Check box A square box in a dialog box that can be clicked to turn an option on or off.

Clear A command on the Edit menu used to erase a cell's contents, formatting, or both.

Clipboard A temporary storage area for cut or copied text or graphics. You can paste the contents of the Clipboard into any Microsoft program file. The Clipboard holds the information until you cut or copy another piece of text or a graphic.

Close A command that puts a file away but keeps Excel open so that you can continue to work on other workbooks.

Copy A command that copies the selected information and places it on the Clipboard.

Criteria form A data entry window used to set search criteria in lists.

Custom view A set of display and/or print settings that you can name and save, then access at a later time.

Cut A command that removes the contents from a selected area of a worksheet and places them on the Clipboard.

Data entry area The cells in a protected (locked) worksheet that must be unlocked because you need to change them.

Data form A data entry window used to view or add records to a list.

Database A collection of information organized by fields and records. A telephone book, a card catalog, and a list of company employees are all lists.

Delete A command that removes cell contents from a worksheet.

Descending Order Data organized from Z to A or 9 to 0.

Dialog box A window that displays when you choose a command whose name is followed by an ellipsis (...). A dialog box allows you to make selections that determine how the command affects the selected area.

Dynamic Information that updates automatically when certain parts of the workbook change.

Edit A change made to the contents of a cell or worksheet.

External reference indicator An ! (exclamation point) within a formula indicating that the cell referenced is outside the active sheet.

Field A labeled column in a list; it contains the same kind of information for each record, such as a phone number.

Field name A column label that describes the field.

Fill handle Small square in the lower-right corner of the active cell used to copy cell contents.

Find A command used to locate information the user specifies.

Find & Replace A command used to find one set of criteria and replace it with new information.

Folder A section of a disk used to store workbooks, much like a folder in a file cabinet.

Font A collection of characters (letters, numerals, and punctuation marks) with a specific design. Arial and Times New Roman are font names.

Footer The text that appears at the bottom of each printed page of a worksheet; for example, the page number and the date.

Form A data entry window used when working with lists. *See also* **Data form** *and* **Criteria form**.

Format The appearance of text and numbers, including color, font, attributes, and worksheet defaults. *See also* **Number format**.

Formula A set of instructions that you enter in a cell to perform numeric calculations (adding, multiplying, averaging, etc.); for example, +A1+B1.

Formula bar The area below the menu bar and above the Excel workspace where you enter and edit data in a worksheet cell. The formula bar becomes active when you start typing or editing cell data. Includes an Enter button and a Cancel button.

Freeze To lock in specified columns and/or rows to assist in scrolling through large worksheets.

Function A special predefined formula that provides a shortcut for commonly used calculations; for example, AVERAGE.

Header The text that appears at the top of each printed page; for example, the report name and the date.

Insertion point Blinking I-beam that appears in the formula bar during entry and editing.

Label Descriptive text or other information that identifies the rows and columns of a worksheet. Labels are not included in calculations.

Landscape A term used to refer to horizontal page orientation; it is the opposite of "portrait," or vertical orientation.

Linking Referencing data between workbooks dynamically so that any changes made in one workbook are reflected immediately in another workbook.

List A collection of information organized by fields and records. A telephone book, a card catalog, and a list of company employees are all lists.

List range A range of a worksheet that organizes information into fields and records.

Locked cells Cells that are protected so that their contents cannot be altered.

Logical test When the condition is a question that can be answered with a true or false response.

Macro A set of recorded instructions that tell the computer to perform a task or series of tasks.

Macro code The Visual Basic programming language Excel uses to translate your keystrokes and commands into words.

Menu A group of related commands located under a single word on the menu bar. For example, basic commands (New, Open, Save, Close, and Print) are grouped on the File menu.

Menu bar The area under the title bar on a window. The menu bar provides access to most of the application's commands.

Module Workbook area where the macro program code is located.

Name A name assigned to a selected cell or range in a worksheet. *See also* **Range name**.

Name box The leftmost area in the formula bar that shows the cell reference or name of the active cell. For example, A1 refers to cell A1 of the active worksheet. You also can get a list of names in a workbook using the name list arrow.

Number format A format applied to values to express numeric concepts, such as currency, date, and percent.

Operators Perform mathematical functions.

Option button A circle in a dialog box that can be clicked when only one option can be chosen.

Order of precedence The order in which Excel calculates parts of a formula: (1) exponents, (2) multiplication and division, and (3) addition and subtraction.

Page Break Preview Allows you to view and change page breaks manually in the Print Preview window.

Pane A column or row that always remains visible.

Paste A command that moves information on the Clipboard to a new location. Excel pastes the formulas rather than the result, unless the Paste Special command is used.

Paste Special A command that enables you to paste formulas as values, styles, or cell contents.

Personal Macro Workbook A file in which to store commonly used macros.

Point A unit of measure used for fonts and row height. One inch equals 72 points.

Portrait A term used to refer to vertical page orientation; it is the opposite of "landscape," or horizontal, orientation.

Precedence The order in which Excel calculates parts of a formula: (1) exponents, (2) multiplication and division, and (3) addition and subtraction.

Print Preview window A window that displays a reduced view of area to be printed.

Print Title The first row of a list (containing the field names) that appears as descriptive information on all worksheet pages.

Protect An option that lets you prevent cells in a worksheet from being changed.

Range A selected group of adjacent cells.

Range format A format applied to a selected range in a worksheet.

Range name A name applied to a selected range in a worksheet.

Record Horizontal rows in a list that contain related information.

Reference Populate cell data using existing cell content. You do this by typing = (equal sign) and then selecting the desired cell(s).

Relative cell reference Use to indicate a relative position in the worksheet. This allows you to copy and move formulas from one area to another of the same dimensions. Excel automatically changes the column and row numbers to reflect the new position.

Report Manager An add-in program that lets you create reports containing multiple worksheets in a workbook.

Row height The vertical dimension of a cell.

Run To execute a macro.

Scroll bars Bars that display on the right and bottom borders of the worksheet window that give you access to information not currently visible in the current worksheet as well as others in the workbook.

Sheet A term used for a worksheet.

Sheet tab A description at the bottom of each worksheet that identifies it in a workbook. In an open workbook, move to a worksheet by clicking its sheet tab. *See* **Tab**.

Sort To rearrange rows of a worksheet, usually rows in a list, in a particular order. *See also* **Ascending order** *and* **Descending order**.

Sort key Any cell in a field by which a list or selected range is being organized.

Status bar The bar near the bottom of the screen that provides information about the tasks Excel is performing or about any current selections.

Tab A description at the bottom of each worksheet that identifies it in a workbook. In an open workbook, move to a worksheet by clicking its tab.

Tab scrolling buttons Enable you to move among sheets within a workbook.

Template A fill-in-the-blank worksheet(s) that can include any text, formatting, formulas, layout and other workbook elements. You open a template, fill in the missing information, then save the file as a regular workbook, leaving the template intact.

Toggle A button that can be clicked to turn an option on. Clicking again turns the option off.

Toolbar An area within the Excel screen which contains buttons that you can click to perform frequently used Excel tasks.

Values Numbers, formulas, or functions used in calculations.

View A set of display and/or print settings that you can name and save, then access at a later time. *See also* **Custom view**.

Wildcards Special symbols used when defining search criteria in the data form or Find dialog box. The question mark (?) wildcard stands for any single character. The asterisk (*) wildcard stands for any group of characters.

Wizard A series of dialog boxes that lists and describes all Excel functions and assists the user in function creation.

Workbook A collection of related worksheets contained within a single file.

Worksheet An electronic spreadsheet containing 256 columns by 65,536 rows.

Worksheet Menu Bar Also called the "menu bar"; a special toolbar that contains commands you use when working with worksheets.

Zoom Enables you to focus on a larger or smaller part of the worksheet in Print Preview.

Zoom box Option on the Standard toolbar that allows you to change the screen magnification percentage.

Index

Index

Index

titles, adding to X- and Y-axes of charts, EX D-12-13
toolbars
    Formatting, EX A-6
    for macros, EX G-16-17
    Standard, EX A-6
totals, multiple, generating with AutoSum, EX E-6-7
truncated labels, EX A-10
2-D Column Charts, EX D-8

▶ U

Underline button, on Formatting toolbar, EX C-6-7
Undo button, restoring records with, EX H-11
undoing sorts, EX H-12
unfreezing, columns and rows in worksheets, EX F-2
unlocked cells, EX F-8, EX F-9
unprotecting worksheets, EX F-12

▶ V

values
    alignment of, EX A-10
    defined, EX A-10
    entering in worksheets, EX A-10-11
    formatting, EX C-2-3
vertical page breaks, EX F-14
views
    custom, of worksheets, saving, EX F-12-13
    defined, EX F-12
    multiple worksheets, EX D-7
Visual Basic Editor, EX G-12
    editing macros with, EX G-8-9
    starting, EX G-8-9

▶ W

what-if analysis, EX A-2, EX B-15
wildcards, in searches, EX H-9

workbooks, EX F-1-17
    closing, EX A-16-17
    defined, EX A-6
    inserting and deleting worksheets in, EX F-4-5
    linking, EX F-7
    opening, EX A-8-9
    protecting, EX F-9
    range names in, EX B-5
    saving, EX A-8-9
Worksheet menu bar, EX G-14
worksheets
    alignment, EX F-16-17
    automating tasks with macros, EX G-1-17
    borders in, EX C-12-13
    color in, EX C-12-13
    column width adjustments, EX C-8-9
    conditional formatting, EX C-14-15
    creating, EX B-2-3
    defined, EX A-2
    determining formulas needed for, EX B-2, EX B-3
    determining output for, EX B-2-3
    dummy rows and columns, EX C-11
    editing cell entries, EX B-4-5
    entering formulas, EX B-6-7
    fonts, EX C-4-5
    footers in, EX F-10-11
    formatting, EX C-1-17
    formatting values, EX C-2-3
    functions in, EX B-8-9
    headers in, EX F-10-11
    hiding areas in, EX F-8-9
    hiding/unhiding, EX F-9
    inserting and deleting in/from workbooks, EX F-4-5
    inserting and deleting rows and columns, EX C-10-11
    label attributes and alignments, EX C-6-7
    margins, EX F-16-17
    moving, EX B-16-17
    multiple, viewing, EX D-7
    naming, EX B-16-17
    navigating, EX A-11
    page numbering, EX F-14-15

    pages breaks in, EX F-14-15
    patterns in, EX C-12-13
    planning and designing, EX B-2-3
    point size, EX C-4-5
    previewing and printing, EX A-12-13
    printing in landscape orientation, EX E-16-17
    protecting areas in, EX F-8-9
    referencing data in, EX F-6-7
    saving custom views of, EX F-12-13
    spell checking, EX C-16-17
    splitting into multiple panes, EX F-2-3
    unprotecting, EX F-12
working with ranges, EX B-4-5
worksheet window, defined, EX A-6

▶ X

X-axis
    adding title to, EX D-12-13
    in charts, EX D-3
XY (scatter) charts, EX D-3

▶ Y

Y-axis
    adding title to, EX D-12-13
    in charts, EX D-3

▶ Z

Zoom, for Print Preview, EX A-13, EX F-12, EX F-14